REBORN

ASTRAGENESIS BOOK 1

CHARLES A CORNELL

THE Q NEBULA PRESS

EPWORTH UK

THE Q-NEBULA PRESS
An Imprint of Astra Novellus Ltd

Contact: AstraNovellus@runbox.com

REBORN – Astragenesis Book One -- 1st ed.
ISBN 978-1-0687344-0-3

This story is dedicated to
those who love imagination and
cherish the freedom to express it
in whatever form their hearts desire.

—Charles A Cornell

ACKNOWLEDGEMENTS

I'm very fortunate to have as friends and colleagues a tremendous circle of talented, award-winning authors to draw inspiration from. Imagination is infinite. They prove that every day they write. It is with great appreciation I acknowledge their assistance in critiquing my stories, providing their precious time and expert literary insight in order to make their telling more enjoyable for my readers.

Reborn and the *Astragenesis* series are based on my short story, *Children of the Stars*, published by the Alvarium Experiment in the anthology, *Return to Earth*.

Special thanks to my developmental editors, Ken Pelham and Vic DiGenti, whose advice was so important in getting *Reborn* on the right path.

To all my editors—too numerous to mention, but you know who you are—I thank you!

— Charles

REBORN

AUTHOR'S NOTES

REBORN is set in the western part of the North American continent in the year 2097. The story is written in American English.

The International Space Agency was founded in 2032. All space-related communications and measurements were metric at that time and this convention was continued after the Federation of Western Military Districts took over the agency's administration in 2042.

1 - HAZMAT CODE EIGHT

2097 AD
Free-Port of Los Angeles
Palos Verdes Military District

Dr. Nikki Akaju sipped the bitter coffee like a thirsty sparrow stuck in a nervous daydream. *That call-out was a glorious shit-show*, she thought. *I feel so lucky to be alive.* She clasped the mug with unsteady hands. A single tear trickled down her cheek. Images of chaos flashed by, begging more tears to flow. A clinic under siege. Medical staff clinging to life. Ambulances on fire. Lifeless faces. Blood and dust.

A friendly hand fell on Nikki's shoulder. The new intern from the Marine Medical Corps sat down across from her. "Need company?" Dr. Bryan Leysson asked, his bright blue eyes probing. "You okay?"

Nikki leaned back. "My mom says I should quit this gig, get a job at some clinic in an agri-settlement, and lead a quieter life. People who grow vegetables aren't likely to be violent, she said. And she should know." Nikki tied back her braided black hair. "That sounded really boring. But after yesterday, I could take a little boring right now."

"We all could."

Outside Malibu Heights Hospital, the midday temperature had reached a stifling 115F. The hospital, perched high on a cliff in the Santa Monica Mountains, overlooked a cityscape that shimmered with a ghostly blur under a veil of oppressive heat. The Long Beach Barrier seemed to float over Los Angeles like a giant tombstone.

Bryan swigged his chicory coffee and flinched. "Where do they get this awful shit from?"

Nikki scowled. "Your biggest problem is our *coffee*? I know you're used to luxuries in the military, but real coffee in Palos Verdes might as well be gold dust. You should know that by now. If it's a strong dose of caffeine you need, get an injection."

"Hey, hey...where's all *this* coming from?" Bryan placed his hand over hers. "Geez, Nikki, face it, coffee isn't the issue, is it? Your escape from death bordered on the miraculous. Do I need to prescribe anxiety meds? Anti-depressants? You shouldn't be ashamed to get help."

"I need another life. Prescribe that." Nikki pushed her mug away. She straightened her back and took a deep breath. "Sorry, about the coffee thing, Bryan. I guess I'm looking for an excuse to vent. Whatever *this* is, it's been building up for a long time. Way before you arrived. Astrid Stenmuir is the newest idiot in a long line of clueless administrators. This hospital needs stability. Instead, we're constantly kept off balance with incessant turnover. Something was bound to break and yesterday, I guess it did. But I'm not suffering from PTSD. That's not me. My anger will pass. It always does."

"Palos Verdes isn't a war zone, but it might as well be."

"I forgot to thank you for all you did out there," Nikki said. "The learning curve here isn't just steep, it's vertical, even for a military guy. You made some pretty brave, life-or-death medical decisions while being shot at. Everyone knew Ward 6 was too dangerous to respond at street level and our security is shit because of staff cuts. What was Stenmuir thinking? Once we crossed into the Wards, our route was tracked every step of the way to the vaccination clinic. This wasn't the first time an IED was used to steal medical supplies. The proof of her dumb decision lays face-up in the morgue. Stenmuir's on some kind of damn efficiency crusade that's going to get everyone killed. It's like she planned that call-out to fail so she could justify her request for another air ambulance."

"Well, it worked. Apparently, we're getting one."

"You're fucking kidding me. People died, Bryan. They were my friends."

"As far as Ward 6 is concerned, Nikki—I'm not sure how much I can tell you, but my contacts in the military say—"

"They're going to clear it out, aren't they?"

Bryan leaned his tall frame forward and lowered his voice. "Not so loud. How did you know that? It's a classified operation."

"Too many staff here have military clearance to keep anything juicy like that a secret. Your idea of 'classified' lasts about five minutes in this hospital. They've always wanted to turn Ward 6 into a parking lot. Is it any wonder the migrants stormed that clinic? They knew what the military was planning. Where's Ward 6 being sent? Las Vegas?"

Bryan ran his fingers through his curly blond hair and nodded.

"Well, doesn't that explain everything," Nikki said. "There are no emergency services in the Vegas Closed City—none, zip, zilch. Depopulation by neglect. There's a thriving black market in Vegas for our medical supplies because treating sickness is a hugely profitable business. The stuff they took has probably changed hands several times by now. They killed two paramedics yesterday, Bryan. Three more are in the ICU. Our people paid for her mistake with their blood. And our flimsy security detail barely got the rest of us out alive."

"I'm sure it's a mistake Dr. Stenmuir won't repeat."

"No shit. But she can't dispense replacement staff from a vending machine, however efficient that might sound."

A rumble shook the glass of the cafeteria's atrium roof. Vibrations moved down the walls and thumped the floor. A giant black shape moved over the glass, blotting out the sun. The ARV or Aerial Response Vehicle—a bulky, gray-metal monster with four tilting rotors—landed on the parched ground in front of Malibu Heights with a heavy thud. Its rotor wash rattled the hospital's windows. This wasn't an air ambulance or police aero-cruiser. This flying behemoth was far too big. Blacked-out windows. Bristling gun-ports. Logo of the Federation of Western Military Districts.

"Oh shit." A red light flashed in Nikki's eyepiece. "We've got a military emergency. And not just any military, Federal Marines."

Bryan received the same message...*Hazmat Code Eight, Potential Unknown Infections*. "What's this about?"

Nikki pulled out a crystal data-tab and checked the notes from Dispatch.

"Container ship," she said, scanning the images. "Anchored ten miles offshore, southwest of the Catalina Prison Island." She rose from her chair. "Coffee break's over. If aerial police escorts are going to be the new norm, I guess a military gunship is even better. Perhaps we won't die today after all."

The pair scrambled down the hallway to Emergency. Nikki tapped the sat-link on her wrist. "Prep Class A trauma kits, portable molecular diagnostics, and two bio-hazmat suits. Dr. Nikki Akaju, senior on-call. Dr. Bryan Leysson, assisting."

Outside the hospital, the rotors of the ARV kicked up eye-stinging dust. "That ARV is one big mother. Right in your wheelhouse, Bryan. Like a home away from home."

"In the desert, we patrolled in dune-jeeps, protecting road-trains from nomads. There are many times I wished we'd had one of those."

The aircraft's ramp lowered. Two marines ran over and grabbed their emergency kits, then escorted them into the cargo hold. Quick retinal scans confirmed to the gunship's duty sergeant the right people were on board. She directed them to jump seats near the door to the flight deck, then joined a row of black-clad marines that sat as rigid as statues. As soon as the doctors stowed their hazmat gear, the ramp closed, and the ARV took off with a powerful thrust from its rotors. With the gunship sealed against chemical, biological, and nuclear attack, a tomb-like silence enveloped the ARV's cargo bay.

"Who's running this show?" Nikki asked the duty sergeant.

"Major Ozzie Armstrong," she replied, stone-faced, as if saying anything more would get a reprimand.

A tall, broad-shouldered husky of a man with two raised welts across one of his black cheeks entered from the flight deck. A fortyish giant with a shaved head, his face was a gnarl of little muscles that flexed as he spoke. Pleasant introductions on a military call-out were a luxury. This one was no exception. "We made contact with the ship after it sent out a distress call," Armstrong said. "The details are sketchy, but whatever came over them, came on suddenly."

"Time to fess up. What's on board that ship, major?" Nikki asked. "Military stuff—nerve agents, chemical weapons?"

"The ship is civilian. Copper ingots. Lithium concentrate. Bananas. That kind of thing."

"I wish I could believe you. Why treat us to this deluxe limo ride for a ship you could quarantine for a couple of weeks?"

"Believe what you want, sister. All I know is that you're going to do your job and help Vandenberg check it out. You got a problem with that, then take it up with Dr. Veron." Armstrong pressed his hand against his ear-piece. His eyes drifted away. "I gotta get back to the flight deck. Get comfortable."

The gunship flew over the hot city and caught a rising thermal. It bounced with a sickening shudder. The ARV banked hard right and the Long Beach Barrier filled the view through the window.

"It's even more impressive from the air," Bryan said.

"My mother remembers the Barrier when it was a pile of bricks delivered by a single truck," Nikki replied. "You could plug a volcano with the concrete they used to finish it."

Thirty-feet tall, twenty-eight miles long, the Long Beach Barrier ran from the Pacific to the hills of the Santiago Canyon Security Zone, cutting the Palos Verdes MD in half. On one side were LA's free-citizens; on the other, the densely populated migrant wards of the South LA Closed City, an endless landscape of dusty hovels and crowded tenements that stretched all the way to San Diego.

"For someone new to the city, it's a monument," Nikki said. "For someone like me, it's a monstrosity. I lived in the shadow of that awful Barrier all my life. It's part of my DNA."

Bryan looked away from the window. "Your family were migrants?"

"My family are *not* migrants." Nikki's voice was a notch short of incandescent. "Who told you I was a migrant?"

"Hey, cool it. You know what gossip is like. You said you lived in the shadow of the Barrier, so I assumed—"

"On the free-citizens' side. I'm tired of that old rumor. What's wrong with people? Don't they have anything better to do than cook up a fairy tale about the poor migrant who fought all the odds to get a medical degree? Because it's all bullshit, Bryan. Didn't happen like that. I was born a free-citizen. So was my mother and father. It was my grandfather who was born in the East. But he was *not* a migrant either. He moved here before all that shit kicked off."

"As far as I know, my family have always lived in the Western Districts."

"That's what your parents back in Denver might have told you, but what are they *not* telling you? No one wants to admit their family members had any connection to what happened. Your long dead relatives probably lived in the same places the migrants came from. They were just lucky to move west before it all started."

"People in Denver accept the way things are. They say we need to move on from the past."

"Move on, Bryan? If the migrants could have moved on, believe me, they would have gladly moved on by now. Who's stopping them? Answer that."

"We don't have the resources to feed everyone. That's a fact."

"So that's it? Let them starve? Life may be hell on our side of that wall, but god knows what you'd call it on the other side. Only a handful of the original migrants are still alive. Their grandchildren shouldn't suffer just because they were born on the wrong side of a Barrier."

"People in Denver think differently. Perhaps because there are no migrant wards there."

"Bingo. I rest my case."

"I'm sorry they feel that way, Nikki, really I do, but I can't change how they think. From what I've seen since I came here, the consequences of removing every Federation Barrier would mean chaos. You can't deny that."

"Denial is another privilege in a world where counting your privileges means everything. But we can't keep treating migrants like forever criminals, simply to justify our security measures. You've worked those wards. You've seen what it's like. They're not all criminals. They just want to build a better life. But it's hard to build solutions on a foundation of mutual fear."

"Is there a solution? Maybe. But we're doctors, Nikki, not politicians."

The door between the cargo bay and the flight deck opened. A slender woman dressed in military fatigues stepped in. She was a few years older than Nikki—mid-thirties, green eyes, auburn hair tied back under her cap. "Dr. Liana Veron. Vandenberg Lab-15. Call me Liana."

Veron buckled in and shook hands.

"Lab-15? The military's chemical warfare lab?" Nikki said. "Don't be surprised I know. I've dealt with you guys before."

"A pleasant experience, I hope."

"Let's say you're not good at feedback. You disappear behind the Secrecy Act of 2042 like it was some sort of magic curtain. So, what shit-storm are we dealing with here?"

Liana's face broke into a semi-genuine smile—the condescending look the military gave civilians who'd muscled in on their party. "The crew experienced symptoms all at once—seizures, within minutes of each other. When the container ship missed its scheduled course correction, that raised alarm bells with the Maritime Guard. We learned the entire crew had been out of action, so we ordered them to weigh anchor and stay put until we got on board to investigate what made them sick. Any idea what might have caused that?"

"You're asking *me*? Why the hell are we even here?" Nikki replied. "Hazardous materials have been hidden in a shipment of bananas before. If Lab-15's involved, that ship must have military cargo. Leaking barrels of something toxic would be my guess."

"My team will check the ship for chemicals and nerve agents. But viruses and pandemics are Malibu Heights' baby. And they say you're the best, Dr. Akaju."

"I'm only the best because my older colleagues died from the infectious diseases they treated. Otherwise, I'd be a nobody."

"I get it. A different kind of war, but casualties still occur. And Dr. Leysson," Liana checked her data-tab. "Leysson, Bryan, captain, trained at the Sagebrush Veterans Hospital in Denver, posted to the Desert Rangers Medical Corps in Flagstaff, now with the Federal Marines, two-year secondment to Malibu Heights. Sounds like you're on the fast track. Battlefield triage in an urban setting?"

"It's Major Veron, right?" Bryan gestured to the insignias on her jumpsuit. "Yeah, I guess that sums up Malibu Heights, major." He nudged Nikki. "I have a fabulous mentor. We may have some disagreements, but nothing medical."

"Please tell him there are no medals for what we do as civilians," Nikki said. "And we're not allowed to shoot back. As much as we might want to sometimes."

"Good to note."

"Do you two mind if I have something to eat?" Nikki said. "I skipped breakfast and with this turbulence, it's not polite to wretch on an empty stomach."

Dr. Veron unzipped a pocket on her jacket. "I've got some cricket protein bars."

"Yeah, but no thanks. They always stuff that cricket-jerky bullshit in our emergency bags. It's a poor excuse for a meal. I feed it to the birds. If I can find a bird."

Nikki opened her belt-pack and took out a plastic bag containing some unleavened flat-bread, a small jar, and a spoon. Nikki broke the bread in half and dolloped jam on it. "Want some?" she said, holding it out. "It's my mom's. Cassava bread. Homemade kumquat jam. From her own garden. Can't buy this. Not affordably. C'mon, treat yourself."

Bryan took a sample. "Kumquats? Never heard of them."

"Not every fruit is extinct. Some trees have adapted better than others. They just need some love."

"Not for me," Liana replied. "Your mother has her own garden?"

"Garden and an orchard. Pretty rare these days with the agri-domes. Mom works in one part-time. I don't see her as often as I should. I could blame my insane schedule, but that's not the main reason. Getting to mom's place isn't easy—two cross-town shuttles, then an unreliable tram service from Rossmore Station. If you don't time it right, you'll get caught in the middle of shift-change. There's always a security problem when visa-migrants cross the Barrier for work. Who needs that after a day at Malibu Heights?"

"Rossmore Station?" Liana noted. "Your mother *lives* in West Garden Grove? I thought that area was mainly industry."

"There's an enclave of die-hard residents. And if you knew my mom, she's someone who's going to fight change until her last breath. Mom's lived in our family home for over sixty years. She won't move, bless her eccentric old heart. But for me, growing up in West Garden Grove was one long, bad memory. My father died in an accident at the recycling plant near Rossmore Station when I was young. Every time I visit my mom, I can't pass by that plant without thinking about him."

Nikki chewed on the tough bread. She paused and smiled. The sweetness of her mother's jam brought back better memories.

"All right, my blood sugar is up to par. Let's follow the idea of a virus and see where it leads. First rule: infections never respect barriers. Viruses slip through every time visa-workers cross into the Free-Port. That's how the recent avian flu pandemic started and with low vaccination rates in the migrant wards, how it spread so fast. The Barrier has its purpose—as much as I hate what it does—but stopping infections isn't one of them. If we have a new virus on this ship, keeping the bug offshore until we figure this out, is the right answer. Where's the ship coming from again, Liana?"

"The United Andean Republic. It makes a monthly trip from the UAR to the Free-Port. It's one of the few trade routes left that hasn't succumbed to pirates."

"They've had an outbreak of South American hemorrhagic fever in Santiago." Nikki finished her bread and packed away the jar of jam. "Any bleeding from the eyes or ears?"

"None reported. Could it be dengue?"

"Seizures are not atypical for dengue. It doesn't present with neurological symptoms. Sudden onset of symptoms is unusual for any kind of infection. Viral outbreaks progress from person to person. A few would have the early stages of the disease while others are bedridden. With a lot of open space on a container ship, you wouldn't expect the crew to get infected and present symptoms at the same time. To have something happen this quickly, and to everyone all at once, tells me it's not a viral outbreak. The ball's back in your court, Dr. Veron. I'm going to place my bet on a chemical leak."

"Maybe, it's something they'd eaten," Bryan noted. "Food poisoning?"

"A possibility," Nikki replied.

Liana pointed to their kit bags. "Your hazmat suits from the hospital won't cut it if a nerve agent is involved. I think we've got Bryan's size, but what size are you?" she asked Nikki. "I'd say a 14-Tall?"

"That'll work."

Major Armstrong emerged from the flight deck. "ETA five minutes." He pushed a military data-tab into Nikki's hands. "But first, sign this."

The screen displayed a form with the letterhead, 'Federation of Western Military Districts Secrecy Act of 2042'.

"Not this again. We already have security clearance," Nikki replied.

"Not this kind—Level Five."

"Because, why? Your transport may be the best way to get there, but I've responded to dozens of hazmat incidents like this with the security clearances I already have."

"Not this time. Not this case. Now sign."

"What the hell, Major?"

"You don't sign," Armstrong said with a scowl. "And you don't return to Malibu Heights. Those are my orders. It's that simple. There's a migrant field hospital opening up in the Joshua Tree Military District. Care to go?" He tapped the data-tab. "This is Top Security, Level Five, Hazmat Code Eight. Understand? That's as big as it gets. So, do I have to tell you again? What's the issue?"

"Issue?" Nikki sneered. "There's always an issue when the military's involved." Her eyes glared at the marine major as she placed her thumb on his data-tab. "The devil is in the details."

"The devil," Major Armstrong said as he passed the data-tab to Bryan, "may be on that ship."

2 - THE CONTAINER SHIP

As the day heated, the winds grew stronger. The ARV bobbed and weaved over the container ship, the Andean-flagged *Espiritu de Lima*. Marines rappelled down to the deck near the wheelhouse to secure a line. A caged platform swung out from a boom on the ARV to lower the three doctors and their medical equipment.

The ship's captain braced against the handrail in the gusty wind. He was a short, stocky man with dark hair, dressed in a freshly-pressed uniform as if he'd been waiting for a presidential inspection not a black-clad SWAT team. The military's hazmat suits were black, tight-fitting affairs—rubberized protective outerwear, black gas masks, and hoses attached to a compact backpack. The marines carried laser-sighted weapons, the distinctive ion-pulse assault rifles only the military could have.

The captain said in his thick Spanish accent, "The crew's assembled inside."

Nikki and Bryan picked up their gear. Four marines removed Geiger counters from a large black case that had come down with it. The marines descended down a gangway to the deck where the sea containers were stacked. Nikki grabbed Veron's arm. "Have you got intel you're not sharing? Radiation? That's why the crew had seizures?"

"Why do you think I insisted on using our hazmat suits and not yours?"

"A third-year med student could tell you a virus was unlikely to be the cause, so what's with this pretense? We could have been back in Palos Verdes doing real work."

"You deal with your side of things Dr. Akaju, and I'll deal with mine. Your job is to confirm or eliminate a biological reason for these symptoms."

Nikki pressed her mask close to Veron's. "Have there been more incidents like this?"

"Get the fuck out of my face."

Nikki scowled. "I don't like it when someone wastes my time. You know more than you're saying."

"Since when did liking something become a job requirement? You're in emergency response. This is an emergency. So respond."

"Okay, then...I don't like *you*."

"And I don't fucking care."

Veron stormed down the gangway toward the sea containers.

"You heard the lady. Let's go, Akaju. Time to respond. Move it." Major Armstrong pointed to the wheelhouse and waved his men forward.

Inside the helm, a back hatchway led down a metal staircase to the crew's quarters. A crew of twenty-two filled every available space inside a room no bigger than a large classroom.

"Everyone feels fine now," the captain said. "See for yourself. We're all fit and healthy."

"Wait a minute," Armstrong said, his voice muffled behind his mask, his tone angry. "On the CCTV footage you sent, we saw your crew writhing on the floor, having seizures. Others were bouncing off the walls, tongues out, eyeballs turned backward. So, what are you telling us? There was no emergency?"

"Yes, there was. Four hours ago. When we sent the alert." The captain shrugged his shoulders. "But we collapsed and fell asleep. In the hallways, on the deck, didn't matter where. Just like that. Boom, asleep. Then, maybe after a half an hour, we woke up, like it was a bad dream. Everyone back to normal." The captain picked out a crewman standing nearby. "This is Miguel. You saw his seizure on the transmission. Here, check for yourself. Miguel is fine now. See?"

"Step into the corridor." Nikki backed the crewman out of the cramped room. "Bryan, can you set up the diagnostics station please?"

Nikki checked the sailor's forehead with a temperature gun. She swabbed the crewman's mouth and put the stick into a plastic tube which had a tiny needle at one end. She pricked his finger and drew a blood sample. A laser device on the gun etched the sailor's retinal data in barcode form onto the tube's exterior. She handed the tube to Bryan. "Insert it into the instrument here. A reagent coats the throat swab and it's analyzed while the blood sample is being extracted from the other end. Molecular diagnostics in thirty seconds. After the cleaning cycle, we're ready for the next tube."

"That's pretty slick," Bryan observed.

"It may seem that way when you only have a few dozen people to test." Nikki processed the next crew member. "Try doing this with a thousand people. Or more. It gets tedious, real fast. With a mass contagion event like the last bird flu, a virus can spread faster than we can test for it. Believe me, this part of the job is no fun when that happens. Boring as hell."

"I thought you wanted boring."

"The problem with 'boring' is that you soon forget how really boring that can be."

Several minutes into the sampling, a marine ran up the corridor. He pushed past the crew members in line. "Major Armstrong, you're needed on deck. There's a situation in one of the containers."

"UAR migrants?" Armstrong took his pistol from its holster. "No one leaves this area until I get back."

Armstrong's heavy boots clanked on the metal staircase as he climbed up and disappeared from view.

Once they'd sampled the entire crew, Nikki packed the instrument back into its case. "Captain, we need somewhere private to assess the results."

"My office, next to the helm."

Nikki zipped up the bag containing the samples, motioned to Bryan, and proceeded to the staircase.

A marine stepped in front of her. "No one leaves this area." He pushed her back with a stiff-arm thrust. "Those are my orders."

Nikki grabbed the marine's gas mask before he could react and released the suction. "Do you want to know what you've just been exposed to? Maybe I should let you die right here, right now. Because unless you let me through to check these results, I don't know what expert medical care you might need to save your sorry ass. That is, if I feel inclined to give it to you. So, back off, Jack."

The marine slumped against the corridor wall. He wrestled with his mask to restore its tightness.

"Not so brave now, are you, jerk? Now, get out of my way!"

The marine waved them through.

"Gutsy," Bryan said as they climbed the stairs to the helm. "He could have shot you."

"I wish. It would have been a blessing."

* * *

Nikki studied the test results on her data-tab. "Blood chemistry is negative for bio-toxins and parasites, and bacteria-caused food poisoning. There are no unusual viral antibodies in their blood. They all tested positive for avian flu type AVF-7, the typical global variant."

"That's not too surprising, is it?" Bryan replied. "The captain said they'd boarded extra crew members on their last journey from the Free-Port back to the UAR. They had an outbreak of avian flu but everyone recovered well from it. Another bout of flu, nothing special."

"I'm not sure about that," Nikki said. "I detected many different accents. Commercial sailors are mercenaries. They call at ports all over the Pacific on different ships. With a crew as diverse as this, a small percent should have contracted a different strain of the bird flu virus. But in every case, their antibodies indicate they caught type AVF-7. That may be statistically significant."

Liana Veron entered the captain's office. "The report from Lab-15 came back. The molecular data is negative for chemical warfare agents, at least for known toxins."

"Did your Geiger counter goons find anything?" Nikki asked.

Veron scowled. "You mean my highly trained, highly qualified nuclear warfare technicians? Thanks for asking. They didn't find any stray radiation signatures, either below decks or leaking from containers. We can eliminate contraband isotopes or a terrorist dirty bomb. You can sleep better tonight, Dr. Akaju, knowing the military has your back."

"You can call me Nikki."

"So, where does all this leave us?" Bryan asked. "We've got a crew that suffered some kind of attack on their nervous systems, went into debilitating seizures, apparently fell asleep, and then made a full recovery. This is outside any textbook I've ever read."

Nikki shut down her data-tab. She leaned back and rolled her neck to loosen stiff shoulders. "Somebody's not telling us something," she said. "Did you see their eyes? The sailors were frightened. A squad of jackbooted, masked stormtroopers rappelled down—I mean, who wouldn't be scared? But then I noticed their expressions. They ignored the marines, rarely looked their way. They've been boarded many times before—by police, customs officers, the military. Searches like this are a way of life. They were looking at each other, then back at us. I've seen that kind of face in the migrant wards. It's a look that says—shall we tell them, about what really happened? They were checking each other to see who might talk first, who might spill the beans. But no one did."

"We need to interview them," Bryan said. "Today, while their memories are fresh. Before they can cook up some collective bullshit to cover up the truth."

The captain's office door opened with a violent bang. A marine barged in. "Get your gear. You're done."

"But we're not finished here," Nikki said.

"Major Armstrong says you are."

The marine hauled Nikki to her feet. Two others entered and grabbed their instrument cases.

"What's going on, Liana?"

"Our investigation is complete."

"*Your* investigation may be complete. But ours isn't. We need to interview the crew."

"You can do that at the quarantine center."

The marines hustled Nikki and Bryan out of the wheelhouse onto the quarterdeck. The stiff breeze had calmed. Gulls hovered over the ship. As Nikki was frog-marched to the drop platform, shots rang out, the muted *thup, thup* of ion-pulse weapons fire. The sound drew Nikki's eyes to the containers. A group of marines raced across their tops. Two bodies lay prone and motionless. When the marines reached them, they lifted the bodies by the arms and legs, swung them back and forth, and pitched them overboard.

Nikki gasped. "Oh, my god!"

"Up, Dr. Akaju," Major Armstrong said, pointing to the platform. "Show's over."

3 - BONANZA PEAK

Early June, the Spring Mountains
Fifty miles west of the Las Vegas Closed City

Chenzi's lithe, athletic legs ached. Sweat poured down her face as the summit of Bonanza Peak came into sight. Tiny spotter drones flew like insects through the gnarled trunks of the bristlecone pines, encircling her route as she hiked up the switchback trail. High above, an armed counter-threat drone was ready to respond if a mountain lion crossed her path.

"I can't shake this feeling something is watching me," she confided to Emma, her Digital Omni-Companion.

"The drones are watching you," the soothing AI-implant replied.

"Not them, something else."

"Scanning...scout drones confirm you are alone."

"I was alone yesterday. It's the same feeling."

The mountainside was vibrant with yellow rubberweed, bright blue flax, and fiery red paintbrush. As Chenzi reached the summit, the temperature fell from baking hot at sea-level to air-con cool. To the southwest, the residential complexes at the heart of the sprawling eco-habitat of Nova Mercurius stretched from one end of the high desert plain to the other. To the north sat SpacePort Centrum with its prominent rows of rocket gantries.

Chenzi dropped her backpack on the trail, retrieved a flask of water, and sat down on a slab of weathered rock. "Were any security breaches reported during the mission prep yesterday?" she asked DOC-Emma.

"No reports of unauthorized access," Emma replied.

"I still can't seem to shake this feeling. Medical status?"

"Your heart rate, breathing, and pulse rate are elevated. Normal, due to exercise. Detecting abnormal adrenaline levels."

"Like yesterday. Why do I have this persistent feeling of dread?"

"No explanation for the increase in adrenaline. No threats imminent. Deep brain-wave analysis would be required to assess neural abnormalities."

"I'm not crazy, Emma, am I?"

"No comment," the DOC replied. "Unscientific characterization of an undiagnosed behavioral condition. I suggest psychotherapy. Your partner is a psychologist. Do you want me to schedule an appointment with her?"

"I don't need an appointment, dummy. I live with her."

"I do know that."

"How can I avoid telling Marisol about this? Shit—why now? What's wrong with me? I'm an astronaut, Emma. I love the unknown, the unexplained. It usually excites me, but this feeling—what should I do?"

"Sorry, Dr. Zhu. Unable to process. No recommendations."

"That's okay. Thanks anyway."

"You're welcome."

Chenzi closed her eyes, laid her back on the warm rock, and absorbed the sounds of the mountain. The calls of ravens and jays, and the hushed whisper of the pines, filled her ears. She moved her palms across the rock's gritty surface. Tomorrow she would be free of gravity's pull. There was important scientific research to be done and new worlds to explore.

Through closed eyelids, Chenzi imagined the vast dark heavens sparkling with stars, a universe eager to give up its infinite secrets. A burst of blue light wiped the celestial slate clean from her mind. She felt a pressure, like a hand being placed on her stomach. Startled, she bolted upright, her cheeks clammy, her heart racing. Her fear had manifested into something physical and inexplicable.

This is craziness. The thought terrified her. Disqualification from the mission. *No, no. Don't think that.*

Her plan wasn't working. However beautiful the mountain vista, however serene Mother Nature, Dr. Zhu Chenzi couldn't shake the feeling she was being haunted in broad daylight.

Fuck this.

She gathered her stuff, turned her back on the eerie isolation of the wilderness, and scampered back down the trail as if outrunning her fear was the only solution.

***

Chenzi walked into the living room from the small galley kitchen, cocktail in hand—tequila, lime juice, and homemade prickly pear liqueur. The view from the third floor of their apartment in Habitat Urania faced west. The setting sun had fallen behind the rugged peaks of the Nopah Range and the sky was rich with layers of orange and blue.

Marisol Nevis, her partner, strode in from their son's bedroom, her pigtail of dark hair bouncing. "It took three stories to get JoJo to sleep. He's inherited your hyperactive mind." Marisol noticed the V-shaped glass in Chenzi's hand and snatched it away. "You can't have that! What are you thinking? You're on the launch pad tomorrow."

"I'm thinking how sexy you look when you're mad at me. I made it for you, silly. Not me." Chenzi kissed Marisol and pushed her toward the sofa's arm. Marisol smiled, tipped over, and fell into the plush leather cushions. Chenzi slid on top and nibbled Marisol's ears. "There's nothing like sex before a rocket launch to chase the demons away."

"I'd love to meet these demons, but you're guarding them from me," Marisol said, rubbing Chenzi's cheek with hers. "As much as you want to seduce me, talk this through, sweetie. It's the last chance I'll have to get inside your head."

"Talk? Oh, boy, can't that be avoided with an alcoholic aphrodisiac and an erotic grope?"

"That's not how it works. You know that. Speak to me, space imp—or you won't get any of this in bed tonight."

Chenzi kissed her and sat up. "Well, that's a mood killer."

"A famous astrophysicist once said the universe is under no obligation to make sense to you," Marisol replied. "From what you've told me so far, that sums it up."

"That's it?" Chenzi replied. "That's the best you got?"

"No, but I think you need a cuddle." Marisol placed her arm around Chenzi's shoulder and pulled her close. "Let's talk it through. Something new will pop up. It always does."

Chenzi snuggled in. "You know me, when I get in my zone, I'm like a robot. Nothing will stop me unless someone pulls the plug. Yesterday, we were in the capsule doing final checks for the mission, things were going as planned, routine. I'm humming a tune, oblivious to what anyone else was doing. I hadn't noticed the other crew members had finished their work and left. For a few minutes, I was alone in the capsule, three hundred feet above the ground. I was running through some diagnostics when I felt a presence."

"How do you 'feel' a presence?"

"I know. Sounds weird, doesn't it? The feeling was like a heavy stone weighing on my mind. I thought someone was watching me. That broke my concentration. Then I felt as if something was sitting next to me in the capsule. The feeling overwhelmed me. I kept busy and tried to shrug this weirdness off, but I couldn't. My stats spiked and Emma was ready to call a paramedic, which would have bumped me off the mission for sure."

Chenzi sighed, eyes fixed on the stars as the landscape turned dark. "I got out, went to the railing, took some deep breaths. That seemed to work. Emma shut up. Then the whole thing passed. I decided I needed some time to myself, take in some fresh mountain air to revitalize my mind and body."

"Ground Control didn't like the idea of you going off on a hike the day before a launch. It shows how important you are they'd even let you do it."

"Yeah, well, I had an army of drones with me. So much for being alone. But the feeling resurfaced as I climbed the mountain. Despite what the drones kept saying, I was sure I was being watched. I got to the top, sat down, and closed my eyes. Out of nowhere, there was this flash of blue light through my eyelids. And I felt something pressing on my stomach, like a firm hand. It felt so real. You're not going to ground me over this, are you?"

"You can wipe that look of horror off your pretty little face," Marisol replied. "I work with shuttle pilots and lunar colonists and I hear worse things than that. Everyone's human, Chenzi. We're not AI. There's an infinite number of ways we process our fears, and I think I've heard all of them. Most of the time, once whatever adventure they're going on starts, their anxiety goes away. The subconscious builds anticipation. It's an adrenaline pump. If I thought there was any real danger with the reaction you had, I'd have to ground the entire space program."

"It's just a simple case of pre-launch jitters?"

"You have to be a special person to do what you do for a living. Where would we be without pioneers like you, sweetie?" Marisol stroked Chenzi's hair as she lay in her lap. "Adventurers that left Earth's orbit for the first time. Landed on the moon. Colonized it. Those old-time space pioneers weren't any different from the ones that sailed away centuries ago to explore the oceans, discover new lands."

"And kill indigenous people."

"Okay, how are you going to do that with a telescope? Out-stare them?"

"Six months is a long time to be away." Chenzi lifted her head and nestled into Marisol's shoulder. "I'm so going to miss this."

"That statement gets to the core of this. You've always had a problem with distance. Not physical distance, the emotional kind. Yes, you're annoyingly brilliant and hyper-focused, but this anxiety could be caused by pending separation from loved ones. It's not making you dysfunctional, is it? You still code as if you're on meth, right?"

"God, you know me so well."

"Are you afraid that when you come back, we won't be here? Is that it?"

A tear trickled down Chenzi's cheek. Marisol caught it with her finger.

"It is, isn't it? That's what you're afraid of?" Marisol squeezed her tight. "You big softy. So that's what's been bothering you? A little subconscious ferret inside your skull has been telling you, if you stayed here on Earth with us, you'd keep what you have, but if you go, you risk losing everything."

Chenzi's lips pouted in agreement as she fell under the spell of Marisol's deep brown eyes.

"So, this brain ferret, for want of a better word, is trying to frighten you into making the simple choice, which is not to go. Only your whole life has been about making tough choices and succeeding. Frustrated, this fear ferret has invented some kind of 'ghost' that can decide for you, so you won't feel guilty about staying and losing out on the biggest honor of your life, and so you won't blame yourself for betraying who you're meant to be. It was the ghost's fault, not yours."

"Are fear ferrets a real thing in psychology?" Chenzi asked, tickling her partner's chin. "And would they really fit inside a skull? I mean, would there be room for them, with all that other gooey brain stuff, too?" She smiled. "I know what you're doing. Mind tricks. But I'm a scientist. There must be more to it than that."

"Chenzi, you have two PhDs. You don't need another one to figure this out. You are one of a kind—a big dork with a heart of gold. And I love you so much. Get your little ass inside that rocket and jet off to supercharge your calling. In the meantime, JoJo and I will live our mundane lives here on Earth, thinking of you every single minute of every single day until you return. And we will still be here when you do."

4 - EMERGENCY

Sunlight glistened off the solar panels of the International Star Observatory. The cupola windows of the Telescope Dome—a globe at the center of its superstructure, forty meters in diameter—sparkled like diamonds as the ISO traversed its medium Earth orbit in majestic silence.

Light streamed into Zhu Chenzi's sleeping pod in Module Alpha, one of two cylindrical living quarters on opposite sides of the Dome. The patch on her arm triggered a small electric shock and administered a tiny dose of stimulant to wake her. Science Officer Zhu was the only member of the ISO's four-person crew that needed medically-induced sleep. When awake, her mind fired at a thousand amps per second. She'd needed sleep aides since she was a child.

Chenzi checked her pulse rate and blood pressure, arched her back to stretch her spine out of its zero-gravity dormancy, and pushed out of bed.

Emma chirped in her sweet sing-song AI voice, "Good morning, Chenzi."

Chenzi scanned the schedule of her day's assignments. She turned on the communications panel. Three images appeared on the split screen. The station's commander, Cody Brinksen, was eating breakfast on the flight deck located above Module Beta. The flight engineer, Su-mae Scott, was performing routine checks on the oxygen generation equipment in the Life Support Module. And Chenzi's research colleague, Parminder Chadra, was in the Telescope Dome reviewing data from the Pan-Cosmos Super-Array Telescope, or as the crew had affectionately named it, Leonardo.

The 'fifth' member of the crew was the station's main AI interface, nicknamed Boris. Boris was a craft-wide system that oversaw the DOCs of each crew member, managed the station's diagnostics, and connected the ISO to Ground Control.

A light flashed on the comms panel. "Incoming message from Earth for Senior Science Officer Zhu Chenzi," Boris droned.

Chenzi tapped the screen and her six-year-old son's beaming face appeared.

"Hi Space Mommy!" JoJo said. "We been camping."

"Where, bunny?" Chenzi asked.

Her son's head turned. "Where are we?" JoJo paused. "Earth Mommy says Los Animals."

"Huh? You mean Los Alamos?"

"Yes. That's it, Mommy."

"What have you been doing?"

"We been counting lizards."

Chenzi scanned the schedule of her day's assignments as she spoke. "Well, that sounds like fun."

"It's fun. But it's hard."

"Why's that, bunny?" she asked, distracted.

"They hide. So, we have to go out at night. We seen your stars. We saw you!"

She smiled back. "You did? I waved to you. Did you see me?"

"No. You're too far away."

"I know," she said in a faux-sad voice. "I miss you."

"I miss you too, Space Mommy. When you coming home?"

"I've only been gone a few days. It's a long time, sweetie, I know. But you have fun with Earth Mommy while I'm away. We'll be together soon. Love you."

"I love you too."

Marisol's face appeared on the comms screen. "How's it going up there?"

"Great. What are you doing in Los Alamos?"

"My department's been monitoring a group of field researchers based near Santa Fe. They're a good proxy for lunar explorers—

same isolation, similar survival risks. A team was assigned to a follow-up psych evaluation but someone went out sick. I said I couldn't go because of JoJo and they said, that's okay, bring him with you. It's a great experience for him and he's having so much fun. He's busy. He takes after you. How are you coping? Any more bad dreams?"

"No, I'm fine. The drugs help. The crew up here is tight. We're getting a lot done."

"That's good. Keeps your mind focused." She paused. "Hey, I've gotta go. Our son—" Marisol's face blurred as she left the screen. "JoJo, no—"

"What's wrong? Is he all right?"

"Yeah, he's seen a scorpion, and he's trying to pick it up. JoJo, it will sting you. Don't go near it, okay? I gotta go, Chenzi. Love y—"

The transmission ended.

Chenzi floated to the window. The Earth's curved surface with its oceans and clouds was a never-ending source of wonder. She scooted over to her locker and put on her flight suit. The comms panel lit up again, this time, Science Officer Parminder Chadra. Chenzi had studied astrophysics with him at the Nova Mercurius Institute of Technology. As a child prodigy, Chenzi was five years younger, but they graduated in the same year. They'd worked with each other once before, on the moon, before her pregnancy with JoJo sent her back to Earth.

"Didn't you get my message? Leonardo found something interesting," Parminder said.

"A new galaxy? Supernova? Dwarf star?"

"Not saying."

"I hate you, Parminder Chadra," she replied.

"Why are you up so late?"

"Someone messed with my patch."

"You need your sleep," Commander Brinksen said from the flight deck. "You went twenty-four hours without it. That's the last time you lie to me, Officer Zhu. Your activity log ratted you out."

"Damn. Can't you turn that thing off?"

"Setting a record for the longest time awake is not a thing."

"An International Space Agency regulation?"

"No, an order from your commanding officer."

"You're a stuffy old coot."

"It takes all our energy to keep you alive, Chenzi," Brinksen said. "Do us a favor and make it easier."

Chenzi giggled. "So, the regulations allow someone to sedate another crew member? Great! I need Parminder to nap for a few days so I can catch up with his discoveries. It's not fair."

"Stop whining and check out your new galaxy," Parminder replied. "It's in the sector you programmed Leonardo to explore yesterday."

"The Coma Berenices constellation?"

"Hidden behind two galaxies in collision. Your hunch something else was there paid off. Really cool X-ray images. I'll send you the renders."

Chenzi grabbed her data-tab from the charging pad and loaded the files Parminder sent. Flight Engineer Su-mae Scott called from the Life Support Module. On the comms screen, Su-mae probed a sensor panel with a diagnostic wand. "Chenzi, have you experienced any loss of oxygen in Alpha?" she asked.

"Can't say I've noticed anything. Why? Have we got a problem?"

"Boris detected signal faults with Module Beta's air filtration system. But I can't find the cause. Must be an intermittent issue, maybe a power surge through a circuit breaker. I'm worried it could be interference from cosmic radiation. But you're our expert on that."

"That doesn't sound good. I'm on my way to the Dome. Do you want me to make a detour?"

"No, you do your thing. I don't want to interrupt your work. Boris is still trying to help locate the fault. But his advice is annoying, like I'm some kind of dummy."

"He's always like that."

"I'd appreciate a human second opinion on the radiation possibilities after he's completed the diagnostics."

"Sure."

Chenzi pulled her way through Module Alpha toward the Telescope Dome. She called out to Boris, "Display X-ray image, recent Parminder discovery." Her headset projected a hologram of the new galaxy in the space in front of her.

"You have experienced a mild heart palpitation," DOC-Emma said. "Are you okay? Pulse rate is elevated."

"It's called excitement."

"Logged," Emma noted.

Chenzi grabbed the frame of the Telescope Dome's entrance and somersaulted into the large open space.

"Double twist, in a pike position. Nice," Parminder remarked, clapping.

"She's pretty, isn't she?" Chenzi said. "A barred-spiral galaxy, Type SBc. What shall we call her?"

"Maybe it's a him."

Chenzi frowned. "Are we going to have that argument again?"

"How about the Parchenzi Galaxy? Credit to both of us."

"Yuck, that's a super-ugly name. Maybe something Greek or Latin?"

"They must be running out of those names by now. What about Hindu?"

"Okay, Mandarin it is."

Parminder shook his head. "You're impossible."

"How about Fangun de Xiongmao? The Tumbling Panda," Chenzi said.

"You mean *you*?"

"Okay. What about Xiongmao Baobao? Is that better? The Baby Panda galaxy."

"You, only smaller. Okay, I like it."

Parminder had kind eyes and a quick wit, all of which made their partnership special from day one. Chenzi thumped his arm and scooted over to the large control panels tied into Leonardo's data processor.

Code zipped down the screen as Chenzi scanned the data from Leonardo's recent exploration of Coma Berenices. This part of the constellation contained a quadrant rich in massive galaxy clusters, many of which researchers had never studied before. Leonardo's ground-breaking software—programs Chenzi had developed—analyzed the telescope's radio-wave and X-ray data to identify the mass, orientation, and star content of galaxies like Baby Panda, celestial bodies previously hidden by gravitational lensing.

She called up a CGI rendering of the new galaxy and rotated the image. "Oh, Baby Panda, you're so beautiful."

Chenzi spotted an unusual pattern in the data feed and stopped it from scrolling. "What the hell is this?" She partitioned the dataset and asked Boris, "Activate Leonardo's modeling sequence on this star cluster. Report its Cepheid variables and provide preliminary analysis."

"The anomaly is not a star cluster."

"Anomaly? What anomaly?" Chenzi frowned. If an AI didn't know what something was, however strange or new, that was a big concern. The term 'anomaly' was applied only when all possibilities had been exhausted after the AI had processed a shit-load of observations and data, faster than a human could pronounce the word, 'anomaly'.

"Do you want a visible light model of the anomaly?" Boris asked.

"Visible light? But that means whatever this data represents, it's really close—like 'inside our solar system' close. Is this a solar flare?"

"Negative," Boris replied. "Direction of approach of the anomaly precludes solar radiation. Detecting gamma rays within high-energy plasma clouds. Solar system radar places these clusters at a distance of 2.87 astronomical units from the ISO. Plasma clouds are currently inside Jupiter's orbit and approaching Earth at two-thirds light-speed. Calculations indicate collision with the ISO."

"*What*? What are you saying? This anomaly is on a collision course with us?"

"Affirmative. The orbital trajectory of the ISO will intersect with the anomaly in thirty-six minutes and thirteen seconds."

"Parminder? Come and look at this. The data's gone crazy."

"Crazy? Is that a new scientific term I should know?"

"If I knew what this was, I'd find a more suitable adjective for it. Right now, 'crazy' is the best I have. Get over here and look at this. Quickly!"

Leonardo's 3D rendering software produced an image of blue plasma clouds dispersed in clusters in front of a larger, roughly circular energy field of bright yellow light.

"Have you ever seen anything like that before?" Parminder asked.

"No. And whatever it is, we'd better find out soon. It's four hundred and thirty million kilometers away and approaching rapidly. Boris programmed a countdown clock. Telemetry says we're going to be in its path in less than thirty-six minutes."

"Oh, shit. We need to get our heads around this, Chenzi."

"Boris," Chenzi instructed. "Initiate emergency alert on all comms channels. Link me with Commander Brinksen. Send Leonardo's files to ISO Ground Control then patch all crew into a conference call."

The console flashed as the station's emergency signal activated.

"We can run some more models," Parminder said.

"We don't have time for that. Thirty-five minutes and counting," Chenzi replied. "What more do we need to know? We need to assume the worst—a destructive radiation field is on a collision course with the ISO. Ground Control better give us a clearly defined exit strategy or we're going to be the newest cluster of space junk orbiting Earth.""

"Crew status check, emergency protocol, step one," Boris chimed in. Each astronaut's Digital Omni-Companion acted essentially as Boris's 'children'. Communications with him were seamless. "Commander Cody Brinksen located in the Docking Bay. Biologics normal. Flight Engineer Su-mae Scott outside the ISO on EVA, solar panel inspection, heart rate elevated but acceptable. Your requested connection with ISO Ground Control is active and data files sent."

Commander Brinksen appeared as a hologram. "What's up, Chenzi? What's the emergency? I don't see any system malfunctions."

"An unknown high-energy radiation field is approaching the ISO at two-thirds light speed. Kinetic damage is likely and catastrophic. The energy field is closing in on the ISO in thirty-four minutes. We need to get Flight Engineer Scott back inside, now!"

"Roger that. I'll abort her EVA." Brinksen's hologram disappeared.

"The broadcast link with ISO Ground Control is live," Boris announced.

Chenzi and Parminder's heads-up displays projected an image of Dr. Simon Belledeau, Director, Astrophysics, International Star Observatory Program. "The anomaly was picked up by a ground telescope in Cascadia," he said.

"What are we dealing with?" Parminder asked.

"It's possible it's the afterglow of a gamma-ray burst. It's eighty kilometers wide," Belledeau replied. "Leonardo's data models indicate unstable pi mesons decaying into muons, with a high density of neutrinos at their core. It will take time to determine if the source was a black hole, or if it's some kind of stellar flare from outside our solar system. But in either case, we should have seen it enter the solar system before now. But there's no record that Cascadia or any of the other ground telescopes detected it."

"Uh...Control, Chenzi here. Not helpful. We don't have time for a science lesson. Less than thirty-two minutes to impact. What can we expect when it hits us?"

"Roger that. The larger energy field behind the clouds seems to generate a gravitational pull that's disrupting matter that gets in its way. It's dragging asteroids behind it, likely taken in from the dark side of Jupiter when it passed by the planet. They've being sucked into the anomaly's core and then vaporized."

"Well, that's really encouraging," Chenzi quipped. "Last time I checked, we're matter too. We need a plan. Unless you have more important things."

"Stand by, ISO. New data coming in..."

"Su-mae is back inside the ISO," Commander Brinksen reported as the screen displayed the pair in the Docking Bay. "Prepare to evacuate the ISO."

"Evacuate?" Chenzi replied. "But this thing will vaporize the station and with it, Leonardo. Can't the ISO take some evasive measures?"

"This anomaly is coming in too fast," Brinksen said. "And it's enormous. You heard Ground. It's eighty clicks wide. We barely have time to prep the Crew Rescue Vehicle."

"Chenzi," Parminder interjected. "Your countdown clock is going backwards. It now says thirty-nine minutes."

"Going backwards?"

"The anomaly is decelerating," Simon Belledeau said from Ground Control. "Its inbound velocity has reduced to less than one-half light speed."

The countdown clock continued to move up, adding to the calculated time of impact: forty-two minutes...forty-three....

"If the anomaly is slowing down, we have time for a Plan B to save the station," Chenzi replied. "What can we do?"

"ISO Ground," Brinksen said. "Can we accelerate the station out of this thing's way?"

"Stand by." Forty-five seconds seemed like a lifetime before Ground Control responded. "You would need maximum burn on all thrusters, but it's possible."

"Roger that. Boris, work out the vectors with ISO Ground. Su-mae and I will prep the Crew Rescue Vehicle."

"I need to shut Leonardo down," Chenzi said.

"Do it quickly. Emergency protocols take priority. Helmets on. Everyone needs to focus and be ready to evacuate," Brinksen replied. "Control, we need re-entry co-ordinates for the CRV in case we need to use it."

"Countdown has peaked at forty-eight minutes, but the clock is ticking down again," Chenzi said. "The anomaly has attained a new stable velocity."

"Then we'd better get to work," Brinksen ordered.

5 - FAMILY SECRETS

Inside the kitchen of her small bungalow, Nikki's mother, Marcia Akaju, scraped a cassava root and slipped the waxy tuber into a pot of water on the floor. She discarded its peel into a wicker basket and picked up another. Behind her, large containers of cassava flour filled the shelves. The flickering light from a single candle bounced from one glass jar to another. Shadows from the movement of her arms danced across the ceiling.

"Mom, what are you doing?" Nikki said as she entered.

The old woman grumped without breaking stride. "You think cassava peels itself?"

"That's not what I meant." Her mother was getting frail despite the strength in her arms. She'd lost weight since the last time Nikki saw her, and she could tell her mother's eyesight was failing. Nikki glanced at her sat-link. "It's getting late. Don't you have work tomorrow? You need your rest."

Marcia ran the knife over the tuber's rough brown rind. "Work makes you strong. Keeps you alive and feeling young. Hard work never hurt anyone."

Nikki placed her hand over her mother's to still its feverish pace. "Stop, Mom. Bedtime."

Marcia looked up with sheepish eyes. "Are you staying tonight? You never stay. Why don't you ever stay with your mother?"

"You know I can't. I wish I could, but I'm on call in a few hours."

"It's dark outside. The streets are dangerous. How are you getting to the hospital from here? You can't take a night tram. They're full of crazy people who ride them all night without getting off."

"The hospital arranged a police cruiser to pick me up and take me to Rossmore Station. It will be here soon."

"The police? No, you can't trust the police, Nikki. No, no, you can't ride with them."

"Mom, not that again. If this neighborhood is so dangerous, and you can't trust the police, why don't you move? You could stay with me in Malibu Heights until an apartment comes available."

"An apartment? What, no yard? No garden? How would I feed myself? How would I earn money from cassava?" Marcia waved a tuber at her daughter. "It's okay for you. You're a doctor. Good pay. You can live anywhere you want. This is my home, Nikki. My friends are here. My life is here. It's not just a bed to sleep in. Who would tend my plants if I didn't? Who even knows how to do that these days? What about the people I sell my flour to, that depend on cassava for their food? The markets don't have enough food as it is. I'm so lucky your grandfather bought the extra land behind this house. It would be spitting on his grave if I left everything he and your father built together."

"I know how important this place is to you."

"Do you? I was only four when we moved into this house. The garden was nothing like it is now. It took years for your grandfather to dig up the rubble and stones, and bring in proper soil. Years and years. After I got married and we moved in with your grandparents, your father helped him plant those trees. Lemons. Kumquats. It's not like anything can grow here, in this heat, in this dry soil. We were blessed when the well was dug, and blessed again when it didn't dry up. How else could we grow cassava? After your father died, this garden fed the two of us. Have you forgotten? The extra income put you through med school. Leave here? No, I couldn't. And you shouldn't want me to."

Marcia rose stiffly and picked up the basket of cassava peels. She shuffled to the kitchen door. "Those marks on your face—have you been mugged?"

"It's nothing. I told you, it's my job. We go to rough places so I can expect to get roughed up sometimes. It's not a big deal. An occupational hazard."

"I don't believe you. I'm your mother. You think I don't know? Has someone been following you?"

"*No*, Mom. Don't worry yourself."

Marcia opened the creaky back door into the garden. She dumped the basket of peels into the compost pile, then stood in silence, empty basket in hand, staring into the night sky. The desert air had chilled. She shivered.

Nikki rubbed her shoulders. "What's wrong, Mom? Is this about Dad? I forgot it's the anniversary of his death. It's not good to dwell on these terrible memories, things you can't change."

"Some days, memories—even the bad ones—are my only companions. I have a good reason to be worried. Nikki. They've been *here*, in my neighborhood. I've seen them skulking around, peering into the garden. I didn't think they would ever find me."

"*Who* Mom? They're just envious neighbors. You've talked like this before, about some kind of conspiracy, a secret society following you. I wish you'd stop being so paranoid. We looked into this months ago and the police said they found nothing. Then they said they would charge you if you didn't stop harassing them. That's when you decided you couldn't trust them anymore."

"You can't. They're everywhere. You can't trust anyone in authority."

"Oh, not this *again*." Nikki hugged her mother and stroked her hair. "Nothing has ever happened to you, or to me—not now, not before, never, right? No one has raided your garden, have they? The police have done nothing but keep you safe."

Marcia's face tensed. She touched her daughter's cheek. "I can see it in your eyes. You didn't believe what I told the police back then, and you don't believe me now." She sighed and turned back toward the candlelight coming from the kitchen. "My own daughter—you hear what I say, Nikki, but you don't listen to the words being said. Always in such a hurry. Always pre-occupied with what's going on around *you*."

Marcia went back inside, a scowl on her face. She opened the tap on the sink and washed her hands under the slow drizzle of the District's tepid water. "It's not just about me. You're in danger too."

"Why?"

"It's been a long time since Grandma Adriana passed. Have you been talking to someone about her? I thought I'd been so careful all these years. I didn't think I would ever need to warn you."

"This is about grandma? Warn me about *what*, Mom?"

Marcia fell silent. The edges of her lips bent. Her eyes watered. She squinted and tears rolled down her cheeks. "I thought Uncle Dante's secrets had died with your grandmother. How foolish of me to think that."

"Uncle Dante?"

"He was your grandma's uncle but that's how I knew him when I grew up. You were only two years old when Uncle Dante died. By then, he was a frail man in his late nineties. After his death, your grandma realized how important it was to disconnect all of us from his research."

"Disconnect us?"

Marcia sat down at the table and swiped scraps of cassava peel into the basket. "This all happened a very long time ago. She didn't want these things traced back to us."

"What things? Mom, you're tired and you're making absolutely no sense. You've always been so reluctant to talk to me about our family's roots in Brazil. Is this why?"

"Uncle Dante Parks wasn't from Brazil. He was an African-American like your father. He and his identical twin brother Amare were both doctors, experts in fertility. They were interested in the genetics behind why some families produced twins, generation after generation. They met Ana, your great-grandmother, and her sister Zella during a trip to a village in Brazil filled with identical twins like they were. Zella and Ana were more than just a part of their research studies. They became Dante and Amare's guides and translators. They were very close and soon it grew to be more than that."

"Your grandmother Ana had a twin sister? You never told me that." Nikki pulled up a stool and sat beside her. "I've always wanted to know more about how she came here."

"Dante Parks visited Brazil several times and every time he came home, he realized he couldn't leave her sister Zella behind. They got married, then Dante sponsored Ana to come to America to work at the fertility clinic the brothers ran at a place called Adobe Park near Santa Fe. It wasn't long before his brother Amare fell in love with Ana. She became pregnant with my mother, your Grandma Adriana. But there was a problem. A big one. Amare was already married and his wife was pregnant, too."

"That never ends well."

"No, it doesn't. And it got worse for all of them. In 2006, Amare went to Japan on a research trip and never came home. Uncle Dante believed people who wanted to suppress their research murdered him there. You might call these people members of a 'secret society', but they're more than that, Nikki. Call them what you want, but they're *evil*. They will kill anyone that finds out the truth."

"Truth about what? Why haven't you explained all this to me before?"

She squeezed Nikki's hands. "I thought it best you knew *nothing*. Because knowing puts you in danger. But open your mind, Nikki. Then you will truly hear what I'm saying." She grabbed Nikki's hand and drew her close. "It's time to listen, Nikki. Really listen."

"I don't like to see you this upset, Mom. Of course, I will."

"After Amare was murdered in Japan, Ana moved in with her sister and Uncle Dante in Santa Fe. They looked after Ana and her new baby, your Grandma Adriana. Twenty years later, Uncle Dante paid to send my mother to medical school in Denver. That's where she met Grandpa. After they got married, they moved here, the old state of California, and I was born a few years later."

Her mother's eyes wandered into the dark past. "In the 2030s, it was not a good time for people of science like Uncle Dante. His research had found something so dangerous he tried to get the old American Congress to understand what he'd discovered. People inside the academic world branded him a lunatic whose theories should be ignored because they didn't want anyone to know what he'd found out. In those days, you could tell lies louder and louder as many times as you wanted until people believed you. I remember my father saying the world had descended into madness. I was only six and I didn't really understand what he was talking about. I just remember my parents being very afraid."

The candlelight reflected in her mother's moist eyes. "Those were the years when millions and millions of people were dying all around the world. I was far too young to understand what a famine was, or a pandemic, or a nuclear war. Then one day, my mother said people in America were choosing sides and preparing to go to war with each other. I asked why and she said they wanted to die for the lies they believed in. That confused me even more."

"This was how the Constitutional War started?"

"Yes. California didn't want any part of what was about to happen and declared its independence. The national government fell apart and Uncle Dante's testimony to Congress was never heard. The war between the states of the East and the South began a few weeks later."

"When did Uncle Dante come to live with Grandma?"

"Many years later. After Zella and Ana died during the typhoid outbreak in Los Angeles. It was terrible. It started in the migrant districts and spread like a brush fire. No one was vaccinated back then and thousands died. Vaccination clinics are the only free medical services we provide the Wards. Not to protect migrants, but to protect *us* from them."

"I'm not sure how long that will last, Mom. These marks on my face—it happened in Ward 6. They overran one of the clinics to steal supplies."

"Can you blame them? Anyway, Uncle Dante didn't really live with Grandma. She let him stay in her obstetrics clinic so he could continue his research in secret. He moved from one safe house to another, hidden by people in the medical fields who were open-minded about his work, people who understood its significance. Grandma helped him write up his final research papers before he died."

"When I was a little girl, I remember Grandpa saying he tried to find his family who lived in the East when the war started. He was sure they joined the migration. But he didn't really want to talk about it."

"No child should hear what it was like, it was too terrible to put into words. So many died from radiation sickness. You're a doctor, you would know what kind of suffering that was. Thousands of others starved to death or were murdered for the shirts on their backs. When the war ended, survival was the only goal. What else could the migrants have done, except cross a thousand miles of unforgiving desert to find safety, to find somewhere no bombs had been dropped?"

"Did Grandpa ever find any of his relatives?"

"No, it was hopeless. A big tidal wave of chaos had swept in from the desert. Refugees were constantly moving from camp to camp. Communications were poor and there were no records. And because they weren't segregated, they acted like animals to each other. Neither side could accept defeat even though both sides lost everything in that war. Our military was forced to clamp down hard to restore order. The Closed Cities were created and the Barriers built. For many years after that, access to the new migrant districts was impossible. Your grandfather died never knowing if any of his family made it."

"Was the hatred between them so great, they started a nuclear war? What reason could they possibly have, to do something as disastrous as that?"

"When I was little, Nikki, teachers said the war started over a misunderstanding, an accident. But how could dropping a nuclear bomb be an accident? But that's what we were taught. Accidental or not, my father said it turned neighbors arguing over the fence into something way more dangerous than telling lies. By the time you started school, those history lessons were dropped. It was left to older people like me to pass down what we remembered. And that guaranteed this history would be forgotten. People today have no idea how it began, just that it happened, and it was awful."

Nikki's sat-link pinged. Its screen flashed a message. "Oh, no. I've got to go, Mom. My ride will be here in five minutes. But I want to hear more. I want to know everything."

Marcia limped to the door that led out of the kitchen. "Before you go, I want to show you something very important."

Her mother's bedroom was down the hall. It was a humble room with little decoration. Next to her bed was a wardrobe made of the wood from old pallets. Marcia opened its doors and removed a pile of blankets from the lower shelf. "Under here." She knelt down and winced. "My knees aren't what they used to be, Nikki. Pull on that for me, will you?"

At the back of the cupboard was a wooden panel with two metal handles. Hidden behind the back of the wardrobe, in an opening cut out of the brickwork, was a rectangular space about three feet wide and a foot tall. Tucked inside was a narrow metal box—a long gray container with a lid hinged halfway down its length.

Nikki took out the box and placed it on the floor. "What's this?"

Her mother wiped the dust off the lid with her apron. "Back in the old days when we had something called banks, they had a special vault for boxes like this. They called them safety deposit boxes. People used them to keep jewelry and cash, and old paper records like birth certificates and land deeds. Paper and cash are obsolete ideas now. When the bank closed, they gave her the box."

Marcia opened its hinged lid. She lifted out a faded photograph and gave it to Nikki.

"I've never seen this one before. This is me...with Grandma. How old was I?"

"You were six. The contents of this box are all that's left to remember your Grandma Adriana." Marcia's hand gripped her daughter's arm. She lifted out some yellowed folders. "These papers may look like junk to you, but believe me, they're not. If something was to happen, promise me, Nikki, you'll not throw any of it away."

"Nothing's going to happen to you, Mom. Stop saying things like that." Nikki gave her a hug. "Memories of Grandma are precious to me, too. If you're saying this stuff is important, of course I'll treasure it. I promise."

The doorbell rang. Nikki checked her sat-link. "The police are here. I'm sorry, Mom. I really have to go. Think about what I said. Come live nearer to me."

Marcia smiled. "And leave my cassava plants? They would die. Then I would die. Now that you're on your own, these are my babies. They need my protection."

"Oh *really*, Mom? I'll always be your number one baby."

Marcia wandered back to the kitchen and grabbed several jars of homemade jam from the cupboard.

At the door, she kissed Nikki on the cheek. "Go, hon. Do your doctor stuff. I'll be fine. There's probably nothing to worry about. Just don't forget about your mom again. And take some kumquat jam with you. It's freshly made."

6 - THE ANOMALY

Chenzi repositioned the cameras outside the Telescope Dome. "The area in front of the anomaly has filled with what looks like semi-transparent dark blue clouds. Do you see them?" She aligned Leonardo's external boom and focused its gamma-ray detectors on the strange clusters of plasma. "What are they?"

"Copy that," Director Belledeau said from ISO Ground Control. "We're calling them Jupiter clouds, after the anomaly's origin. They have a unique radiation profile, unlike anything in our database. We have no idea what they are."

"That's not good," Chenzi replied.

"Control," Commander Brinksen said from the flight deck. "Orbital vectors programmed. We are go for thruster burn on your command."

"Roger that, ISO. The countdown clock is going back up, which means the anomaly has slowed its approach again. You have fifteen minutes to impact."

"It's slowing down?" Brinksen asked. "Do we need to recalculate the CRV's escape vector?"

"Negative, ISO. Initiate thruster burn in five minutes with full CRV evacuation protocols in place."

"Chenzi, I'm sorry, you're out of time," Brinksen said. "Lock Leonardo down and leave. Crew, proceed to the Docking Bay. We'll fire up the station's thrusters once we're inside the CRV. If anything goes wrong with the burn, we can jettison from the ISO."

Parminder exited the Telescope Dome through a cross-access tunnel that led into the Docking Bay. On her way out, Chenzi patted

Leonardo's massive housing. "Just a slight detour in space-time, buddy. Don't worry. I'm coming back."

A strong vibration shook the ISO. Red warning lights flashed across every panel on the wall. An alarm sounded, a pulsating siren. The jolt knocked Chenzi away from Leonardo. Inside the Telescope Dome, lights flickered and died, plunging the entire chamber into darkness. The heads-up display in Chenzi's helmet flashed with alerts. "Commander, what's happening?"

No answer.

Chenzi clung to Leonardo's console as the ISO shook again. "Boris, comms are down. Situation report."

"Critical power failure."

"I can see that. What are you doing about it?"

"Primary comms channels damaged. Re-routing to back-up circuits. Station integrity checks underway. Emergency life support engaged."

Strange colored lights streamed through the observation cupola, a section of windows at the top of the Dome where the massive telescope projected into space. Chenzi crouched her body against the console, pushed up to reach them, and looked outside. The anomaly—previously an amorphous swirl of vaporous yellow light—had coalesced into a distinctive aqua-blue ring. Inside the ring, strands of darker cobalt-blue energy rotated around a central black void. Suddenly, a bright yellow dot appeared in the center of the void, expanded in a violent rush of light, and pushed the Jupiter clouds of blue plasma toward the station.

"Radiation alert," Boris said. "Unknown radiation field approaching ISO in T-minus ten seconds, nine, eight, seven..."

"Oh geez, no!" Chenzi exclaimed. "What the—?"

The observation windows filled with the intense blue light of the advancing Jupiter clouds. Chenzi pushed back from the window. A swirling blue mist penetrated the station's walls, covering her in a rush of colored gas that flowed from one side of the Telescope Dome to the other. Her skin prickled like she was being stung by bees.

"No, no—" she cried out. "Emma, help!"

No answer.

She clutched at her helmet, a reflex, a vain attempt to soothe the stings on her face. "Boris—what's happening?"

No answer.

The blue mist inside the Telescope Dome disappeared through the opposite wall as quickly as it had arrived. The prickles that crawled across her skin faded away. "Boris—are you there? Where'd you go?"

Silence.

Chenzi pushed away from Leonardo to reach an observation window that faced Earth. Swirling blue Jupiter clouds were moving rapidly away from the ISO, heading toward the planet's atmosphere. Her mind raced as she tried to process this strange event. *What the hell was that?*

The flashes from the emergency lights inside the Dome ceased. The siren turned off. A moment of absolute silence stopped her racing thoughts.

"Commander Brinksen? Are you there?"

No reply.

"Parminder? Su-mae? Anyone? Boris?"

Cabin lights and computer screens came back on.

"Medical emergency," Boris droned. "Crew DOCs reporting in. Commander Cody Brinksen—seizure, neurological malfunction. Flight Engineer Su-mae Scott—seizure, neurological malfunction. Science Officer Parminder Chadra—seizure, neurological malfunction. Analyzing bio-data. Seizures are generalized tonic-clonic. DOCs are synthesizing sodium channel blockers. Activating auto-injection via transdermal patch. Patients injected."

Chenzi pushed off to reach the cross-access tunnel, a padded link three meters in diameter, four meters long. Su-mae floated inside, her body jerking from the waist. Her arms flung back and forth, banging uncontrollably against the tunnel's roof. Chenzi grabbed her suit and pulled her off the ceiling. Her eyes had rolled into the back of her head. Foamy spit floated out of her mouth and coated the inside of her helmet. She tried to pin Su-mae's arms, but they refused to settle. Her flailing forced Chenzi to let her go.

"Boris, get Sue-mae's DOC working on her!"

"Anti-seizure medication ineffective," Boris replied.

She pushed Su-mae's body out of the way and entered the main chamber of the Docking Bay, a cube five meters high with multiple hatchways. Commander Brinksen and Parminder Chadra floated around its assembly area like untethered balloons in a strong wind. Their bodies twisted and jerked, springing off the Docking Bay's walls as they made contact.

"All patients unresponsive to treatment," Boris's voice droned. "Blood pressure and pulse erratic. Applying sedatives. Inducing coma to protect vital organs."

"Damn it, Boris! That will render the crew useless."

"Transdermal injections complete. DOCs reporting... patient seizures now under control."

Chenzi pulled the limp bodies of Brinksen and Chadra down to floor level and pinned their safety harnesses to a strut. "Boris, have you restored comms with Ground Control?"

"Affirmative. Medical records generated and transmitted. Crew members Cody Brinksen, Su-mae Scott, and Parminder Chadra, stable but comatose."

"Comatose? Thanks for that, Boris. Just what I always wanted."

"You're welcome."

To Chenzi's left was the docking port for re-supply shuttles, to her right, the EVA air lock, and in front of her, the hatchway that led to the Crew Rescue Vehicle. "Ground Control, this is Science Officer Zhu Chenzi. Some kind of energy burst has hit the ISO. One of those Jupiter clouds passed through us. Damage to the ISO unknown. Radiation exposure has left the rest of the crew incapacitated. I need help with the thruster burn sequence."

"Negative on the thruster burn. Can you get the crew's bodies into the CRV?"

"Ground, the ISO risks collision with the anomaly. Repeat, I request new timing for a thruster burn."

"You are authorized to abandon the ISO, Chenzi."

"That's a big fat negative, Control. This station took a decade of aerospace engineering and three years of orbital construction. I can't abandon it. Are you crazy?"

"The anomaly is still on its collision course with the ISO. You will be outside the envelope of safety in five minutes, Chenzi," Belledeau said. "Get everyone, including yourself, into the Crew Rescue Vehicle. We will coordinate with Boris to control your re-entry descent."

"Damn it, we have to move the station out of the way of this thing's path!"

"You can't initiate thruster burn and deploy the CRV in the time available, Chenzi. You can only do one of those things, not both."

"Just watch me."

Chenzi scooted out of the Docking Bay and retrieved Flight Engineer Scott. One by one, she pushed the limp bodies of the crew through the access hatch into the CRV, placed each in a seat, buckled them into safety harnesses, and connected their helmets to the CRV's on-board oxygen supply.

"Time's up, Chenzi," Belledeau said. "Get out of there!"

"Fuck, do you not understand English? I'm not going anywhere. Initiate CRV life support monitors, Boris."

"Initiated. Complete."

Chenzi left the CRV, closed the hatch behind her, and decompressed the air lock connecting the escape pod to the Docking Bay. "Boris, apply auxiliary station thrusters to align the CRV for re-entry."

The ISO rotated. "Aligned," Boris replied.

"Initiate undocking sequence. You are go for CRV separation and auto-descent."

"Sequence commenced. Crew Rescue Vehicle has detached from the station."

"Control, this is Science Officer Zhu Chenzi. I have deployed the CRV, and it's under auto-control for re-entry into Earth's atmosphere. Three crew members aboard. Damn it, I'm staying with the ISO. So, unless you help me with the thruster burn, I'll have a ringside seat for a very personal and terminal fireworks show."

"What the hell are you playing at, Dr. Zhu?" Belledeau said.

"Thruster burn, Control. *Now*—damn it!"

"Find a place to strap in."

She flipped down a jump-seat. Its harness buckle clicked. "Way ahead of you. I'm secure."

"Boris, this is ISO Ground Control. We are go for thruster burn. Initiate ISO re-positioning program."

"Program loaded. Sequence started."

Several short bursts from small auxiliary jets rotated the ISO. Chenzi's view through the Docking Bay's windows changed from an aspect that directly faced the bright ring of the anomaly to one that displayed a broad vista of Earth.

"Re-orientation complete," Boris said. "Main thruster burn in T-minus ten seconds, nine, eight, seven..."

The station's rockets engaged at maximum power. Once the burn completed, the feeling of acceleration faded. The only indication the station had accelerated was visual—the Earth below the ISO passed by her window at an ever-increasing rate.

"Burn complete," Boris announced. "Thrusters shut down. Target velocity reached and stable. High Earth orbit in T-minus two minutes."

"Okay, Control," Chenzi said. "I'm just a passenger now. Status please? Did the burn work? Has the ISO avoided collision?"

"Stand by, ISO."

"Stand by? Are we still on a collision course with this thing or not?"

"Stand by, ISO."

"What the hell, Control?"

"We have a change in the anomaly."

"A change? What kind of change? Has it changed direction? Is it still on course to hit the ISO or what? Give me some idea of what changed, damn it!"

"The energy anomaly is no longer moving toward Earth," Belledeau reported.

"Say again, Control?"

"The energy anomaly has stopped its approach and is holding a fixed position at a distance of thirty-six thousand kilometers above Earth."

"Which means I'm safe, right?"

"Affirmative. The burn is now irrelevant. Collision has been avoided."

"What about the CRV? The crew?"

"They're re-entering Earth's atmosphere now. Life Support says they're still comatose but not critical, unresponsive to our communications. We will assess them as soon as we recover the capsule."

"And the anomaly? Any more information on what it is? Its origin?"

"Chenzi, how are you feeling? Your blood pressure is elevated. You had quite an ordeal."

"I was fine until you changed the subject. The anomaly—what are we dealing with?"

"Everyone on the ground is trying to answer your question. In the meantime, gather as much data on the anomaly as possible."

"What the hell? In other words, keep doing what I'm good at?"

"Affirmative. For as long as the anomaly allows. Get some rest, Chenzi. You're going to need it."

7 - THE SIGHTING

Outside Malibu Heights Hospital, a gentle wind rustled the leaves of the acacia trees that surrounded a solitary figure sitting on a bench. The lights of the communities along the coast flickered in the cooling air as Nikki watched the setting sun cast a shimmering glow across the waters of the Pacific Ocean. Behind the hospital, wind turbines, perched like sentinels on the hillsides of the Santa Monica Mountains, slowed to a crawl.

The sudden wail of curfew sirens startled her. In ten minutes, the nightly power-saving blackout would begin. Nikki had lost track of time. *Must try calling again,* she fretted. Her sat-link connected with her mother's number. *Pick up, Mom.* No answer.

Footsteps echoed down the gravel path.

"There you are," Bryan Leysson said. "Where have you been all day?"

"Yeah, sorry. I got home late yesterday from visiting my mother and changed my shift to get some sleep." Nikki straightened and shook off her fractious daydream. "I've called her several times tonight, but she's not returning my messages. I'm worried. She thinks someone's been following her. I thought she'd calmed down, but being alone, she could have worked herself into a panic again."

"Has she called the police?"

"She thinks they're part of the problem. Maybe I shouldn't worry so much. She's probably at a neighbor's and her sat-link's battery has run down. I need to get her a new one. Anyway, how about you? I heard you checked out the crew from the container ship. How are they? Any recurrence of symptoms?"

"No, they seem healthy, just pissed off. I guess they were expecting a few nights out on the town. Instead, they're in quarantine under armed guard, stuck in the nastiest part of the Free-Port I've seen. It's not a whole lot better than the Wards."

"Did they say anything more about the incident that got them quarantined?"

"None of the crew said a word. Nothing important. But I noticed the same odd looks again. You were right about them knowing something. Whatever it is, they're still not telling. The results from their latest blood tests indicate we don't have any medical reasons for holding them. I've told the authorities to shorten their quarantine."

"I can't help feeling there was something suspicious lurking on that ship. I just can't put my finger on what."

The distant sirens stopped wailing. As the blackout began, the lights of the Free-Port of Los Angeles went out. Critical facilities like Malibu Heights were exempt. The building behind them dimmed as its generators kicked in. As the night air cooled, the gentle wind that had rustled the trees withered. The orange-tinged sunset faded, and the coastline became a black, winding void under a cloudless, starlit sky.

"How are you doing, Nikki?" Bryan said, breaking the moment of quiet. "You know, after what happened in Ward 6?"

"Forgotten. That's the best strategy to keep sane—forget. You can't change anything really big, so I try to be thankful for the little things that come my way." Nikki gestured to the darkened city. "Is there a tiny slice of heaven buried inside that massive blob of hell? My mother's found one, bless her. It's her garden. You were right about me. Maybe my own slice of heaven comes with every new shot of adrenaline. The next call-out makes me forget the pain of the one before."

An unexpected gust of wind picked up the dead leaves in the park—a sudden swirling wind that rocked the trees back and forth. Patches of blue light appeared high in the night sky. Static electricity raised the hairs on the back of Nikki's neck. She stood up. "What is that?"

Clouds of sparkling blue lights descended on the Free-Port, up and down the coast, settling like squalls of fluorescent rain in dense patches. All over Palos Verdes, strange lights illuminated buildings. As the sparkles dimmed, total darkness returned. An uneasy silence haunted the night. Rays of moonlight danced across the ocean's still waters as if nothing had happened. Time seemed to have stood still.

The bright flash of an explosion lit up the streets near the Barrier. Flames billowed skyward, casting their light over the industrial area near Rossmore Station. A few moments later, the sound of the explosion arrived. Distant sirens wailed as the flashing lights of emergency vehicles crept through the cityscape.

"My adrenaline's kicking in. I have a feeling my shift is about to start."

"And mine isn't ending," Bryan said.

The doors at the main entrance of Malibu Heights Hospital opened and Dr. Astrid Stenmuir ran toward them. "Suit up! I need as many emergency response teams as possible. We're getting multiple call-outs, all over the Free-Port. Traffic accidents. Heart attacks. Seizures. All over Palos Verdes. Weirdest thing. What could cause that?"

"Seizures?" Nikki said. "Did you say *seizures*?"

***

Bryan pressed his nose against the window of the air ambulance and scanned the sky. "The military will try to convince us that what we saw with our own eyes, we didn't actually see."

"We saw those lights. The whole city saw them."

An alert flashed in Nikki's heads-up display, notes from Dispatch. She leaned against Bryan and looked out the window. "We've got company. Over there. A heavy transport flying alongside, with ground jeeps and military paramedics."

Nikki's sat-link flashed—incoming message. She tapped and Astrid Stenmuir's hologram appeared.

"Whatever fell from the sky caused a riot at shift change in the walkway between Rossmore Station and an aerospace component factory," Stenmuir said. "Supervisors panicked and fled to a security office for shelter. Work-visa migrants shed their tracking bracelets and looted a food warehouse. The situation escalated as more migrants shed their tags. They torched a fuel depot. Several buildings nearby are in flames. The situation on the ground is dynamic and getting worse."

"Dispatch says we're responding to seizures," Nikki replied. "Riots and burning buildings don't cause seizures."

"A fire brigade found people in a state of what they described as epileptic fits. The Los Alamitos Military Base declared a Hazmat incident, and we were called in. That's all I know."

"Are we going to walk into another Ward 6 shit-storm, Astrid? We have no security detail this time."

"The area is being flooded with military. Everything with a laser-sight has been mobilized. Look, I have to go. We have incoming trauma patients. Do what you can, but don't take any unnecessary risks. I can't lose any more personnel."

"Thanks for the love, Dr. Stenmuir. My life is a catalog of risks, whether you label them unnecessary or not."

Nikki closed the comms-link. "Asshole."

The air ambulance descended and bumped down hard in a supermarket parking lot. Nikki was the first off. On the ground, columns of armored personnel carriers had disgorged heavily armed police who fanned out in search of looters. Across from the parking lot, the Long Beach Fire Service struggled to contain the spread of a fire that had engulfed two adjacent factories. Flames soared into the night sky. The largest of two air ambulances sent from Malibu Heights landed next, in the last remaining open spot, right in the middle of a group of APCs and police aero-cruisers. Every available patch of asphalt was now occupied.

Nikki activated her sat-link. "Dispatch, this is a total cluster-fuck. We're stuck in a traffic jam that's blocking us from unloading our jeeps." She shouted across the parking lot. "Bryan, tell the medics to unload their kits from the jeeps. We've got to go on foot from here."

"On foot? Out there? Shit, if we're not careful, these security goons might mistake us for rioters and shoot us."

"You're right." Nikki got on the comms again. "We need a dedicated police escort, Dispatch. Don't argue with me. It's not optional. We're not on vacation."

As she helped the paramedics gather their gear from the jeeps, a heavy finger tapped hard on her shoulder. She turned. "Oh fuck, no. Not you. I've got enough problems."

A smile expanded two scars running across one cheek. "You're attracted to danger like a fly to shit, aren't you?" Major Armstrong said. "Protection? My middle name. I'm going to send a big fat bill to Malibu Heights to cover the stench of this one. There'll be a party in the barracks tonight. The booze is on you."

"Look, Armstrong, I don't know where you get your pay from, but we're both paid to help the same people." She pointed toward the crowded street. "This time, I'm in charge. So, no fucking forms need to be signed. I need you to do as I say, and we'll get through the night without any fuss."

He saluted. "Major Ozzie Armstrong at your disposal, doc. Just remember, you can bark at me all you want, but my marines take their orders from only one big dog and it ain't you."

"We're moving out," Nikki yelled to her team of medics. "This is Major Doberman, Federal Marines." She pointed to the squad that had formed ranks behind him. "If anyone has any doggy treats, save them until he and his wolf pack get us back here safely. Let's go, people. We've got patients out there."

Armstrong twirled a finger in the air and pointed. "This way."

"How do you know where we should go?"

"Follow me, lady. Seizures, right?"

"You know about that?"

"You're not the only hound on this trail, Akaju."

"Hey, wait a sec," Nikki said. "Why was an ARV full of marines so close in the first place? This isn't a federal military incident. It's a district civil response."

"You ask some dumb questions, don't you? We're based out of Los Alamitos. This is our neighborhood. We got the first call."

"For seizures?"

"Like I said, lady. We got the first call. Now get your ass in gear."

"Hey, I give the orders, remember?"

"Whatever you say."

Darkness swallowed the industrial zone the further away from the fires they marched. After four blocks, Armstrong signaled with raised fist for his platoon to halt, lowered his weapon, and turned his flashlight straight ahead. Nikki ran to the front to see what his light was pointing at.

A throng of people slowly shuffled toward them as if in a trance. A slim woman in her mid-thirties tottered from side to side and nearly walked straight into a pole. Nikki ran up to her and shone a light into the woman's eyes. "Good. Pupils constricting normally." She checked her forehead. "Temperature also normal. How do you feel?"

"Like I just woke up."

"Bryan," Nikki shouted back. "Tell the medics to check their eyes for pupal dilation. See if anyone appears to be suffering brain trauma. Check for elevated body temperatures, too."

"Got it."

Nikki held the woman's hands. "You have bruising on your arms and your hands are clammy. Did you fall down?"

"What time is it?" the woman asked. "I can't be late for work."

"Don't worry about that now. Have you had a fall?"

More and more people shuffled forward out of the darkness. The woman's head swiveled around. "Who are all these people? What am I doing here? This isn't the normal way I go to work."

"Hey, look at me. Do you remember what happened?"

The woman hesitated. "Clouds. Blue clouds."

"Clouds? What kind of clouds? Did you smell anything? Like chemicals?"

"Smell? No, like a mist. Only not wet." The woman collapsed in Nikki's arms. "I fell asleep. I—I don't remember anything else."

"Okay, sit here, rest. I'll send a medic to give you another check."

"But I'm late—"

Nikki propped the woman against the pole and surveyed the other dazed people. The medics' assessments were the same— weakness, confusion, memory loss.

Bryan treated an elderly man for a cut on his head. "He says he doesn't know how he got hurt, but the dust on his hands and knees suggests he fell over suddenly. Possibly a seizure, certainly memory loss. Pupil constriction is normal. His temperature is fine."

"Like the container ship," Nikki said. "Seizures, sleep, memory loss, recovery. What the hell is happening?"

Armstrong appeared to be in a conversation on his sat-link. Suddenly, he sprinted back down the road in the direction they'd come from and waved his flashlight in the air. A large armored personnel carrier appeared out of the darkness, turned toward them, and rumbled forward. Armstrong yelled to his troopers, "Our wheels are here. Get on board. On the double. Let's go!"

She ran up to him. "Where are you going? What's going on?"

"Security forces are in a firefight about two miles from here in West Garden Grove. Migrants jumped a police cruiser and stole weapons. How they activated them without the correct fingerprint IDs, I don't know. But there's a lot of them and not enough of us. We're not winning. I'm about to change that. And there are civilian casualties."

"West Garden Grove? That's where my mother lives. I have to come with you."

"The hell you will. Look, I'll leave a few of my men to protect your team. You'll be safe enough. Your zombies look tame."

Armstrong boarded the rear of the carrier and waved his marines inside. The door was about to shut when Nikki jumped in. The door closed and the carrier sped off. Armstrong moved to the back, his face like thunder. He picked Nikki up by her jumpsuit and slammed her against the tank's back door. Nose to nose, he yelled, "I've got a good mind to throw you off this rig, lady! What the fuck are you doing?"

"You need to calm down. And you need to brush your teeth. Doggy breath."

"What the fuck—"

"Civilian casualties and medics at your disposal? But you didn't take us? Shame on you. Anyway, you got me. Be thankful."

"Look, lady, we don't operate that way. If we need a clean-up crew, we'll send for one later."

"I've seen how you operate."

"Then you should fucking know that you're the last person I want on this mission."

"Good. Drop me off at my mother's house and come back for me when you're done."

"This isn't a taxi service, lady. You want a ride? Okay, I want the pleasure of seeing you take a pulse round." He grabbed an assault vest from a hook on the side of the carrier. "Put this on. One size fits all. Morons included."

The APC raced through streets Nikki Akaju knew so well from her youth—the primary school she went to; the park she played in; the community center. The same graffiti was scribbled on the brick walls; the grounds were still as parched and bare—a small working-class neighborhood of free-citizens, a stone's throw from the Barrier that separated West Garden Grove from the crawling ant nests of the Wards.

The APC took a turn down the street her mother lived on. It swerved to avoid an obstacle. The flames of a burning jeep flashed by the window. The carrier bumped as it mounted a curb and came to rest. A marine opened its rear door. The sound of ion-pulse rounds zipped through the air. Incoming fire glanced off the armored vehicle with hollow thuds.

"Stay in here, doc," Armstrong barked.

The marines leapt out and ran for cover behind the wall of a home. Nikki heard Armstrong issuing orders as the squad crept up the street, returning fire. She had a clear sight between two houses of her mother's backyard with its distinctive kumquat trees. The sound of weapons went quiet. Whoever had been firing at the marines was on the run. Confident, she jumped out of the vehicle and ran across the road, through an alley, reached the wall around her mother's yard, and scaled it.

"Mom! Mom!" she yelled as she ran through the bungalow's back door into the kitchen.

Her mother's jars of cassava flour had been ripped from the kitchen shelves and lay shattered across the floor. White powder marked a trail of footprints. In the front room, furniture had been toppled; books removed from shelves. Drops of blood had splattered on the floor that led to the bathroom. Nikki cautiously opened the bathroom door. No one was there. The window had been smashed. Had the intruder cut themselves on the broken glass? Or was it her mother's blood as she tried to escape?

She went back into the living room. "Mom, are you hiding? Where are you?"

No answer.

A dark shadow passed by the closed curtains. Someone was outside the window. She ducked behind the overturned sofa. The front door was kicked in.

"Akaju, you moron. Are you in here?"

Major Ozzie Armstrong burst into the front room, weapon raised, laser sight bouncing from wall to wall.

Nikki stood in the glare of his flashlight.

"What the fuck are doing?" he grunted.

"This is my mother's house."

"So what? I told you to stay put."

"My mother's gone. Look at this place—it's been trashed."

"Yeah, well, this and every house on this block. It's called a riot for a reason. My guys are doing a house-to-house. If I hadn't seen you running in here like a frightened rabbit, you would have been shot as a looter."

"You'd like that, wouldn't you?"

"Look, I got plenty of trophies. I don't need your head mounted on my wall. As much as that idea gives me a hard-on. Let's go, before I change my mind."

Armstrong grabbed her by the arm. Nikki swung loose and marched toward her mother's bedroom. "Rioters don't have the time to search like this. Not with goons like you around," she yelled back. "Whoever ransacked this place was looking for something specific."

The bed had been tipped over, its mattress and pillows sliced open with a knife. The floor was covered with scattered clothing and blankets. The wardrobe's doors were open and its contents emptied. Nikki bent down. The panel at the back had been removed. The box was gone.

A loud explosion rocked the house. The sound of shattering glass echoed from the kitchen. A moment later, something big and solid hit the roof with a thud. Plaster fell down from the ceiling.

Armstrong bolted into the bedroom and grabbed Nikki by the waist. "We have to go, dickhead! Like now!"

"Wait...no!"

His grip was too strong to fight him off. Armstrong dragged her through the front door. Outside, an orange light flickered across the buildings. The APC was in flames; a mangled wreck, nearly unrecognizable, its hull ripped open. "Rocket grenade. The motherfuckers. How did they get that? Stay here until I come back for you."

Armstrong sprinted across the street; weapon drawn. A new firefight raged, ion-pulses streaking back and forth.

An arm pulled Nikki back inside her mother's house. "Not that way. Out through the back," Bryan said. "Go!"

"Bryan? How—?"

"No time. We need to get out of here."

Nikki and Bryan ran through the kitchen. Shards of broken glass crunched underfoot. Flames from the burning APC lit up the backyard. They raced through the garden, their shadows moving like phantoms through the rows of cassava shrubs. Bryan helped Nikki over the orchard's wall and they dropped into the street. He hustled her to a military scout car parked on the other side.

"You didn't think I'd let you wander off with Armstrong's marines, all on your own?" he said. "I followed the APC. What were you thinking, Nikki? You have no combat experience. In the military, the mission is everything. You may think you work in a battlefield but in a real one, the rules of engagement are different. Civilian lives like yours are a secondary consideration."

The sharp zip of ion-pulse rounds resounded in the street around the corner. As the jeep pulled away from the curb, a dark-clad figure ran toward it, jumped in front of the headlights, and slapped the hood.

"I've got wounded," Major Armstrong said, out of breath. "Can you take a look?"

Nikki stepped out of the jeep and pushed Armstrong in the chest. "I thought you didn't want me along?"

"I'll make an exception for my dearest friend."

"Yeah, right. Okay, show me where they are, big man. Then go find a place to sit and lick your balls like a good little doggy while I take care of your pups."

She turned to Bryan. "You coming? And by the way, fuck your military rules of engagement. Nothing has changed, marines or no marines. This is my neighborhood, and it's been my battlefield since I was a child."

8 - THE DESERT CAMP

Chenzi's hands trembled as she adjusted the station's solar panels. She wiped her palm across her forehead, wet with perspiration. Her T-shirt was soaked, her breathing rapid and shallow.

Need to keep busy. Keep my mind occupied.

It had been two days since the emergency on the ISO, two days filled with urgent repairs and inspections. First priority was restoring the oxygen generation equipment to its pre-panic state. A complete check of the other life support systems followed, then a day-long, laborious trudge to re-certify the station's electronics. Chenzi conducted system reboot after system reboot. Boris wanted to know why no one trusted him when he said everything was fine. Then she shut Boris down and rebooted him too, just to be sure.

EVAs had been performed to check for exterior damage. The station had lost a few gold-plated solar cells which had to be replaced. Body drained of energy, mind a weary mess, Chenzi struggled to stay on task. "Okay Boris, one last time and we should be done. Systems check, please."

"Solar panels optimally aligned. Power generation normal. Oxygen production normal. Communications operational. Air filtration in Module Beta is still intermittent. Electrical fault. Circuit breakers activated."

She sighed. "Not again. Seal off Beta's sleeping quarters. I don't need them. Shut down its air filtration system to save power."

"Beta sleeping pods sealed. Filtration terminated."

Damn, I feel so hot.

"Detecting increased heart rate and abnormal blood pressure," DOC-Emma said. "High levels of cortisol hormone and glucagon secretion indicate nervous system imbalance. Body temperature elevated."

"It's called stress, Emma. The fight-or-flight response. Right now, my body wants to do both."

"Rest is indicated."

"No shit." The screen in front of her blurred. She couldn't read the data. "Oh damn, I can't concentrate."

"Rest is indicated."

"Okay, okay, don't nag."

Chenzi fussed with the station's controls again but gave up. "Boris, take over Leonardo. Let me know if anything unusual is detected with the anomaly."

"Parameters set. Data analysis switched to Auto-Screen."

Chenzi left the Telescope Dome and entered her sleeping quarters in Module Beta. She switched on the comms panel. Signal strength with Earth was good. The ISO hung over the Western Districts. Night had fallen. She sent a comms request to Marisol's sat-link, geo-located to her team's campsite in an area of desert northwest of Santa Fe.

"Hi there," came the cheery response. "I didn't expect to hear from you."

A lump formed in Chenzi's throat at the sound of Marisol's voice and the sight of her pretty face. "I, uh... you're up late. You okay?"

"I'm fine. But you sound strange. Is everything all right?"

"It's, well...," Chenzi paused, clammy sweat dribbling down the side of her face. "It's complicated. We've had a tough day up here. Had to reposition the station. Um...lots of multi-tasking. I'm a bit tired."

"You sound stressed."

Oh no, Emma. Don't you dare comment.

"Yeah, I admit, I am tired. But I thought I'd give you a call before I went to sleep."

"Hi Space Mommy!" A beaming little face appeared on the screen next to Marisol.

"JoJo? What's up? Why are you not in bed?"

"We had a campfire and sang songs."

"That's so nice." A tear formed in the corner of Chenzi's eye.

"And then we saw the lights."

"Lights?"

"Earth Mommy called them 'ora borries'. They're very pretty."

"He means the Aura Borealis, of course."

"What color are they?" The lump in Chenzi's throat tightened.

"They're bright blue," Marisol replied. "And they're not in ribbons like I've seen before. They're more like clouds, you know puffy."

"And they sparkle," JoJo said. "Like fireworks!"

"First, there were a few small clusters dotted around the sky," Marisol said. "But it's grown bigger. Do you know what it is, Chenzi?"

"Get out of there, Marisol. Get out—*now!* Take shelter. Quickly! Somewhere like a cave."

"*What?* It's just the Northern Lights, honey."

"It's not. Trust me, it's not!"

"A cave? We're in the middle of the desert. It's just cactus and sagebrush. Hey, what's going on? You sound really agitated. Are you having bad dreams again?"

"It's not about me, Marisol. You need to find shelter—quickly!"

"Shelter? We're in tents. Where else can we go?"

"Marisol, *oh no*, please listen to me, *please*—"

"Mommy, look! The ora borries are falling from the sky. Is it raining?"

"Marisol, what's happening?" The audio feed buzzed with static. Images on the comms display distorted, broke up, then the video feed turned into a fuzzy haze. "Marisol! No, oh *no*—!"

Chenzi frantically adjusted the signal. Nothing improved. "Boris, comms check."

"All frequencies active. Receivers and transmitters fully operational. Your link is experiencing signal interference at planetary level. All ground relay stations within one hundred miles of that sat-link responder are no longer broadcasting. Intense electrical storm indicated. No adverse meteorological conditions were predicted. Source of interference unknown."

"Keep trying."

"Link unresponsive. Will initiate comms sweep until connection restored."

Why did I stay here? Chenzi thought. Why didn't I go back with the others? This is my fault. They need me.

"Get me Spaceport Central, Boris."

"Earth communications interrupted. Electrical storms over the Joshua Tree Military District."

"What about Vandenberg?"

"Initial comms message restored, proximity Santa Fe, Great Texas Desert. Relay station back on line."

The visuals coming from the camp were distorted, but Chenzi heard the signal's audio. "Mommy, Mommy! Please stop!"

The video feed re-appeared. It struggled to settle, then disappeared again. When reception returned, Chenzi strained to make out what was going on. Images from the sat-link strapped to Marisol's wrist bounced around the camp, up into the sky, then back down to the ground. JoJo's face flashed past. He was crying, his face contorted.

"JoJo—" Chenzi yelled. "Grab Mommy's wrist. Grab her wrist. Can you do that for me? JoJo, can you hear me?"

"Mommy's sick," he sobbed.

"JoJo, grab her wrist."

The images settled, but the sat-link pointed up. Wisps of blue sparkles drifted over the camp.

"I can't see you, JoJo. Turn Mommy's hand."

The side of her son's face appeared. Tears wet his cheeks. His mouth was curled down as he cried. Over his shoulder, Chenzi could see members of the desert research team laying on the ground, their bodies jerking.

"Mommy's sleeping now." The video feed shook. "Wake up, Mommy! Wake up! Why you not wake up?"

Chenzi heard a groan. Oh no, please, don't tell me—she's not dead!

JoJo's face disappeared from view. She heard Marisol's voice in the background. "I'm okay, sweetie. I'm okay now."

Reception was lost and the display turned black.

Chenzi slumped forward in tears, her face pressed against the comms screen as if she could crash through and transport herself back to Earth.

I'm such a selfish fool.

9 - MALIBU HEIGHTS

Dawn arrived and the halls of Malibu Heights Hospital buzzed with activity—gurneys with burn victims; head injuries; smoke inhalation. Bryan Leysson had finished tending to a firefighter with a severely broken leg when Nikki tapped him on the shoulder. "Where are the people who suffered seizures?" she asked. "The desk has no record of admitting them."

"The paramedics left them behind when that building collapsed," Bryan replied. "I should have gone with our team as well, but more air ambulances arrived, so I followed you instead. The rest, you know."

"We let seizure patients disappear into the night like they were just fine? We needed to check them for neurological damage. How can we find them now?"

"If I were you, I'd cook up a story to account for why you didn't stay with our emergency response team."

"What Stenmuir thinks of me is the least of my worries. We assumed the crew of the container ship had been exposed to something already on board. But maybe what happened to them was caused by something else. Maybe the ship was hit by the same kind of clouds that fell on the Free-Port. If the ship's crew hasn't been released from quarantine, we need to bring them back here, run tests and MRIs. We need to find the cause of these seizures. The Wilmington Park Quarantine Center is a one-hour straight shot from Malibu Heights. You coming to help me?"

"Leave? We're on-call."

"We haven't slept, Bryan. I'll tell Stenmuir we're taking a break, buy us a little downtime. Surely, she isn't so cruel she'd deny us sleep."

"Don't bet on it."

"I'm going, regardless. Are you coming with me or not?"

He disposed of his surgical gloves. "Okay, go Nikki, ask her. What are you standing around for?"

Nikki sprinted out of Emergency. When she arrived at Stenmuir's office, her boss stood in front of a large screen displaying a map of the emergency call-outs in process across the Palos Verdes Military District.

"Got a minute, Astrid?"

Stenmuir briefly acknowledged Nikki's presence with a sideways glance and gestured for silence. She was in conference with a medical team on the ground.

"You've done enough. Return to base," she said over the comms-link.

"Triage isn't complete," the doctor leading the call-out responded. "We have injured migrants."

"Your job is to take care of our security guards, not their side of this fight. They'll find a way out without our help. Evacuate our dead. The fire will cremate the other bodies. We're not their funeral service too."

Dr. Astrid Stenmuir wasn't just new, she was a complete enigma to everyone on staff. What was her background? What hospital had she come from? She wasn't telling and no one dared to ask. Gray-streaked short dark hair, prominent cheeks, a lithe figure that was a bundle of boundless energy. People assumed she must have been in the military at some point. Maybe she still was. She fitted the mold of a battalion commander perfectly, Bryan said. Analytical, tough, uncompromising, and above all, mission-focused. Today, with the Free-Port in flames, Dr. Astrid Stenmuir was in her element.

She expanded a dot on the map with a swipe of her hand. Drone footage filled the screen. "The Newport Beach Desalination Plant,"

Stenmuir said, without looking Nikki's way. "Built before the Barrier went up. Now a federal armed fortress surrounded by Ward 10, a tinderbox of street vendors and temp housing. Food stalls with vats of cooking oil. Vehicle fuel dispensed from barrels. You can hear it scream, 'fire trap' from up here."

She manipulated the drone feed and panned across the migrant ward. Thick plumes of black smoke rose into the sky. At ground level, bright flames consumed block upon block of densely packed wooden shacks. "Migrants always shit in their beds. The fire services aren't even trying to contain it. Their orders are to let the Ward burn to the ground."

"People may be trapped inside the buildings. What about them?"

"For every migrant that believed this fire would be the end of their world, ten others saw opportunity in the chaos." Stenmuir glanced away from the screen. "I have no idea how the fire started and I don't care, but once it did, it torched a black-market liquor distillery bordering the desalination plant. The stills exploded. That created a breach in the desalination plant's barbed wire perimeter. Hundreds of migrants fled into the grounds to escape the blaze."

As flames licked the perimeter fence, a mini-city of humanity huddled anxiously under the desalination plant's overground pipes. Mothers draped clothing over their children's faces to prevent them from inhaling the swirling smoke.

"What possible 'opportunity' could be in that chaos?"

Stenmuir controlled the drone camera and zoomed in. "A gang drove a water truck through the opening in the fence and in the middle of a raging inferno forced their way into the pumping station. They were in the process of siphoning off what to them was liquid gold when plant security intervened."

An air ambulance had set down on a patch of wasteland next to the desalination plant. Paramedics tended to several injured security guards. At the side of the pumping station, the front cab of a water truck burned, its doors and windscreen riddled with holes. Two bodies were slumped inside with others laying prone on the ground.

"Once we've stabilized the injured guards, we'll evacuate the staff and the military will secure the perimeter."

"What about those migrants?"

"What about them? They can stay where they are until the fire dies down. We have other priorities, unless you haven't noticed. I would have sent you on this call-out if you'd been here. Where the hell were you? Your team said you'd disappeared."

"I was with a squad of marines. They took fire from rioters near Rossmore Station. Some of the marines were shot."

She swiped the drone footage away and pointed to another dot on the map. "The incident with Major Armstrong's unit?"

"Yeah."

"Why? You weren't assigned to support the military. They have their own medics."

"Not last night. The situation was...well, let's say, fluid. We got separated from the paramedics when rioters attacked. Astrid, I'm here to ask you for...Bryan and I need to get some sleep."

Stenmuir pointed to the dot on the screen, the location of the desalination plant. "Two dead guards and the rest with gunshot wounds." Her fingers moved to other markers. "And there are new riots flaring up every hour, on both sides of the Barrier. The security services are stretched and so is our medical response."

"Bryan and I are exhausted. We're beyond useful. A fresh set of trauma doctors and nurses have just started their shift. They're rested. We're not. We've been up all night. We just need a few hours' sleep before we go back on call."

Stenmuir cast her cold, piercing blue eyes in Nikki's direction. She looked her up and down. Nikki's scrubs were covered in blood. "Don't leave the hospital, do you understand? The situation in Palos Verdes is getting worse. I need everyone on duty. *Everyone*."

"I understand."

Other incidents flashed up on the display from all over Palos Verdes. Stenmuir's face resumed its focus. Nikki backed out of the office, raced to her locker to change into a jumpsuit, then scurried back through corridors filled with patients to Emergency.

She spotted Bryan collapsed on a chair. "Let's go."

"She okay-ed it?"

"I worked my charm."

"Charm doesn't work on her."

"Dispatch has only one jeep available. We need to go before someone else takes it."

"And sleep?"

"You can nap in the jeep."

"Said like a true adrenaline junkie."

***

The jeep turned off the coastal road from Malibu Heights onto Military Highway 10. Four miles later, the jeep's transponder allowed access to the Culver City Super-Freightway, a multi-lane toll highway that ran from the Getty Center, the district government's main offices, south to the Free-Port of Long Beach. The super-freightway had been shut down to anything except military and police traffic. Their medical jeep, racing at high speed with a flashing blue siren, slipped by the security forces unnoticed.

Toward the Long Beach Barrier, a flat pall of brown smoke and reddish dust lingered in the sky over West Garden Grove where the factories had burned. Further down the Super-Freightway, a steady stream of military ARVs and heavy-lift transports cast their shadows across the road as they took off from the LAX Security Forces Aerodrome.

Nikki exited the freightway at Alameda Street and headed south past the chemical plants and warehouses of the Torrance Industrial Zone.

"We're being followed," Bryan said. "It pulled off from the hard shoulder just after LAX and it's been keeping its distance ever since."

Nikki checked the rear camera on the dash. Behind them, a black land-cruiser with darkened windows and a heavy bull-bar hung back several car lengths.

Alameda Street was deserted. The security emergency had shut down the factories. Nikki slowed the jeep, expecting the land cruiser to do the same, but it closed the gap. "No sirens. So it's not wanting to pull us over."

The land-cruiser accelerated and rammed the back of the lighter jeep with a jarring thud.

"Shit! I get it. You're not friendly."

Nikki picked up speed as the bigger vehicle kept tight to their bumper. She swerved from side to side across the empty street and the cruiser followed suit.

An overhead sign pointed left into the entrance of Wilmington Market. "Hold on, Bryan. I've done call-outs here before. It's a crazy maze of alleys. This big motherfucker will have trouble following us."

As Nikki swung the jeep sharply left into the marketplace, the jeep tilted on its side, its tires struggling for traction on the pitted, gravel-strewn side road. After it settled back on all four wheels, Nikki floored it.

Wilmington Market was closed, stalls locked up, shutters rolled down and clamped shut. Empty food sacks bounced across the path of the racing jeep like tumbleweeds.

She jinked down an alley and glanced over her shoulder. "Did that do it?" she asked.

A split-second later, the reply came, "No, it's still with us."

They reached a junction between the narrow alley and a wider street. Nikki threw the jeep into a skid and spun it completely around. They emerged from a cloud of dust and accelerated back up the alley toward the land-cruiser, forcing the bigger vehicle to slam on its brakes. Just as collision seemed inevitable, Nikki jinked right, down another tight alley. They entered a cramped pedestrian market lined with corrugated metal shacks. She slalomed through the empty stalls at high speed until a barricade of old pallets and tires appeared and blocked the way.

"Oh shit!"

Nikki jumped on the brakes, but they couldn't hold traction. The jeep veered from side to side and came to a violent, sudden stop, slamming into a wooden pillar that held up one side of a shuttered food stall. Nikki was thrown forward into the airbag as the stall's roof collapsed on top of the jeep. Dazed, she leaned out, fell to the ground, and stumbled away from the wreck.

At the far end of the alley, a black-garbed figure shouldered a tubular weapon.

"Get down!" Bryan yelled.

A rocket-propelled grenade whizzed down the alley. The food stall exploded in a shower of wood and twisted metal, covering Nikki in a deluge of debris and dust.

She pushed up with her elbows, but the weight on her back forced her down. She drew her knees under her stomach and pushed as hard as she could until the splintered wood fell away.

Blood streamed down the side of her face. Her ears rang with a high-pitched whine. Coughing, she wiped the dust from her eyes, got to her feet, and staggered forward. A pair of firm hands reached under her armpits and dragged her under the shelter of a concrete archway.

Someone laid her against a wall—a stranger with a thick beard, brown unkempt hair. Rough hands gripped her face. The stranger opened her eyelids with his fingers, checking if she was conscious.

She heard another voice, a woman's voice. The man answered back, their words muffled by the ringing in her ears. The only thing she heard was, "She's alive."

The man lifted Nikki up like a doll and placed her over his shoulder. Images swirled in front of Nikki's eyes—a beige dust blotting out the sun; the blurred face of the woman as she ran behind them; black smoke and orange flames billowing from the burning jeep. Blood dribbled down her face, its iron taste making her feel nauseous. And then everything went dark.

10 - ALONE

Living alone on the ISO had become unnerving. The slightest extraneous sound made Chenzi twitch. Without the camaraderie of the crew, the Telescope Dome had become an eerie echo chamber. Boris, an emotionless interface with no sense of humor, was a poor substitute for a soul with flesh and blood. She never realized how important the presence of another human being was. She needed sleep, but didn't look forward to it. Her nightmares had returned.

The excitement and anticipation that had marked her first days on board the ISO were gone. The distance to home and her loved ones was a huge, unreachable chasm. Her mind kept wandering back to that patch of empty desert northwest of Santa Fe, to Marisol and JoJo. Their anguished faces haunted her. The SpacePort had made brief contact with the research team after the incident with the Jupiter clouds. There had been injuries from the seizures but Marisol and JoJo were fine. The group had broken camp and were on their way back to the Adobe Park Desert Research Center when communications were lost again.

Chenzi scrolled through the data stream from Leonardo, a monotony that was strangely calming. It settled her mind and kept her busy. Outside the station, the anomaly, with its bright-blue outer ring, rotating middle, and central black void, had not changed shape since the event that had sent the crew into seizures. Why Chenzi had not suffered from the Jupiter cloud exposure was a mystery. The crew were safely back with their families on Earth, with no aftereffects from the event.

Chenzi set Leonardo's data-mining to Auto-Screen and left the dome to get some rest in Module Alpha. The short tunnel into Alpha had two observation windows. Through one of them was Mother Earth—azure oceans dotted with white clouds, continents with swathes of desert where green forests once lived. In the Western Military Districts, night had fallen. Along the coastline, the distinction between land and ocean had faded. One by one, the clusters of lights that marked the communities of the Federation blinked off as the blackout commenced.

Through the other window, the moon shone brightly, a white and gray orb. Lunar Base Imbrium was more than humanity's first permanent base on the moon—established before the Constitutional War started—it had grown into a nation-state in its own right, with ever-expanding mining colonies, aerospace factories, and a launch port for future deep space missions. Her time at Imbrium, early in her career, had been a disappointment. She was young and enthusiastic, smart enough to lead a research team but too immature to survive the suffocating culture that came with too many people living in small spaces with little privacy. Her escape from that stress had been a regrettable one-night stand that sent her back to Earth to give birth.

She'd just settled into her bunk and closed her eyes when the comms panel lit up with its unique beeps. Her heart skipped a beat. *Marisol?* She bounded out of bed and tussled her short black hair. The incoming call was from Lunar Base Imbrium. An unmanned supply shuttle had been sent from the moon to the ISO to refuel the station's depleted thrusters and act as a replacement for the Crew Rescue Vehicle.

"Boris, what's this about? Do you know?"

"Negative. Encrypted security protocol. To proceed, the recipient's retinal profile is required."

Chenzi acknowledged the incoming signal and the transmission opened.

On the screen, a short stocky man with a pie-shaped face sat with an officious-looking woman in a small bare room with white walls.

From her time stationed on the moon, Chenzi recognized the pair's distinctive uniforms—the Pan-Lunar Internal Security Force.

"I'm Agent Terao Vinh," the man said. "This is Agent Petra Maroska."

"Is this about the shuttle? It's a little beat up and was tricky to dock. Fuel transfer went smoothly but—"

"It's not about the shuttle. We got a report from some guy named Boris. No last name."

"Yeah, he's some guy all right. So, who are you?"

"We work for Edison Denard."

Lunar Base Imbrium was the lifelong obsession of the founder of Pan-Lunar Exploration, Edison Denard. He was also commander of the Joshua Tree Military District where SpacePort Centrum was located. Edison Denard's immense wealth and political muscle stretched beyond the borders of the District he ran like his own private kingdom. Only the Governor-General of the Federation, Addison Dray, held more apparent authority. But as a former VP of Pan-Lunar, Governor-General Dray worked for Denard, not the other way around. Edison Denard played second fiddle to no one. It was the Federation's dirty little secret. A secret everyone in power knew. Constitution be damned.

"I work for the International Space Agency," Chenzi said.

"The ISA is a subsidiary of Pan-Lunar Exploration," Agent Petra Maroska replied. "So you work for Edison Denard too. We're not here to teach you Pan-Lunar's org chart."

Her face was angular, her nose and cheekbones pronounced; jet black hair, dark brown eyes. She reminded Chenzi of a hawk—sharply focused once it spotted its prey. Where on the moon did they grow such ugly goons like these two?

"So, to what do I owe this pleasure?"

"You experienced something recently and we would like to know more about it," Agent Vinh said.

"You're talking about the Jupiter clouds?"

"We'd like to understand how it felt," Maroska added.

"Wait a minute—why does the Pan-Lunar Internal Security Force want to know how I felt when some strange cosmic radiation tickled my bones?"

"It's not a lunar security issue. This is for Edison Denard, personally."

"Personally? How did you get this comms frequency? Does SpacePort Centrum and Director Belledeau know about this conference call?"

"Edison Denard owns SpacePort Centrum. He runs it. They work for him. He doesn't need permission from anyone to ask questions, any time he wants."

"Even so, I think you need clearance from the SpacePort for this conversation."

A document appeared on a side screen. "Like this one?" Maroska said. "We're here to ask the questions, if you don't mind, Dr. Zhu."

"I mind. In fact, my mind is why I'm on the ISO. And my mind likes answers."

"Let's get started, shall we?"

"Tell us what happened from the first moment," Agent Vinh asked.

"Okay. I looked up. There was a face looking down at me."

"A face?"

"Yeah. Couldn't tell if it was a he or a she, what with the surgical mask. Then someone slapped me on the ass and I let out a big wail. That was my first moment. It was great."

"You keep this up," pie-faced Vinh said. "And it will not go well for you."

"I answered the question. You need to be more specific. I'm a scientist. I respond to specifics. It's my alma mater. I have no clue who you are and why you're asking for this. Didn't you read the incident report? It details everything that happened. The report is SpacePort property so Edison Denard owns it, right? So, if he didn't understand what was written, you need to be way more specific with your questions."

"We're interested in what you saw outside the ship," Agent Maroska said. "You described it as a swirling, blue, cloud-like formation."

"Right so far. Still not a question though."

"Can you estimate its size and shape?"

"It's in the report."

"Remind us."

"Forgetful? Okay. My guess was, and still is, easily thirty meters in diameter, roughly organized, but generally concentric. It was moving pretty fast, so my estimate of its size might be conservative."

"What happened next?"

"It accelerated quickly after passing through the station. It had this odd change in color, dark blue in the middle of the cloud, getting lighter toward its edges. It was semi-transparent. I could see the Earth on the other side. There was a lot of distortion. Because of that, I'd say the cloud had areas of different density. Specific enough?"

"How did you feel afterward?" Maroska asked.

"How did I 'feel'? You must have seen the biometric data from my DOC, Emma. Who cares how I 'felt'? There isn't anything about my body that Emma doesn't know. In fact, she knows more than I do, in real-time. Have you looked at that data?"

"An AI interface can monitor brain activity and measure the electrical impulses in your nervous system," Maroska replied. "But she can't see inside your mind. She assumes you're angry from your blood pressure. Sad from your serotonin levels. Excited from the secretion of adrenaline. But those are crude algorithmic assumptions. Extrapolating emotions from biofeedback is an art, not a science, even for the best AI. So, I'll ask you again, how did you feel?"

"And you've been warned about the quality of your answers," the pie-faced man said. "If you're as smart as you say you are, you'll know your career at the International Space Agency—which Edison Denard owns—can easily be *shortened*."

"Okay. Whoa, stop. Message received." Expressing herself in non-scientific terms was not Chenzi's forte, especially when she was so tired. "All right," she said. "I guess I could sum up the whole experience as feeling invaded."

"Invaded?" Vinh asked.

"Yeah, like two people were occupying my body at the same time. I reported it as prickles, like bee stings, but I got the sense that another—I don't know what to call it—another 'being' or presence had been inside me."

"And?"

"There's an 'and'?"

"Keep talking about what you felt," Maroska said. "After that kind of trauma, the subconscious can suppress your recollection to prevent further distress. The more you talk through it, the more you'll recall."

"That's what my partner always says. But it's always better if my subconscious has downed a few cocktails and I'm lying on her couch. Sadly, none of that is aboard this galactic cruise ship."

"Careful, Science Officer Zhu," Vinh hissed. "No more warnings."

"All right, I get it. You're serious." Chenzi closed her eyes for a moment, then said, "I felt wanted. Objectified. Not in a sexual way, but definitely not in a loving way. Like being the object of someone's desire, the recipient of someone's envy. Like someone coveting what they wanted to own or control. Like a child wanting another child's toy, and that toy was me. When the prickles ended, that feeling stopped, leaving me drained, weak. You can check my bio-data. Maybe my blood sugar dropped or something. It didn't last long. Boris set off the alarm about the oxygen supply and my adrenaline soared. It was action stations after that."

"Thank you, Ms. Zhu," Vinh said, his pie-face expanding even further as he smiled. "That's all."

"That's all? Hey, aren't you going to tell me why Edison Denard wants this information? I mean, you already seem to know enough about what happened to ask some pretty pointed questions."

The pie-faced man and his hawk-like companion remained silent.

"Oh, wait, how stupid of me. In my state of exhaustion, I've overlooked the obvious. I get it now—in spite of owning the non-irradiated world, your boss isn't getting answers to his questions back home. Loyal employees like Dr. Belledeau haven't told him everything he wants to know, right?"

"He just wants to hear your version of events, not theirs."

"No, he doesn't. The official version is in a report everyone has access to. He wants to know something no one else knows."

Vinh smirked. "And we'd like to keep it that way."

11 - THE FACTORY

Nikki woke to the caress of warm air blowing across a thin bed sheet. She rubbed her face and sat up. She was in her underwear, but didn't remember undressing. She'd slept on a simple cot, no mattress, just a bed of canvas, like a hammock on a frame. The rest of the room was just as sparsely furnished—another cot like hers; a rusty metal chair with her jumpsuit draped across its back; bare walls, peeling paint. In the far corner, a crudely built air conditioner rumbled softly as it cycled. Above her, a ceiling fan whipped the stale air with a monotonous *whoosh, whoosh*. The room smelt of rust and oil.

Where am I? A hospital?

Nikki tossed the bed sheet off and placed her feet on cool concrete. She massaged her stiff neck. Bruises covered her legs and she had a bandage on one side of her face. The sun's rays streamed through a wooden blind covering the room's only window. She peeked through the dusty slats. Outside was an empty parking lot and a brick wall. Someone had taken her sat-link from her wrist. She picked her jumpsuit off the chair, shook the dust off, and checked its pockets. Her data-tab was gone too.

Nikki felt faint and braced herself against the wall.

The explosion. Where's Bryan?

A loud grinding sound vibrated the walls. It broke the stillness of the bright morning. The grinding stopped, then started again, its high pitch stinging her ears. "Oh boy," Nikki moaned out loud as it went quiet. Her head pounded. "This hospital has some weird wake-up calls." The sound of grinding returned. "Okay, enough of this."

Nikki got dressed, went to the bedroom door, and it wasn't locked. She pulled the door slightly ajar, just enough to peek outside.

Acrid white smoke drifted into the bedroom. The room she'd been sleeping in was just a small part of a large factory. Tall ceilings, metal struts holding up the roof. Naked bulbs under wide industrial shades. The factory had several rows of workbenches, all much lower than normal; some covered in electronic components, strands of wiring, and partly finished solar panels; others with scraps of tubing, old gears, and rusty sheet metal. There was a metal lathe, a drill press, and a table-saw. Reclaimed wood was heaped in a pile beside pieces of furniture in various stages of completion.

A female voiced emerged from the other side of the smoke. "Good. You're up."

A woman stepped through the white fog, wafted it away from her face, and took off her welding goggles. Younger than Nikki, early-twenties, she was taller, maybe six feet; buzz-cut hair, pierced lips, pale skin covered in tattoos. She wore a camo-colored tank top, muscular arms. "Just a small electrical fault. But we'll get it working."

A very short man peered under a riveted stainless-steel drum elevated on metal legs. He flipped down his face-shield, crawled under its base with a stick of metal and a welding torch, and said, "Last one. Then I think it will work." Bright sparks shot out, followed by a plume of white smoke.

"It's a bread dough mixer," the woman explained. "After what's been happening, we're expecting an influx of people seeking refuge in Ward 13."

"I know you—the explosion—you were there." Nikki looked around the cavernous factory. "Who are you? Where am I? A migrant ward?"

"You're still in the Free-Citizens Zone. My name is Echo. And this is Brother Mikey."

Mikey, a dwarf, removed his safety visor and gloves. He had a bright smile, a stubby nose, and a shock of sweaty brown hair. "Okay, let's try it now."

Echo flicked a switch on the drum's side and a steady whirring sound replaced the grinding noise.

Mikey jumped onto a stool and peered into the top of the drum. "A misaligned shaft caused the motor to vibrate. New bracket did the trick. Shaft and motor repaired, good as new."

"You stayed in our bedroom last night," Echo said. "I slept here on the couch. Mikey's my partner." She pointed to sheets strewn over an old leather sofa next to a metal lathe. "He prefers to sleep next to his projects so he can tinker in the night when the mood strikes him." She yawned. "Damned annoying. Up and down. Talks in his sleep. Snores too. Makes for a fitful night. He says I'm the one that snores. Yeah, right."

"You do. It's a fact." Mikey wiped his hands on a rag. "You guys want breakfast? I'm starving."

"Breakfast? Not until I get some answers," Nikki said. "Where's my comms? My sat-link? My tab? I want them back!"

"Hey, hey, settle down," Echo snapped. "Don't be so ungrateful. We saved your ass yesterday. Big time. Don't worry, your comms are in a safe place—shielded, so the security services can 't track their signals. Believe me, you don't want to be found right now."

"The fuck I don't. And where's Bryan?" She paused. "He's not—is he?"

"No, he's alive. We took him back to Malibu Heights."

"That's where I should be. Not here in this, *this*—whatever this place is."

"Careful, sister," Mikey said. "You're lucky to be here. And you're stuck with us until we get some answers."

"*You* want answers? To *what*?"

"What does the Association want with you?" Echo asked.

"The *Association*? Who the fuck are the Association?"

A sliding metal door at the opposite end of the building opened. A tall man with a shaggy beard checked the street before he stepped inside. He was in worker's clothing—dark-colored T-shirt, cargo pants, heavy boots. "I don't think anyone followed me." He strode through the maze of work benches. "But surveillance drones are everywhere. They're searching for somebody and we know who."

"This is Muldoon," Mikey said.

"I remember you. You're the guy that pulled me away from the explosion."

"Don't expect gratitude," Echo said. "Not in her vocabulary."

Muldoon pulled a data-tab from his hip pocket. "The police database is red hot with activity. Someone's taking a special interest in yesterday's camera feeds down by the Free-Port. At some point, facial recognition will spot you getting in our jeep and the cameras will track your movements here. We've got maybe half an hour before we have to move you again."

"Move me?" Nikki shuffled toward the exit from the factory. "Thanks for rescuing me, but I don't know who the hell you people are. I need to call the hospital." Her legs wobbled. "And I need my sat-link—" Nikki lost her balance and slumped to her knees. "Oh, shit, my head."

Echo lifted Nikki to her feet. "Look, sis, you had quite a day. You need to get your strength back. We're not your enemies. You're not our prisoner. But I can guarantee you this—if the Association finds you, your time with them will not be quality time. You'd tell them what they want to know. I guarantee you."

"Tell who—what?

"Your mother is Marcia Akaju and you're her daughter, Dr. Nikki Akaju, right?"

Nikki steadied herself on a work bench. "My mother? Do you know where my mother is?"

"Sit down," Muldoon said, drawing up a metal chair. "Why do they want to kidnap you and your mother? Ask yourself, what do the two of you know that no one else knows?"

"Wait—my mother's been kidnapped?" Nikki's eyes darted from one face to the other.

"No, don't worry," Echo replied. "The Cassava Lady is safe. She's with our people, in Ward 13."

"The Cassava Lady? So, you know her?"

"Everyone in Ward 13 knows your mother. She trades her cassava flour with us."

"Ward 13?"

"Both of you are on an Association hit list," Muldoon explained. "It was their people that ambushed your jeep at Wilmington Market. They aren't just any thugs. They're highly trained operatives. When the Association puts an operation in motion, they don't piss around. Things happen in the blink of an eye. And they're still hunting you. You've survived one attempt. But there will be others. They get what they want. Your mom reached out to us for protection and we helped her escape. For some reason, both of you are special people to them. Why else would they want to kidnap you?"

"Kidnap us? I don't know what this is all about. I just know it sounds crazy. Who are you people? If you're not with the security services, how do you know all this stuff?"

"We have our sources. Several days ago, they said Association operatives would arrive on a container ship from the United Andean Republic. Federal marines landed on that ship to intercept them."

"A container ship? You mean, the *Espiritu de Lima*?"

Muldoon nodded.

"I was there. It was a medical emergency."

"Then you know marines shot several stowaways. But not the right ones. We believe their operatives had already escaped, probably by mini-sub before Armstrong's men arrived."

"Then again," Echo said. "Perhaps that whole exercise was just for show. Perhaps the marines were sent to ensure the safe arrival of the Association's team and the people they killed were just in the wrong place at the wrong time."

"You're kidding, right? It was a genuine medical emergency," Nikki replied. "Are you implying the emergency on that ship was faked?"

"It could have been a false flag," Echo added. "The Association has a nasty habit of staging one thing to look like another, to cover up what's really going on. Their agents have infiltrated the security services. When you got on board, did you find a lot of sick people?"

"They were sick, we think. But—" Nikki paused. "Your source? It's Bryan Leysson, isn't it?"

"He's a lot more co-operative than you are."

"I'll ask you again, who are *they* and who the fuck are *you*?"

"Do you know Lewis Temple?"

"Who in the Federation doesn't know Lewis Temple? Are you kidding?"

"We work for him."

"Doing what?"

"Protecting people like you from the Association," Echo said with a scowl.

"Oh, geez, you're kidding?"

"Do I look like I'm fucking kidding?" Her swagger confirmed it.

"For years, the Association has been looking for an archive of lost research," Muldoon added. "Anyone who knows about it tends to disappear and stay disappeared. You were doing research work before Malibu Heights, right?"

"It wasn't a big deal. I was still a student. Mostly blood analysis and genetic sequencing. My grant paid med school bills, but out of nowhere they cut off funding. I had to work part-time as a paramedic to make that up. That gig got me the job at Malibu Heights after I graduated."

"Genetic sequencing? That'll put you in their cross-hairs, for sure."

"A contract with who?" Echo asked.

"Temple Research, the BioSciences Division. So yeah, I know who Lewis Temple is."

"What kind of research?"

"A new gene therapy to treat auto-immune disease. I was super-disappointed when Temple Research withdrew its funding for my project."

"We know Lewis Temple. His heart is in the right place," Muldoon remarked. "No one wants to unravel the secrets of the Association more than he does. It might have been Temple's decision to begin the research, but you can blame the Association for ending it. As important as he is, they always find ways to disrupt what's not in their interests."

Mikey dabbed sanitizer on his hands. "I'm getting something to eat before we all die of starvation." A door between two sets of metal lockers led into a small kitchen.

Nikki's head dropped into her hands. "I feel like shit. Maybe all this Association drama is your 'normal'. It's not mine. I'm confused. I just want to find my mom, go home, have a shower, get up tomorrow morning, and make a sick person better."

"They won't let you do that—until they get what they want."

"What the hell do they want from an emergency physician, Echo? Shit, if I knew more about this Association crime gang and what they do, I might be able to figure it out. Stop being so shit-ass vague. Unless you haven't noticed, we have much bigger problems than this." Nikki pointed to the factory's ceiling. "Those—whatever the hell those clouds were—that's what we should really be talking about, not *this* shit."

"They're one and the same," Echo said.

"They're *what*?"

Brother Mikey returned from the kitchen, his little frame struggling with a large wooden platter stacked with bread, carrot sticks, and apples. He plonked it on the workbench. "Get some food in her, mountain man. Before our guest faints again."

"We need to watch the time." Echo pointed to her sat-link. "We should think about moving her."

Muldoon passed the platter to Nikki. "Eat. We have to go soon."

"You have apples? Who has apples?"

"Ward 13," Echo replied.

"A migrant ward has apple trees?" Nikki's stomach growled at the sight of food. She broke off a hunk of bread. It was soft and had the smell of home.

"What do you know about Dante Parks and his genetic research?" Muldoon asked.

Nikki's hand froze as she was about to take a bite of bread.

They know about Uncle Dante?

Her mother said it was important to disconnect them from his research. Maybe her paranoia wasn't an unfounded fear after all. She said you can't trust anyone.

What was in that box Mom had? Did these people ransack her mother's house? Is this whole thing just a trick? Are they actually...the Association?

"Never heard of him," Nikki replied. "Why?"

"Genetic diversity threatens the Association," Echo added.

"What do you mean by genetic diversity? We're all human beings. Regardless of skin color, we share the same genetic code."

"That's where you're wrong, doctor," she replied. "It's not a question of ethnicity."

"The human genome is a fact, Echo."

"Are you sure, Dr. Akaju? Do you test every birth?"

"Of course not. I don't have to."

"Then maybe you should start," Muldoon said.

A red light flashed on an electrical panel on the wall. Mikey took a data-tab from his overalls and a hologram of an aircraft popped up. "My homemade and highly illegal rooftop radar system says a police aero-cruiser is imminent."

"Good, I can go back with them," Nikki said.

Echo put her hands on her hips. "Haven't you learned anything yet? For someone smart enough to be a doctor, you sure are fucking dumb. They may be the police. Then again, maybe they're not."

A second hologram popped up. "If you didn't order these taxis, you'd better get off the street before they run you over," Mikey said.

"So, doc, do you want to see your mother or not?"

"Okay," Nikki replied. "What now?"

"Just follow me."

"Don't forget this." Mikey opened a locker and tossed a small backpack to Echo.

"Your comms, doc," she said. "You'll get them back when it's safe."

Mikey ran over to a table-saw. He tripped a switch and the heavy equipment moved out of the way. Below the factory floor, a metal staircase descended underground. Echo took Nikki by the arm and hustled her to the hatch. Heavy banging shook the factory's service doors.

Muldoon yelled, "Down! Now!"

They scurried down the staircase. The saw moved back in place to cover up their escape.

"What about Mikey?" Nikki asked in the pitch darkness of the underground chamber. "He's not coming with us?"

"He'll stay and deal with the police," Echo said. "They're not looking for him. They're looking for you."

12 - WARD 13

Echo grabbed a flashlight from the wall and led the way down the staircase beneath the factory. At the bottom, a small landing opened into a circular tunnel, eight feet in diameter.

"This is one of the old storm-drains under the Free-Port." Rats scampered away from the oncoming light. "It will take us to Ward 13 on the other side of the Long Beach Barrier."

"Migrants use this to get into the Free-Citizens Zone?" Nikki asked.

"Decades ago, the drainage system under the Wards was supposed to be sealed off from the Free-Port when the Barrier was built. But contractors didn't have the right plans. This storm-drain was missed. Ward 13 bricked off the other connections to this forgotten tunnel. It's the only one with a direct passage under the Barrier."

They picked their way through a cluster of rotted steel drums, metal carcasses emptied of once precious contents and then dumped underground. The further they went, the more obstacles blocked their way—old gas pipe regulators, rusted wastewater valves, switch panels for buried network cables; obsolete equipment long since stripped of any useful metal and wiring. The air in the tunnel was stagnant and bone dry. Every now and again, a ray of light peeked through a break in the concrete to let fresh air blow down.

The group trekked underground in sweaty, airless conditions until they reached a locked gate. Echo retrieved an old-school metal key from her pocket. "This is where we'll cross underneath the Barrier."

Beyond the gate, the passage followed the old grid pattern of the roads above ground, a streetscape that in many places had long since disappeared, especially in the Wards where shanties and tents filled every inhabitable space between buildings.

Nikki asked Muldoon, "Mikey called you 'mountain man'. What did he mean by that?"

"I'm from the north," he replied. "Cascadia."

"I thought so. It's your accent. And you're ex-military. I can tell."

"Mount Hood Forest Rangers. In some ways I miss Cascadia, and in others—well, there ain't no hell on Earth like thousands of acres of burning mountain forest. Winds that blow like the Devil's breath. Nothing grows back for years, if ever. It's a strange landscape— islands of green forest separated by high alpine desert."

"People here would like to see Cascadia join the Federation."

"I doubt that will ever happen. Cascadians are fiercely independent."

"So why did you come here?"

"Our political ties with the Federation are close. Getting a residency visa was relatively easy and there's no migrant stigma about people from Cascadia. Why did I leave the land of my birth? After I met Pastor Harold, I just followed him where he led me. Which brought me to Palos Verdes and Ward 13."

"Pastor Harold?"

"He's the regulador of Ward 13," Echo said. "And Mikey's twin brother."

"Regulador? So, he's a migrant? That would mean Mikey is a migrant too. But his factory is on our side of the Barrier? I don't get it. That can't be. The authorities wouldn't allow it."

"The brothers are not migrants. They're both free-citizens."

"Wait—being a regulador is a fast-track way for a migrant to earn credits for residency in the Federation. It's a rare opportunity. Migrant wards choose one of their own for that privilege. If this Pastor Harold is already a free-citizen, he doesn't benefit from holding that position."

"That's not why Ward 13 wants him as regulador. There are bigger reasons," Echo said. "His relationship with both sides of the Barrier is complicated. They're coming back. As sure as shit. And Ward 13 feels safer with him in charge when they do."

"Who's coming back? The Association? No one I know has ever heard of this Association crime gang."

"The Association aren't criminals," Echo replied. "Not in the sense you're thinking of. It would be easier if they were. They cover their tracks to suppress their existence, not just here in the Federation, but in other parts of the world, what's left of it. Your mom seems to know what's going on even if you don't. Maybe she can explain it to you when you see her. She said you were a stubborn dickhead. Well, not exactly in those words. She is your mother, after all."

"Explain what?"

"Let's just leave it, okay? I've said way too much. Maybe you and your mom are Association agents and these kidnap attempts are a false-flag to flush out our connection with Ward 13? We can't be sure, until you're fully checked out."

"How could I have faked the rocket-propelled grenade that hit my jeep? Is this evasiveness just a hobby or do you have a degree in it?"

"I'm ex-military too. So, unlike you, I'm a professional dickhead, not an amateur one. I'm just being careful. The Association are embedded everywhere—inside the government, the military, the security forces. People who talk too much about them disappear. People like you and your mother. Lewis Temple is on their hit-list too. He's survived because he's got a cocoon of security few people can afford. You and your mom certainly can't."

"So, if they're not criminals and they've infiltrated our government, what's their goal? If it's not money or power, then what is it?"

"You're not going to leave it, are you?" Muldoon said.

"I'm not in emergency response to sit back and twiddle my thumbs, waiting for the world to fall in my lap. So, wrap your shit in a bow. I can deal with it. I've dealt with far worse."

"Really? Okay, how about answering this question first, smart-ass," Echo said. "After the nuclear wars, why did our small part of the world survive while other countries were set back centuries?"

"We were taught some kind of sanity returned to the world."

"Oh sister, please," Echo scoffed. "By what miracle did thoughtful diplomacy end all that madness?"

"How else did it stop? Someone, somewhere, must have seen reason."

"That's our modern fairy tale, isn't it? We desperately want to believe ordinary people decided they'd had enough. That they talked it out."

"Why not? Diplomacy works."

"Well, that dumb idea is certainly a load of shit wrapped in a bow. Despots and warlords bombed the world back to the Stone Age. Europe and Asia went from the most populated places on Earth to the least and their people now live in caves. So, what kind of depraved fucking miracle saved the Western Federation from that chaos? We have the most advanced technologies of anyone left on this planet. We even have a moon colony, for fuck's sake. You think that happened by pure blind luck?"

"Yes, I guess we were lucky. What's wrong with that?"

"What's *wrong*? Do you honestly believe all that gift-wrapped shit they taught you in school? That enemies with their hands on each other's throats, and their fingers on nuclear buttons, miraculously saw *reason* because cooler heads prevailed? Is that what you believe? Is that the truth, Dr. Akaju? And whose truth, is it?"

"What other truth is there, Echo?"

"Truth and lies are born from the same facts, but separated at birth by angry, warring minds," Muldoon said. "Naked facts are pretty ugly things to look at. People prefer to believe lies because they love the intoxicating dreams they produce. But when we pass those lies down to our children, they build a set of myths barely recognizable from the facts they came from. In the end, people have always believed whatever comforts them."

"Doesn't answer my question."

"Nuclear wars around the world had become too awful to count," Muldoon replied. "But what did the old America do? It started its own. Military-engineered pandemics, hunger-driven genocides. Humankind knows how to do death, Dr. Akaju. We're exceptionally good at it. The world was happily going down the path of uncontrolled extinction. What seemed like an inevitability—certain doom for the human race—had to be reversed. It simply had to end. It was counter to the Association's aims. It didn't fit their plans. The Association took back control from those who'd completely lost it."

"Fit their plans? What plans?" Nikki huffed. "There's always been powerful, wealthy people in the shadows, pulling strings. So, what's new? If this Association is real and it saved us from extinction, that wasn't a bad thing, was it?"

"You want to go back to your supposedly 'safe' world?" Echo said. "Where 'your people' will protect you? People like Major Armstrong? Do you think you can rewind the clock, like the last twenty-four hours never existed? Because if you do, you're just waiting for those assholes to find you and finish the job."

Her laughs bounced off the dank passageway. "Great plan, sister. Glad you thought of it. I'll let the Association know."

"Okay, enough with your twisted history lessons. I get it. The world was a crazy place. Still is. Let's say I believe your story. What does this global political shit have to do with trying to kidnap me and my mother?"

"Patience, sis. The Association won't be in the shadows much longer. They've been waiting for the right moment and that moment has arrived."

***

Muldoon pointed to a trickle of light peeking through a steel grate high above them. "We're here."

"Thank god," Nikki wheezed.

Muldoon climbed up a steel ladder on the inside of a narrow vertical shaft. When he reached the top, he lifted the grate, took a quick look around, and called down, "We're good to go."

At ground level, the smooth, wind-worn facade of Ward 13's main entrance gates loomed over the trio. Thirty feet high and twin-towered, the entrance had been crafted of baked mud and crushed red brick. It sat across a narrow bridge on the other side of a deep aqueduct, an old storm runoff now a dry moat.

The towers guarded Ward 13's southern boundary, Echo explained. To the north, an abandoned highway at the bottom of a broad gully met the rising hills of the Silverado Canyon, forming a natural barrier patrolled by District security drones. An adobe brick wall surrounded Ward 13 to seal it off from its neighbors.

"Of all the wards in South LA, this one's the safest to live in," Echo said.

"No doubt," Nikki replied. "I've never seen a Ward like this."

The group crossed the bridge. A small device dangled from a strap on Echo's wrist. She waved it at the vault-style entrance door. It clicked open.

On the other side, an arched roof sheltered an alley that led them into a plaza lined with shops with apartments above them. The pavements were clean; the buildings in good repair.

Two stories above their heads, brightly colored clothes dried in the sun on lines of washing strung from one building to another. Several women looked down with curiosity at the strangers, then hauled their laundry back inside.

"Welcome to Residential Territory Number 13 of the Palos Verdes Immigration Reception District," Echo chirped with a wry grin. "What demented bureaucrat won an award for that fucked-up name? Ward 13. Simple. Descriptive. No wasted meaning."

On one side of the plaza, people sat at outdoor tables shaded by sail-like canvas canopies. Meals had been served in wooden bowls and they drank from earthenware mugs. Hushed whispers. Polite but suspicious glances. Word spread. Someone new had arrived in Ward 13.

"People who live on the other side of the Barrier believe all the migrant camps are ugly and dysfunctional," Echo said. "Now you know at least one that isn't."

"The people here don't venture out much except to trade with the other Wards," Muldoon added as they walked across the plaza. "They keep busy recycling old equipment, making their own clothing and tools, growing fruit and vegetables. One advantage of being fortified like this, no one can break in at night and steal from our agri-dome. Ward 13 has become a reliable supplier of fresh food to the other Wards. Earning a living by doing something legal—well, in the Wards of South LA, that's a miracle in itself."

On the far side of the plaza stood a tall structure with two whitewashed towers, its entrance a massive set of wooden double doors. Above the doorway, multi-colored tiles rose three stories, ending in a curved Palladian arch. Black, onion-shaped domes topped the towers. Behind them, a ridgeback roof extended back until it met a much larger black dome that spanned the width of the building.

"The Cathedral of the Fifth Pathway," Echo said.

"The *Fifth* Pathway? What are the other four?"

"You need to take it first, to understand the rest."

***

Inside the Cathedral of The Fifth Pathway, an oasis of cool air brought relief from the beating sun. The scent of freshly baked bread and burning charcoal drifted from a bakery in what had been a chapel's alcove. Long dining tables hewn from reclaimed planks occupied one side of the church. On the opposite side, men and women worked at tables laden with baled sheaves of grass. They were busy making yarn, rope, and baskets. A communal kitchen at the end of the nave served soup from large metal pots. The residents of Ward 13 came and went, browsing for crafts or sitting for a meal. If they needed some yarn or a basket, they took it. If they wanted sustenance, it was provided. No money or denbits changed hands as far as Nikki could tell, but no one seemed to take more than they needed.

Echo led Nikki to a counter with a stack of earthenware bowls and plates. "You must be hungry. I'm starving."

They were served a meal of vegetable soup so thick it was more like a stew, and given as many bread rolls and fruit as they wanted. Nikki joined Echo and Muldoon at a table, her stomach rumbling. That hunger faded as the first spoonful of hearty stew went down; a simple dish, spicy and rich in flavor, food like nothing she'd ever tasted before.

Echo noticed her delight. "Some of our bread is made with the cassava flour we trade with your mother. In return, she sells our vegetables to her neighbors in the Free-Citizens Zone. Your mother's jams are famous here. She grows spices we use in our homemade beer. This is how it's meant to be—communities across the Barrier in harmony, not divided. People co-operating, not fighting each other over every morsel. People in the other Wards have the same hardships we have, but they've chosen a different path. Your side of the Barrier encourages that because crime justifies the Federation's security measures."

"I know. I've seen us in action more times than I want to remember. But I didn't navigate the sewers for a lesson I've already learned. I came here to find my mother."

"We sent word," Muldoon replied. "Don't worry, she'll be here soon."

Echo explained how deep aquifers had been tapped beneath the Ward's red abode, providing residents with drinking water, sanitation, and irrigation for their agri-dome. Workshops repurposed anything with a moving part, producing the small wind turbines that adorned every rooftop. Kilns made pottery. Blacksmiths forged reclaimed metal. While the other migrant wards relied on power and water rationed from the Federation, a service that could be curtailed as punishment, Ward 13 was a community built around its self-reliance.

Nikki's energy returned as she ate. Her patience waned as the shallow banter continued—hydroponics and the millet harvest, the progress of Brother Mikey's new kitchen equipment. *This idle chitchat needs to be cracked wide open,* she thought. She put down her spoon and pushed her bowl away. "Bread-making? Something weird is happening all across the Federation, on both sides of the Barrier, and you're big priority is how to make more bread? Why are you pretending everything is normal? However shitty that normal is, it just got a whole lot worse and you seem so calm about it." Nikki surveyed the people coming and going in the cavernous church. "Frankly, I'm scared shitless. But they don't seem frightened at all."

Muldoon and Echo exchanged hesitant looks.

"They saw what you saw. All of us saw it," Echo said. "Pastor Harold knew they were coming. He talked to everyone, reassured them, as only he can."

"He *knew*? Knew what?"

"We'll be ready to fight back when they return," Muldoon replied.

"Who's returning? From where? After all the chaos that's hit the city, you'd better explain what you think is going on. Let's start with that container ship, the one you said was a false flag. It wasn't. The crew experienced something that fucked up their biology in a big way. Whatever that something was, it caused seizures. I saw other people last night, miles away from that ship, who'd also suffered seizures. So there goes your 'false flag medical emergency' bullshit. *Something* descended on the city, some kind of radiation clouds. I think it's causing brain damage and seizures. I'm going to take a wild guess and say Pastor Harold's spirituality won't save you if that happens again."

"Look around you," Echo said. She waved her hand at the throng of people in the church. The kitchen hummed with activity. "What do you see?"

Impatient, Nikki glanced around with angry eyes. "What am I supposed to see? We're in a migrant ward. Okay, people here seem cleaner, better fed, and I assume from that, healthier. But like any other Ward, their clothes are handmade, ragged. Their hair needs cutting. Other than that, this place is not much different from any migrant ward I've ever been in, whether I'm welcomed or not. What's that got to do with anything?"

"Nothing seems much different about us on the outside," Echo replied. "But it's always what's inside that counts. You think everyone here is a migrant? How do you know that? Because of geography? Because we're on the side of the Barrier that labels us that way? Would it surprise you to know the vast majority of people who live in Ward 13 are free-citizens of the Federation?"

Nikki huffed. "Yes, it would. It most definitely would. Why would people choose to live in a migrant ward?"

"I agree. Why choose deprivation? Why suffer restrictions here, instead of freedom on the other side? Why don't we live in settlements protected by the police and the military?"

"Yeah, you hit all the high notes. My thoughts exactly—and?"

"If you want to hide from the Association, a migrant ward is the perfect place. The Association has no interest in powerless migrants. Power resides on the other side of the Barrier. And power is what they want. Why do we prefer what you call deprivation? Because here, we have a freedom and security your so-called wealth can't give us. My story is everyone's story. Judge it for what it is. Believe what you want. I don't fucking care."

"I'm listening, Echo."

"I haven't always lived in Ward 13. I was born a free citizen, joined the military at a young age, in the Sequoia Forest Military District where I grew up. I thought preventing the Federation from sliding into anarchy was a noble profession. Preserving law and order in the communities I served, arresting bad guys. Smoked more than a few of them and felt no regrets along the way. I was thrilled when I was selected for officer training."

Echo pointed to her head. "And that's when it all fell apart—up here. At first, they were just bad dreams. But my concentration suffered and I made mistakes. I became hesitant, lost focus. Then the blackouts came, sometimes in the middle of an exercise. That finished me as an officer. Soon after, it completely ended my military career."

"But Ward 13? You're a free-citizen. You could have found another job anywhere in the Federation."

"Those nightmarish dreams drove me to Ward 13. To seek out Pastor Harold. He has a reputation among people who know about these kinds of things. Our people. *My* people now. Just thinking about what those dreams were doing to my mind makes me nauseous. They'd become so vivid, so detailed, scary, lifelike. My dreams were transporting me back to places I'd actually been. Pastor Harold explained I'd buried those thoughts so deeply in my subconscious, my conscious mind had built barriers to shut them out, to help me forget the pain. In the stress of military life, those walls fell, and the dreams took over. The sight of those clouds brings those dark times back, in living color."

"Brings what back?" Nikki asked.

"I was just a small child, six-years-old." Echo's voice faltered as she spoke in a half-sob. "*They* took me, Nikki. I was just a child. *They* took me."

"Who took you?"

Echo's mouth tried to form the next words but when the sound came out her voice cracked with anguish. "*They* did *things* to me— things Pastor Harold helped me remember so I could confront the truth. I'd repressed those ugly images over so many years, they returned not as memories of things I actually experienced in real life, but as dreams, as nightmares. You asked me why people would want to live in Ward 13 if they were free to live elsewhere? Well, the answer is simple."

"I'm confused," Nikki said. "What are you saying?"

"I'm saying, everyone here—we've *all* been abducted by *them*. Every single living soul in Ward 13. We've *all* been abducted by those monsters—the Ceruleans."

"The *what*?"

"I've not just *seen* their spaceships," Echo said. "I've been *inside* them. Seen *them*. Peering down at me, as they did things to my body. Just a child—facing monsters. Large bulbous heads with glassy black eyes. No mouth or nose. And this strange leathery blue skin—that's why we call them, the Ceruleans. I never thought blue could be such an ugly color."

Echo gazed up as if the cathedral's ceiling was open to the sky. "All of us here in Ward 13 were the first witnesses to the evil they will bring. And we will be the first warriors in the coming fight. All of us have fought the memories of our experiences, the things they did to us. To you, the people of Ward 13 may seem peaceful on the outside, but we are a warrior community, Nikki. We're not fighting the other Wards. We're a different kind of survivor and we're getting ready for a much bigger fight. What will it take for the rest of you to fucking wake up? You already know that answer because yesterday it fell from the sky. The Ceruleans are coming back. And they don't just want to 'sample' humans for their gruesome experiments—they're coming for *everyone*. And the Association is going to help them."

"The Association?"

"The Association of the Reborn," Muldoon said. "If we are the failures from the Ceruleans' experiments—call us their 'rejects'— then the Reborn represent their success. Ask yourself, what do you know about genetic engineering that nobody else knows? Because whatever that might be, the Reborn want that knowledge. And want it badly. Not to learn from it. But to bury it. To kill it."

"I don't know anything." Nikki leaned back and massaged her aching temples. "What could I know? I'm nothing special. Believe me. I'm not a genetic researcher. I'm just a doctor. What could I possibly know about genetics that no one else knows? There isn't anything."

"There's everything," a familiar voice said from behind her. "Everything I've tried to protect you from—for your entire life."

Her mother rested her hand on Nikki's shoulder, bent down, and kissed her on the cheek.

Nikki rose and they embraced, and for the first time in a long while, they clung to each other, mother and daughter, as if by holding each other so tightly, their combined strength could defeat anything.

"I love you, Mom. But I don't understand." Nikki sobbed. "Please help me understand. Why us?"

13 - REVELATIONS

Tucked in the cellars below the Church of the Fifth Pathway was a large room with two beds. A battery-powered lamp provided a glimmer of light.

"Mom, was I abducted by aliens as a child?" Nikki asked.

"No, Nikki. Nothing like that."

"I can't tell you how sorry I am for not believing you all these years," Nikki said. "All the arguments we had that shouldn't have happened. I was worried you were slipping into some kind of paranoid dementia, but all this time, you've held these secrets—about this Association, about Ward 13. The people here adore you. You must have been coming here for years and I never knew. You said all that secrecy was to protect me. From what? Why?"

"It's always been hard to explain. Not because the story is complicated. Because in the end, it isn't. Some things in the past needed to be done for the greater good. Things that broke the rules, that challenged authority. I'm not talking about lawlessness or anarchy. After the war, there was plenty of that. No, for Dante Parks, it was about discovering a threat to our existence and wanting to do something about it. That was the struggle he faced, a struggle he hoped we would continue."

"Who? You? Me?"

"You remember me telling you the brothers were experts in fertility?"

"Yes. And that Grandma Adriana helped Uncle Dante with his research."

"This struggle started a very long time ago. Uncle Dante and his brother stumbled upon something unusual with twin births in remote villages deep in the rain forests of Brazil. Women in these villages had superhuman fertility."

"What do you mean, *superhuman*?"

"The length of their pregnancies had been reduced from nine months to as low as four. Healthy twin babies had grown in the womb incredibly fast. Some women were giving birth twice a year. Always to twins. And the age of child-bearing for these women had increased as well. Some were able to bear children when they were over one hundred years old."

"*What?* One hundred? That's impossible. They didn't go through menopause?"

"Not impossible. It happened then, and it's still happening now. You remember the trip Uncle Dante's brother took to Japan, the one he never returned from?"

"You said he was murdered there."

"Yes, by the Association. Amare Parks visited a research colleague, Dr. Mitomi, who found similar women living in an isolated village in the mountains of Japan. Uncle Dante kept his brother's papers. They were in that box hidden inside my wardrobe."

"Where is the box?" Nikki looked around the room. "Do you bring it with you?"

"No, I couldn't. When the Association discovered where I lived, Muldoon and Echo came to my house to warn me. It was the night those clouds fell from the sky. I was packing up when these thugs appeared. They were surprised I wasn't alone. Muldoon and Echo scared them off. I knew what they wanted and grabbed the box. We fled through the orchard but more of them arrived, too many to fight. We had to leave. While they ransacked the house, I hid the box inside the compost heap in case they caught us. On the other side of my garden, a riot started. The military came up the street, searching for looters, shots were fired. There was so much confusion. It was too dangerous to stay. We had to leave it behind."

"I must have missed you by minutes. Is the box still there? Buried in the garden?"

"They took me to Mikey's factory but were afraid we were followed. We came here, through the tunnels, not my usual way. What an awful trip. That journey nearly killed me. The next day, they sent Mikey back for the box. He hid it again, I don't know where, somewhere inside his factory he said. Let's hope the Association doesn't find it. Uncle Dante's research is too valuable to be lost."

"That box can't possibly contain all of his research, it's too small."

"There are papers in the box that explain where his research can be found. That's why I never told you about the box or about Dante Parks. That's how I've been protecting you, Nikki. The less you knew about all this, the better. When I got old enough to really understand what all this meant, my mother told me everything about that trip to Japan, just as Uncle Dante described it to her before he died. It was chilling, something you never forget once you've heard it. That changed everything for me, just as it had done for him and then your grandmother. But you dismissed it as paranoia."

"It connects with what Echo said? About aliens, abductions, experiments?"

"Yes. Eighty years ago, those women in Japan suffered the same ordeal. Amare Parks interviewed them. Horrific stories of abduction. One night, a large spaceship appeared over the village. It projected a beam to the ground, like a tube, and an alien came down it. There's a notebook in the box that describes what they witnessed. The creature was nine or ten feet tall. They followed it into a temple. Inside was a woman giving birth to twins. The alien took the mother and her newborn babies away. Amare Parks and Dr Mitomi fled. Their car slid down a ravine. Mitomi was killed. Amare Parks survived the crash but died the next day on his way to Tokyo."

"Did something like that happen to Echo? Did she give birth to twins?"

"No, but Echo's mother was abducted several times. She was very old when she had her final set of twin girls, Echo being one of them."

"Echo has a twin?"

"Her sister died when they were both six. The aliens came back to find out why. They forced her mother to dig up her sister's body and then they tore it apart, right in front of both of them. They took Echo and her mother away. Echo was returned, alone, just six years old, an orphan. She never saw her mother again. Those are the frightening memories that haunt her. For some reason, children like Echo were rejected for further experiments."

Nikki noticed the fear in her mother's eyes. "You said the Association is everywhere. So, the Reborn—they look like *us*? They live among us?"

"That's why you can't trust anyone, Nikki. I know they say it's safe here in Ward 13, but you still need to be very cautious. The Reborn can communicate with each other in ways we don't understand. Pastor Harold knows more about this than I do."

The lamp flickered, its battery losing charge.

"You look so exhausted, Nikki. You've been through quite an ordeal and you're struggling to stay awake. It's not just the lamp that needs to be recharged. Your mind needs rest."

Nikki yawned.

Marcia opened the blanket on one of the beds. "That's enough for tonight, dear."

The straw-filled mattress rustled as Nikki settled in. Her eyes closed and in less than a minute, she was fast asleep.

Marcia stroked her daughter's head. "Oh Nikki, if only you knew how truly special you are."

***

An eerie sensation woke Nikki from a deep sleep. Her skin prickled. She jolted upright. As her eyes adjusted to the darkness, she saw a strange blue light swirling in circles around every object in the room, including her. Flickering sparks passed through her skin, burrowing inside her body, making her organs vibrate. As she inhaled, the sparks stung her throat. She felt nauseous and gasped for breath.

Her sleeping mother stirred, coughed, and woke with a start. Marcia cried out in shock and threw off her blanket as if it crawled with insects. "Nikki, what's happening?"

The mist of sparks moved quickly through the room like a wave crashing on a shoreline. A few moments later, it faded through the walls. Darkness returned as the blue glow completely disappeared.

A loud bang rattled the door. "Nikki, get up! We need a doctor!"

Nikki put on her jumpsuit. "Stay here, Mom. I'll find out what's going on."

She opened the door and ran into the arms of Muldoon.

"Outside—in the plaza," he said. "Pastor Harold sent out a warning, but it was too late."

Nikki raced with him through corridors of panicked people until they emerged into the plaza in front of the Cathedral. Scattered around were about a dozen men, women, and children having seizures. Sparkling blue clouds drifted high in the air, heading toward the other migrant wards.

Nikki scurried between the victims, giving instructions to those trying to help. "Find clothing to cushion their heads. Move them onto their side. Tilt their head back. Keep them warm."

A woman approached Muldoon in a state of distress. "There are more, inside the buildings," she said, crying.

"I'll go. You stay here, Nikki."

"Remove anything around the patient that might injure them," Nikki said as he left. "Tell them not to put their fingers in their mouths. Let the seizures run their course. Without medication, there's nothing more we can do."

Several anxious minutes passed. The seizures subsided on their own. As the victims relaxed, they appeared to fall asleep. Nikki went from one stricken person to another, checked their breathing, felt for a pulse.

Muldoon returned. "There were five more inside. By the time I got to them, their seizures had stopped. Just like the people here."

Weak voices murmured around the plaza. The victims were waking up, dazed but alert.

"I need to get them to Malibu Heights, Muldoon. They need MRIs, blood work. I need to run every test I can think of. It's the only way to figure out what's going on."

"Malibu Heights? How? We can't take them through the tunnels. Not in this condition. We don't have enough jeeps to take them by road. And it's too dangerous even if we tried."

"Leave all that to me. It's time Astrid Stenmuir made her new air ambulance pay its way for the blood it cost to buy it. It's time Malibu Heights found out where I am. I want answers and I won't get them hiding here."

14 - CROSSBOW-4

"Target altitude for first stage separation is twelve thousand kilometers."

Chenzi peered through the ISO's cupola windows at the speeding object that streaked up from Earth. "Roger that, Control. I have a visual on Crossbow-4."

"We have main rocket separation. Second stage boosters have engaged."

"Copy that, Control. First stage has broken away. I've got a bird's-eye view."

"One thousand kilometers until separation of probe capsule from the secondary stage rocket boosters."

Given the anomaly's power to ingest asteroids, the survivability of Crossbow-4, a hastily improvised satellite, was unknown. The worst it could do was offer a limited period of spectrographic data before the anomaly overpowered it. The best it could do was buy time to build something better.

"Second stage boost engine cut-off. Capsule hull separation initiated."

Glints of sunlight bounced off the outer segments of Crossbow-4's protective shell as it exposed the satellite's internal instruments.

"Control...separation confirmed. She's looking good."

"Firing probe thrusters. Commencing deceleration to target. We are go for intercept with the anomaly." The rapidly advancing probe slowed. "Crossbow-4 has stabilized its approach. Velocity: two hundred meters per second. Altitude: thirty-five thousand four hundred kilometers. Solar panel extension initiated."

"Roger that, Control. Probe has reached its target position in front of the energy field."

"Activating spectrometer. Transferring controls to the ISO. Crossbow-4 is all yours, Chenzi."

"Signal confirmed. Synchronization with Leonardo's radiation analyzer complete. Data stream from Crossbow-4 received. Let's poke this puppy and see what it's made of. Hey, any news about JoJo and Marisol?"

"Negative. Sorry, Chenzi. We've lost civilian communications east of Flagstaff. Military patrols are still searching the area where the group was last seen."

"Searching is not good news, Control. Finding, that's the news I want to hear. I'm trying real hard up here. I need you to be trying just as hard where you are."

"Copy that."

Data streamed in from Crossbow-4's laser and X-ray bombardment of the energy field.

"Control, sending the first data map. The anomaly's outer ring contains potassium, hydrogen, and nitrogen with layers of trapped cesium and strontium. Crossbow-4 detects beryllium and magnesium in small pockets. Leonardo's AI program indicates the anomaly's outer ring is a mixture of Bose–Einstein condensates and some kind of exotic Rydberg matter, comparable to dusty plasma clouds in interstellar space."

"ISO...stand by."

"Control...did you copy that? Leonardo's AI has concluded—"

Sirens wailed aboard the ISO. Emergency lights flashed.

"Chenzi, move to the resupply shuttle immediately. Prepare to evacuate the ISO."

"Evacuate? I'm in the middle of—"

A shadow moved across the windows and plunged the Telescope Dome into darkness. A moment later, a pulsating blue glow illuminated the inside of the dome. Chenzi pushed up to see outside. A long, elliptical spacecraft moved slowly beside the space station. Beneath its translucent blue exterior, pulse-like bursts of energy rippled across rows of triangular panels. The pulses ran from one end of the craft to the other, and then back again.

"Oh shit, is this thing on a collision course with the ISO?"

"That's a negative, Chenzi. Evacuate, now!"

"That's a double negative, Control. We need to probe this anomaly for as long as we can. "

"Chenzi," Director Simon Belledeau said. "This is no time for heroics."

"Then when is it time?"

Strong vibrations shook the ISO. The jolt pushed Chenzi away from the windows. "Did something just hit us?"

She clambered down to Leonardo's workstation. "We're still receiving signals from Crossbow-4." The blue glow intensified. "Boris, activate all external sensors and cameras. Document the spacecraft outside the ISO. Examine every hair on its body."

"Affirmative, documentation sequence initiated. I can confirm the object has no hair."

A second, stronger, more unsettling jolt hit the station.

"What the hell—"

"Warning," Boris announced. "Oscillating magnetic field, strength 2.5 tesla. Low-frequency infrasound waves detected. Potential danger to structural elements. Shutting down all vibration-sensitive equipment."

"No, Boris. Don't do that—"

The lighting in the Telescope Dome went out. Instrument consoles and their display monitors shut down. The streams of data from Crossbow-4 disappeared.

"Control...I feel weird. Oh, geez—"

"Chenzi, are you okay?"

No response.

"Initiate medical diagnostics," Belledeau ordered.

"Bio-status, Science Officer Zhu Chenzi," Emma reported. "Internal organ functions disrupted by molecular level vibrations. Subject's breathing approaching hyper-ventilation. Blood pH rising.

Respiratory alkalosis indicated. Synthesizing mild dose of benzodiazepine.

Emma paused.

"Synthesis of agents complete. Injecting nano-biocytes."

Emma paused again as the transdermal patch on Chenzi's arm did its work. "Patient responding."

"Chenzi...come in. Acknowledge, please."

"Control, I blacked out for a moment. I feel like I'm—like, the whole ISO—that we're inside some kind of giant MRI machine."

The vibrations stopped.

"Reactivating instruments," Boris said.

The lights, consoles, and displays turned back on.

"Chenzi," Belledeau said. "Get to the resupply shuttle and evacuate the ISO while you still have power."

"Negative, Control...I'm fine. Stop telling me to evacuate. I'll be the one to make that decision, okay? But I'll warn you in advance, it may be the other side of never. So, shut up about it."

During her blackout, Chenzi's body had floated back up to the cupola windows at the top of the dome. Outside the station, starlight glistened on a field of pitch black. She peered outside. "Control...this is amazing. The spacecraft has moved away from the ISO. Sections on its side have opened. Oh...will you look at that! Six smaller craft are leaving the mother-ship. They're approaching the energy field. They've split into two formations. One group is veering toward the left side of the anomaly's outer ring. The other to the right."

"Copy, ISO. We're tracking them."

"Control, the six craft have positioned themselves around the ring and are moving in tandem around its circumference." Chenzi glanced down at Leonardo's consoles. "Crossbow-4 is back on-line, and its data stream is going wild."

She peered outside again. "There are flares of bright white energy sparking out of these smaller spacecraft as they accelerate around the ring, leaving behind bright nodes of what seems to be like—I don't know even what to call them—maybe static energy bursts, like ball lightning. These nodes are spitting out even smaller energy spheres which are clustering together. This is the most bizarre thing I've ever seen. It's like six spiders spinning a circular web of starlight, perfectly synchronized with each other. If it wasn't so frightening, it would be beautiful."

Chenzi returned to Leonardo's main console and swiped across the display screen, selecting chunks of data for processing into models.

"Boris," she said. "Duplicate all raw data coming from Crossbow-4 and transmit to Ground Control."

"Copied and transmitted."

"Control...I'm going to let Leonardo continue its modeling of the data feed, but I don't want to lose the raw data if we get into trouble again."

"Copy that, ISO. We are receiving your files now."

"Control...Leonardo is giving us a first look at those spherical light clusters. AI concludes they are ultra-high-density energy fields. There's a large concentration of ionized lead and gold in the areas the spacecraft leave behind as they move around the ring. Transmitting Leonardo's models now. Any idea what's going on?"

"Standby, ISO."

Oh geez, Chenzi thought. Not another emergency.

"Chenzi," Director Belledeau said. "Lewis Temple is here. He's been examining your models."

Professor Lewis Temple? Oh wow.

"Chenzi," Temple said. "It's possible the small spacecraft are using some kind of miniaturized fusion reactors to collide lead and gold atoms. Leonardo is detecting quark-gluon plasma in their wake which then attracts strontium ions to the ring from the larger energy field. What happens next is complicated and theoretical. I'll condense my conclusions into the simplest form I can, but what you're seeing is the encapsulation of this quark-gluon plasma by what I can only call an evolving physical structure of crystalline Rydberg matter."

"What are they doing that for?"

"Lots of theories. No conclusions yet. What we know is that you are the first human being to witness the production of a ring of exotic matter made of particles we thought were only theoretical. The physical properties of this ring may very well violate all known laws of physics. So that's a big concern for your survival and for the integrity of the ISO. But I agree with you. We need to maintain Crossbow-4's data stream for as long as humanly possible. But the unpredictable may occur. You're fully aware what that means, right?"

"Yeah, I do. After the memorial service, I'll get a bronze statue in Nova Mercurius. What are our next analytical priorities, professor?"

"Uh, Chenzi, this is Simon Belledeau. You need to see the feed from one of the ISO's cameras."

"I can see fine through the windows."

"It's not about the anomaly. Boris, show Chenzi the exterior of the resupply shuttle."

The resupply shuttle hung from a port on the Docking Bay like a large trophy fish. It was twenty meters long, with an eleven-meter wingspan and a fuselage width of eight meters. Attached to the ISO, the shuttle presented its upper side to the various windows around the station. The underside of the spaceplane faced Earth and was only visible from an inspection camera attached to one of the station's solar panel booms.

Boris selected the camera viewing the shuttle's underbelly. Chenzi gasped. "What the hell—"

An egg-shaped object clung to the shuttle's underside. It was about half the length of the shuttle, about ten meters long, six meters wide. Its smooth surface was semi-transparent and rippled with waves of blue energy. Tiny sparks of bright white light drifted out of its top, fading into nothing as they floated into space. A large dark shadow, about three meters or nine feet tall, moved behind the opaque surface of the egg-shaped craft. The being had long thin legs and arms, and a bulbous head. It appeared to be manipulating a flat control panel with its fingers, flashes of light emerging from its fingertips as they skimmed across it.

"Shit, Control—that thing's not getting inside here! There's no damn way!"

Chenzi pushed off the console and scurried out of the Telescope Dome. She clambered through the access tunnels until she reached the flight deck above Module Beta, climbed into the commander's chair, and grabbed the joystick. "Boris, camera view of the resupply shuttle, please."

The monitor in front of her displayed the nose-cone of the docked shuttle.

"Initiate first stage, shuttle undocking sequence."

"Initiated. Airlock depressurizing. The resupply shuttle is safe to detach from the ISO."

"Boris, calculate shuttle thrust burn for separation. I need enough thrust to get the shuttle at least one hundred meters from the ISO."

"Calculated and programmed."

"Program a re-orientation sequence to rotate the shuttle. Align its trajectory toward the center of the anomaly."

"Understood. Calculated and programmed."

"Transfer the shuttle's flight controls to my command console."

"Transfer complete. Flight systems connected."

"Control...I'm going to dispense with this thing. Let's find out what happens when you fly that alien egg and whatever the fuck is inside it, right into the center of their energy field."

"Roger that, ISO. As good a plan as any we have down here."

"Initiating second stage separation of the resupply shuttle." Chenzi released the clamps that held the shuttle to the dock. Reverse thrusters engaged, accelerating it away from the ISO.

"Target distance of one hundred meters achieved," Boris said.

"Initiating burn to stop the shuttle." Chenzi arrested its rearward journey. "Here goes, Control. Re-orienting the shuttle."

Jets fired to roll the shuttle over, then fired again to tip its nose up. The egg-shaped object, with its alien cargo stuck on the shuttle's underbelly, came into view through the flight deck's window.

"Control, we are go in ten, nine, eight…" Chenzi gripped the joystick with sweaty palms. Nervous fingers twitched. Her stomach churned. She gritted her teeth and pushed the joystick forward. "Bon voyage, baby."

The shuttle's main engines ignited, sending the craft hurtling toward the anomaly.

"Control, have you come to any conclusions about the black void in the center? Because that shuttle is about to slam head first into it."

"That's a negative," Professor Temple replied. "Consider this a cosmic bench experiment. The bronze for your statue has been ordered. Good luck, Science Officer Zhu."

The resupply shuttle raced past the alien mother-ship.

"Chenzi, the shuttle is sixty kilometers from the center of the anomaly. Impact in twenty seconds."

"Roger that, Control. I'm strapped in." Her fingers gripped the edges of the seat.

"Elevated heart rate."

"Not now, Emma."

The six small spacecraft that surrounded the energy field's outer ring stopped their work and scattered away. As the shuttle approached, the strands of energy that connected the anomaly's black void to its outer ring increased in brightness and expanded in width. Then—as if the aperture of a giant lens opened—the void expanded rapidly until it was three times its original size.

"Impact in ten seconds."

Tendrils of forked energy appeared from a point of light in the center of the anomaly and formed a kaleidoscopic spiral that swirled inside the ring. The shuttle—minuscule in comparison to the energy field—appeared on Chenzi's display as a tiny silhouette set against a bright angry backdrop.

"Five, four, three, two, one…"

Upon impact, the swirling spiral exploded in a blinding flash of white light. The burst of energy collapsed inward as quickly as it had formed, then disappeared entirely, leaving behind the original black void, pulsing as it had done before.

The shuttle and its attached alien payload had disappeared.

"Chenzi, do you copy? Are you there?"

"Affirmative, Control."

"The anomaly has absorbed the shuttle."

"Copy that. Looks like we punched some kind of hole in it. Then it repaired itself. What's your take on what happened?"

"We're still processing the raw data from Crossbow-4," Lewis Temple said. "But everything we've witnessed—all the work those spacecraft were doing—is consistent with building a structure of exotic matter with a negative energy density."

"Okay, got that, professor, I think. But a structure for what purpose?"

"There can only be one conclusion, Chenzi. The anomaly is the entrance to a wormhole."

15 - THE CARAVAN PARK

Astrid Stenmuir's dour face frosted the walls of her office. "You stole a jeep, wrecked it beyond repair, and then somehow ended up in a migrant ward? What the fuck, Akaju?"

"Our jeep was ambushed."

"So you say. Then you sent for a military transport to bring a bunch of grubby migrants back *here?* What for? They don't even appear to be sick. We're a trauma center, not an out-patient clinic."

"I don't care if they're migrants. They were exposed to radiation clouds that caused seizures. Testing them is the right thing to do. Those clouds don't care which side of the Barrier they hit."

"Palos Verdes is in a state of emergency, in case you haven't noticed. That will tie up medical resources at completely the wrong time."

"Wrong time? What better time is there? There couldn't be a better time to do it than now."

"Who the fuck do you think is running this place, Akaju?" Stenmuir hissed. "As soon as I can find a transport that isn't full of critically injured patients, those migrants are going back to whatever shit-hole they came from. You're confined to ward duty until I figure out your real punishment. Just know, it will be painful."

"You could fire me before I quit."

"Firing you is a luxury I can't afford. And quitting is a luxury *you* can't afford. I'd say we're stuck with each other for now."

The comms display lit up. Its flashing signal deflected Stenmuir's ice-cold glare. She scanned the message. "In-bound transport. Joshua Tree Military District."

"Joshua Tree? Those clouds hit the SpacePort?"

A holographic map appeared. "No, some kind of mass casualty incident at a caravan park on the Vegas side of the Mojave Desert. There aren't any other details, except that it's another Level Five Security, Hazmat Code Eight."

"It can't be a virus again."

Stenmuir expanded the military's request for assistance. The mission leader assigned to the call-out was a broad-shouldered major with two raised welts across one of his cheeks. "It's a coordinated response between the Palos Verdes and Joshua Tree Military Districts, led by Federal Marines."

"Armstrong again." Nikki tapped the comms display. "Hazmat Code Eight, but there's no Liana Veron this time? That's strange. I thought Lab-15 was always involved in this kind of stuff. And they've specifically requested Bryan and I on this call-out."

"You're not going. Neither is Bryan Leysson."

"Say what? An infectious disease response? Which needs someone with that kind of expertise...check. And has the appropriate security clearance...double-check. Do you have anyone else that isn't already out on call? So, what's the plan, Astrid? Delay your response to a Hazmat Code Eight incident until someone else is available, like in two or three hours? I wouldn't want to argue with the military on that one. But be my guest. Knock yourself out. Could be career ending, just saying. Let's hope not. I was so looking forward to my punishment. But hey, it's your call. You run this place."

"You are such a fucking nuisance."

"I'll prep my kit. I don't need a hazmat suit. I'll use theirs. They already know my size."

*** *

Thick struts emitted a loud hiss as the heavy military transport landed with an earth-shaking thud on the grounds of Malibu Heights Hospital. The ramp at the back of the transport lowered and a tall figure in military fatigues sprinted toward Nikki and Bryan.

"The doctor with the unfulfilled death wish," he said. "Maybe today your dream will finally come true." Armstrong grabbed their kit bags like they were weightless. "Why HQ asked for you again, I'll never figure out. Guess they like stubborn mules. So if you two asses are ready, let's get airborne." He twirled his hand in the air. They jumped onto the ramp just as it started to close.

Nikki strapped in. "This has something to do with those clouds, doesn't it? More seizures?"

"Not this time. The information we have is sketchy and, to be honest, doc, a little bizarre."

"Bizarre, as in...?"

"As in, there are no survivors this time."

"So, this is a forensics exercise?"

"You could call it that."

"If they're dead, you need pathologists not emergency doctors. Why us?"

"Vandenberg wants to keep this incident quiet. They want to maintain a tight circle of people in-the-know."

"But we don't know anything."

"You know more than you think. You know enough to be useful. And—" He checked his sat-link. "In about thirty minutes, you'll know things no one should ever know."

***

"Prepare for landing," the pilot announced.

The ruins of old casinos surrounded their destination, Whiskey Pete's Caravan Park, located in the ghost town of Primm, a hard-to-reach outpost where the lost treasures of a lost generation lay buried beneath the Mojave Desert's advancing sand dunes. The first indications of what happened at Whiskey Pete's came into view as the transport descended. Abandoned dune buggies and mobile eco-sheds littered the desert outside the campground's perimeter, their tracks fanning out in all directions. Beside each vehicle, a spray of black soot stained the desert sand. Several heli-cars had crashed, the inside of their canopies painted black. The sand around each of the park's huts was charred. Whatever had befallen the caravan park, the residents didn't have time to escape it.

The heavy transport's metal feet sank into the desert. Nikki zipped up her hazmat suit, checked her mask was tight, then hoisted her gear down the ramp.

Armstrong surveyed the campground. He pointed to a structure with thick adobe pillars, its walls of canvas flapping in the wind. Sunlight flashed off large copper kettles. "An illegal agave distillery. Over that ridge, there's a maze of dunes nearly two thousand feet high. Nomads outnumber you and outgun you. So, who in their right mind would want to drive an unreliable government dune-jeep across this empty desert in order to collect a ten percent liquor tax? There are easier ways to risk your life. But this camp's freedom from taxes came with a high price. Take a look around and you'll see what I mean."

Two more military transports thumped down next to theirs. Armstrong rallied his squad of marines. He gave them orders and they moved away from the campground toward the dunes.

"Hey, where are you going?"

"To salvage what's left of their mechanicals, doc. The parts in those wrecks are too valuable to let them rot in the sun. There's more life in their lithium packs than around here. Congratulations, I'm giving you an honorary degree in forensics. That way you don't need me holding your hand."

"And I don't need to be a qualified vet to put down a mad dog."

Armstrong chuckled as he walked away. "Yeah, copy that, soldier. I'd like to see you try."

Nikki and Bryan shuffled through the hard-packed dust. In front of the first eco-hut, a pair of folding chairs sat empty under a shade canopy. Upon closer inspection, the chairs were coated with a thin layer of viscous brownish-black slime. Nikki gagged and stepped back. "Oh, shit."

She retrieved a pair of tongs from her bag and sifted through the ugly residue. "A coating of wet ash. Some charred bone fragments. Small chunks of burnt flesh. But mostly, it's just a pile of goo."

Bryan bagged a similar sample from the other chair. "It's like they melted. Whatever caused this, happened so quickly they didn't move."

Nikki's eyes wandered from one chair to the next. "It can't be possible, can it? I thought this phenomenon was just an urban legend. None of the reported cases came with any sensible explanation. But supposedly, this is the result."

"Are you suggesting spontaneous human combustion?"

"It certainly describes what we're looking at. And it's certainly not a virus. Hazmat Code Eight? Yeah, right." The gruesome scene was the same in front of the adjacent huts. "I don't even know what to call this, a mass combustion event? Even in a nuclear attack, the people at Ground Zero are vaporized until there's nothing left of them to find. And survivors are badly burned, not melted into goo like this."

"Now we know why the military selected us," Bryan said. "A tight circle of people in-the-know."

"When it comes to something like this, I know what you know. Which isn't anything more than I can see with my own eyes."

The pair took more samples of human remains, just enough for DNA identification. The morphology of each victim was identical— a scum of ash, charred bones, and residual flesh. Some victims had combusted where they'd sat or slept. Footprints around the huts traced where some tried to flee, stumbling through the park during the cataclysmic event, whatever it was.

"Heads up," Nikki said. "Our gracious host, Major Ozzie Armstrong, is coming back."

"Okay, docs," Armstrong chirped. "We're going to be on the ground for two more hours. Once my marines have retrieved personal effects for the victims' families, we're going to clean this place up."

"Clean it up?"

"Let's put it this way, by tomorrow morning, Whiskey Pete's Caravan Park will only exist in photographs. You can put your samples in here."

He opened the top of a large cooler bag labeled 'Mead Canyon Research Center'.

"Why do I get the feeling our samples are not coming back with us to Malibu Heights?"

"Two hours, boys and girls—then we torch this place."

Despite their suits' cooling tubes, an hour on the ground in hazmat gear had sapped their energy. They moved beside the concrete skeleton of a roofless, derelict casino to shelter from the wind-driven sand and dropped their gear. The heat was oppressive. The transport had arrived in the morning when the desert was waking from its cool sleep, but as each minute approached high noon, the heat of a breathless new day consumed the hills and dunes.

"I gotta rest." Nikki took off her respirator. Sweat streamed down her face. She splashed water across her forehead. "Just as well we're going soon. We can't last much longer in this heat."

A sound emerged from inside the casino ruins—a loud tap, metallic and repeating.

Nikki holstered her water bottle. "Hey, did you hear that, Bryan?"

The tapping continued. A faint whimper accompanied it.

"Get our trauma kit from the ARV. I'll see if I can identify where the tapping's coming from."

Nikki ran into the abandoned building. A large rubble pile lay where the roof had collapsed. The tapping sound wasn't coming from the rubble. She entered a former gaming room, its roof also open to the sky. A large sheet of corrugated metal lay on top of a crude wall of reclaimed timbers. There had been other makeshift shelters like this dotted around the camp, used to cover the campers' treasure digs. She navigated her way through mounds of excavated rock and found the source of the tapping—a woman, curled up inside the tin-roofed shelter. Dusty sand covered her clothes. Her hand banged a trowel against a metal panel in a mindless robotic movement.

Thirst had turned the woman's parched lips white. Nikki touched the water bottle to her lips and the woman came to life. She grabbed the bottle with both hands. Water spilled down her cheeks and chin, washing the dust away from her face.

"Steady," Nikki said, pulling back on the bottle. "Don't drink too fast."

"Have th-they gone?" she stuttered in a raspy voice.

Bryan scrambled toward them over the rubble.

Nikki checked the woman's neck. Her pulse was weak. "You're safe now. Help is here."

16 - MEAD CANYON

Mead Canyon, the dried bed of a former lake, in places over nine hundred feet deep, crept through the River Mountains east of the Las Vegas Closed City. The Mead Canyon Research Center sat on the edge of the Boulder Cliffs, twelve miles due north of the disused Hoover Dam. Access to the facility ran along a single road cutting across the brownish-red ochre of the desert. Solar panels sparkled in the waning light as the transport flew over and landed at an adjacent heliport.

A slightly built man in a white lab coat stood next to a waiting ground shuttle. He was shorter than Nikki, about five-foot-six, in his late thirties with mid-length wavy black hair that framed dark brown eyes, bushy eyebrows, and high cheekbones. "My name is Dr. Pavel Zharlev," he said.

The survivor from the caravan park deplaned, sedated in a mobi-cradle, drip lines in her veins restoring life.

Rotor aircraft of all descriptions landed and took off all around the shuttle. "I don't think I've been in a heliport this busy," Bryan said.

"Two thousand people work here," Zharlev explained. "We taxi them in and out every day. There's only enough water purified on site to accommodate a small workforce overnight. The rest live with their families near the SpacePort at Nova Mercurius where there's a pipeline from a desalination plant on the coast. You'll stay here at Mead Canyon tonight so we can discuss what you found."

The ground shuttle weaved its way through the landing pads. The Mead Canyon Research Center was a squat, featureless facility with sandstone walls, two stories high. Telescopes, satellite dishes, and weather research equipment broke the starkness of its roof-line. Mead Canyon had ten more floors underground, Zharlev explained, each level with south-facing glass that overlooked the deep canyon, to allow in as much natural light as possible. The logo of Temple Research dominated the front of the building.

"Temple Research?" Nikki said. "I thought this was a military research center."

"No, the brainchild of Lewis Temple and Ansel Denard," Zharlev replied.

"Ansel Denard of Pan-Lunar?"

"You're thinking of Edison, his twin brother. Ansel Denard keeps a much lower public profile. He isn't involved in the management of Pan-Lunar Exploration. Too much power politics with the military."

The shuttle entered the research complex through a large rolling door, stopped inside a vehicle elevator, and descended on a platform. Six floors down, the group exited the shuttle inside a foyer lined with polished sandstone walls. Banded curves of embedded iron oxide contrasted with the industrial grayness of the concrete floor. At one end of the foyer, a glass door-wall opened.

Dr. Zharlev led Nikki and Bryan down a long corridor to Particle Physics, a high-ceiling, windowless laboratory. A compact particle accclerator powered by fusion tokamaks hugged the walls of the large circular-shaped room. Technicians in white lab coats scurried in the cramped space between the accelerator and benches filled with high-precision cutting machines and 3D printers.

"It takes as much time making the parts to keep the accelerator running as it does to conduct the research. Some of our test apparatus is unique, the last of its kind."

Zharlev directed them into an empty conference room with a spectacular view of Mead Canyon. He tapped his data-tab. Shutters covered the window and the conference room lights dimmed. A montage of images appeared on a display screen the width of the wall.

He expanded one of the images to full-screen and said, "Do you recognize these people?"

"The crew of the *Espíritu de Lima*," Bryan answered.

The crew were arranged in the photograph like a college graduation class. In the front row, dead center, was the ship's captain: a short, stocky man, clean-shaven and well-dressed.

"I'd recognize the captain anywhere," Nikki said. "So neat, so proud of making a good first impression. A charming man. Polite, efficient, unassuming."

"How about this photo?"

Zharlev expanded another image, taken inside a dormitory. On a row of cots, white sheets were stained a blackish brown. On the wall behind each bed-head was a spray of black soot. "This happened last night. Same crew, same place—the Wilmington Park Quarantine Center."

Nikki turned her head away and held her hand to her mouth. "Oh god, not them too."

"The crew were about to be released back to their ship," Bryan said.

Zharlev replied in a deadpan tone, "They didn't make it. And neither did most of the staff at the quarantine center."

"Spontaneous human combustion?"

"That's our conclusion, Dr. Akaju. Just like the caravan park. There have been more incidents exactly like this, in quick succession."

She gasped. "*More?*"

Zharlev launched another set of gruesome photographs. "Flagstaff Drone Base, Great Texas Desert Military District. Nineteen victims."

Nikki and Bryan flinched.

"And this one—in Santa Fe, at the Adobe Park Desert Research Station, twelve victims. Same pathology, all of them died from some kind of human combustion phenomenon."

"Seizures, now this," Nikki said. "If a facility like Mead Canyon can't figure out what's happening, how do you expect us to? We're emergency doctors. That's it. But we keep getting side-tracked into all kinds of shit like this. First the container ship, now the caravan park. Why us?"

"Let me show you something else. We've recreated the time-line of those events."

Zharlev minimized the images on the screen and brought up a map displaying the area east of the Palos Verdes Military District, from Los Angeles to Santa Fe. "The first fatal incident, affecting the crew of the *Espíritu de Lima* at the quarantine center, occurred here." He selected the photo of the stained cots, shrunk it with his fingers, and pinned it as an icon above its location in the Free-Port of Los Angeles.

"The second incident happened here, at Whiskey Pete's Caravan Park." He produced a photo of the caravan park and pinned it to its location south of Las Vegas. "One of the heli-cars that crashed sent out an automated distress call, so we know the exact time of the incident."

"The third incident," he continued. "The military's Flagstaff Drone Base in the Great Texas Desert." He pinned another icon on the map. "And finally, the Adobe Park Desert Research Station outside Santa Fe."

Zharlev touched his data-tab again and blue lines connected the pinned locations together. "These incidents occurred in this time order, from west to east across several Military Districts. When you join them up, what have you got?"

"I don't know," Nikki said. "The same mystery, multiplied several times?"

"Not quite, Dr. Akaju. You have a flight path. Radar tracked three Unexplained Aerial Phenomena over a six-hour period." He touched his data-tab again and a red line superimposed over the jagged blue one. The new line hugged it closely, from the first incident in LA to the last one in Santa Fe, a location where both lines ended abruptly.

"Ten miles east of Santa Fe," he said, "the three UFOs ascended to an altitude beyond the stratosphere and then disappeared completely off every radar and satellite tracking system we have."

"They're coming back," Nikki remarked. "What will it take for the rest of us to wake up?"

"I'm sorry, what?"

"Just something someone said to me recently."

"Did those electrical clouds that fell on the Free-Port cause these horrible deaths?" Bryan asked.

"No, this happened later," Zharlev replied. "The Jupiter clouds fell several days before."

"What are Jupiter clouds?"

"Just a name we're using until we can get a better handle on what they are. As far as these incidents of human combustion, no one knows about the container ship crew or the fatalities at the other locations. The incident at the caravan park will be deep-sixed, you can be sure of that. It was remote and anyone who owned property there, and was lucky enough to stay home, will be told it's closed for security reasons. The world is a chaotic mixed-up place right now and telling the truth would put it right over the edge. We need to contain what we know, so what we *don't know* doesn't seed panic."

"What we really need," Nikki replied, "is to convince hospital management at Malibu Heights—specifically Dr. Astrid Stenmuir—to test patients from Ward 13 exposed to those, what did you call them, Jupiter clouds? Given what you've told us, that exercise is beyond urgent."

"We've already had that discussion with her. It's possible there's a biomarker that defines who can survive this kind of extra-terrestrial attack and who can't."

"A bio-marker?"

"There were several survivors of these combustion events—three at the quarantine center and a drone operator at the Flagstaff Base, Lieutenant Zachary Castleton. He raised the alarm right in the middle of the attack. Castleton was taken for a medical examination back at Central Drone Command then went AWOL before he could be interrogated about what he saw. The other three were office staff in a different wing of the quarantine center and didn't see anything."

"More survivors? What kind of bio-marker?"

"Of all the dozens of victims, these four people are the only ones whose medical records show they tested negative for avian flu antibodies. The blood tests from your caravan park survivor came through while you were touring the lab." He pointed to his data-tab. "Her tests confirm she's negative for avian flu as well. Our AI program indicates a high probability of a correlation."

"A correlation of what?"

"Between a negative test for avian flu antibodies and the ability to survive these attacks."

Nikki's face twisted into a frown. "Avian flu antibodies as a bio-marker? That makes little sense. Why would there be a connection between avian flu and spontaneous human combustion?"

"We don't know. But with the test result on this recent survivor, we can't discount anything at this point. If there's a bio-marker that predicts why some people can survive these attacks and others can't, we need to find out what that is, and *fast*. We need doctors with infectious disease expertise to join our team. That's why you're both here."

17 - THE SURVIVOR

"Is she strong enough to talk to us?" Zharlev asked.

"We shouldn't push her," Nikki replied as they walked into Mead Canyon's health wing. "If we hadn't found her when we did, she would have died from heat stroke. She was severely dehydrated. But she's a fighter. "

A tall, broad-shouldered black man in military fatigues, two scars running down one cheek, opened his arms wide to block the entrance to the ward. "This area is restricted access."

"This entire building is restricted access. So what? I made it inside," Nikki said. "But who let you out of your kennel, Major Doberman?"

"Your survivor knows more than the military does," Armstrong replied. "And when that happens, we're not fucking happy." He inched forward into her space until they were nose to nose. "I'm here to change that."

"You get around, don't you, Armstrong?" Nikki placed two hands on his chest and pushed him back. "Now, step aside!"

"Don't fuck with me, doc."

"I wouldn't dream of it," she sneered. "She's my patient. Now get out of my way."

"She's a military detainee."

"Like hell she is."

"What's going on?" Zharlev said. "This is *our* interview, major."

"What a coincidence. Join the party." Armstrong turned his data-tab around and flashed a document with a military logo. "Federal Intelligence Order—priority interrogation of a suspect aiding a military fugitive."

"A fugitive?" Zharlev glanced at Armstrong's ID and the information on the data-tab's screen. "I guess we can conduct this interview together, major. There's no point in putting her through this ordeal twice."

"I'm glad you share my concern, Dr. Zharlev."

"Always willing to co-operate with our armed services."

"You see, Dr. Akaju. Here's a man with the right attitude. You could learn something."

"Fuck you, Armstrong. Let's get on with it."

The survivor from Whiskey Pete's—a young woman named Mackenzie Noor—shifted nervously in her mobi-cradle as the group entered and sat down at a glass-topped table. Young and slim, her eyes were sallow and her short reddish hair matted.

Major Armstrong opened files on his data-tab. "Mackenzie, what were you doing at the caravan park?"

Noor glanced at Armstrong. His eyes had narrowed. His brow had creased. Her words came out in a stutter, "I've been... well... I'm..."

"Mackenzie, you've had quite an ordeal," Nikki said. "A frightening, traumatic experience. It's a wonder you can talk to us at all. You don't have to be afraid. You're safe now." Nikki sensed her reticence to speak. "Look at me, Mackenzie, not at him. Would it be better if Major Armstrong left the room?"

"Hold on, doc," Armstrong said. "She's not in any trouble if she co-operates. But she isn't going anywhere until she does. She was there. She saw it happen. Co-operation isn't optional, Mackenzie. This is too important. Do you understand?"

Mackenzie leaned forward. Her voice choked. "I'm okay with this. It's just that I lost some great friends. They just disappeared before my eyes."

"You shouldn't be ashamed to have survived it," Nikki said. "Tell us what you can. You choose where to start."

Mackenzie Noor placed her forehead in her hand. "Yeah, where to start? Okay, I wasn't supposed to be there. In fact, I wasn't even supposed to be on Earth."

"You were listed as a payload specialist in your last job," Armstrong said. "At Summit Station, Imbrium."

"That's right. Three months ago. The space end of the Lunar Skyway, two thousand kilometers above the surface of the Moon. I loved my job. Never dull. We were always super busy. Shuttles would arrive, dock with Summit Station. All this interesting stuff was unloaded and transferred down the elevator to Aldrin's Crater."

"I see from your medical records; you've never had avian flu?" Nikki asked.

"No, been on the lunar side of life since before all of that started down here. I was supposed to get vaccinated against it when I returned to Earth, but yeah, life on Earth got in the way, big time."

"You're unemployed?"

"Okay, that's where it gets all fucked up. See, I met this lunar shuttle pilot—"

"Lieutenant Zachary Castleton," Armstrong interjected.

"Wait, she knows someone that survived Flagstaff?" Nikki said. "He was stationed on the moon?"

"She also knows where he is now," Armstrong huffed. "I'm sure of it."

"I don't," Mackenzie replied. "I wish I did. We'd have a lot to talk about." She wiped her face. "Look, I wasn't involved with anything he did on the moon. I was just his girlfriend. Our free time together was brief. Since neither of us got much time off, we made the most of what we were given. Sex, okay? Nothing wrong with that."

She caught Armstrong's menacing glare. "I don't know what else he was alleged to have done, but whatever it was, it cost me my job. Pan-Lunar said I was being sent earthbound, that I'd get a new job at the SpacePort. But about a week after I landed back home, the bastards fired me. No explanation. No appeal. Worse than that, I got black-listed with all the contractors. I ran out of savings real fast. Apartments are so expensive in Nova Mercurius. People there get paid way too much. Serving lunches from a food truck couldn't pay my bills. And there were no jobs at the agri-domes. Damned automation."

"So, what did you do?" Armstrong asked.

"Zach got in touch with me again. He'd been investigated, not charged with anything, but he'd been demoted from shuttle captain and sent back to Earth. He said he owned an eco-hut at this neat desert park near Vegas. I could stay there if I wanted to, free of charge. Once I got there, I found plenty of ways to make money. People came and went all the time, rich people. So, I ended up doing all kinds of things—looking after their property, servicing their dune buggies, cooking for them at barbecue parties. It paid well and was rent free. God, I loved that place. During the week it was quiet, peaceful, no one there. Then at weekends, it became shit-face central, as wild as it gets. It was a cool lifestyle, majorly off-grid, pretty great, until—" Her head dropped into her hands. "God, I wish I could forget that night."

"Take a minute," Nikki said. "We've got lots of time."

She asked for a drink of water. The glass shook in her trembling hand. "So, yeah—about that night. It started with some kind of weird sunset. But it wasn't the sun. That had set already. We saw a single light, way up high in the sky. It expanded into this large bright ring. A loud boom followed. It knocked people off their feet. Someone from the SpacePort said it was a shock wave, like from an explosion. What I saw next—I thought I was dreaming. But it was fucking real."

"What did you see, Mackenzie?"

"Spaceships. Not like the space-planes we have. Three of them. Their bodies were thinner, their fronts curved in an arc like a boomerang. There was this strange pulse that ran back and forth on their sides. And these weird panels, with triangles. They flew down over the camp. Then there was this strange hum. It vibrated inside your body; made you feel like throwing up. The humming got intense. People fell over, then—oh, god, no—their bodies jerked and—"

Her face fell into her hands. Her lips curled and she sobbed.

"It was the most *awful* thing to watch. They just...like they were on fire—" She turned her head and gagged. "Oh, fuck—"

"You don't have to describe that," Nikki said. "We know what happened next."

"And then *they* arrived."

"Who?"

"This one spaceship hovered over where I was, like a ceiling over the whole camp. There was absolutely no sound. A blue beam projected onto the ground, a really dark blue. It looked kinda solid, like a giant blue tube. And then these long black shadows fell down to the ground. At first, I couldn't make out what these shadows were. But they were tall, I mean, really fucking tall. Twice my size. Then, then one of them saw me—"

Her eyes widened. Mackenzie shook, clutched her arms around her chest, and hugged herself. She rocked gently; her eyes glazed.

"It's okay. They're not here. They can't hurt you," Nikki said. "Take a deep breath. That's it, nice and deep. Do you need a break?"

"No, no, it's just that—seeing one of those things moving toward me, I've never been so frightened. I don't even want to think about what I saw."

"I know this is hard for you, Mackenzie. But it's so important we know what happened."

"They had these long, thin arms and big heads with black eyes. They walked funny, like in slow motion. And their skin, it shed this kind of vapor. Underneath that, there was this glow, like blue electricity, all over their bodies. They were searching around the burned chairs, like they were checking to see if there were any signs of life."

She drank some water, spilling some on the glass table. "I was a basket case by then. I ran out of the camp. I didn't know where I was going. I'd been drinking. That didn't help. I threw up, until I thought I was turning inside out. I don't know where I ended up. All I knew was, at some point, it all stopped. The blue tubes were gone. The spaceships disappeared. It was dark and quiet. Deathly quiet. I was alone, too scared to move, afraid of my own shadow. I don't remember anything after that, until I woke up here."

"We'd like to monitor you for a while, see if anything develops that needs treatment," Zharlev said. "You can stay here at Mead Canyon. Once you're better, I'm sure we can find some work for you here. We're always needing people. That way, we can keep a regular watch on your condition."

"A job? You're kidding? You'd do that for me?"

"Oh yeah, that's some great warm and fuzzy stuff from Professor Kumbaya here," Major Armstrong said. "But there's still the matter of aiding a fugitive that needs to be worked out first. I'm talking about Lt. Zachary Castleton."

"Zach? What's happened to him? Is he dead?"

"If he was, we'd have found him. Or what was left of him. As far as we know, he's very much alive. He went AWOL from—well, that's classified. Do you know where he is now, Ms. Noor?"

"He mentioned being stationed at some drone training base at the SpacePort. That's why he could see me at weekends. It wasn't far to Whiskey Pete's."

"How did he get to the caravan park?" Armstrong asked.

"He had his own heli-car. We tripped into the desert in it. He's a fabulous pilot."

"I've got an ARV that will test him on that score if he tries to escape again. Did he ever mention being transferred from the SpacePort to a base in Flagstaff in the Great Texas Desert?"

"Flagstaff? No."

"Did he have friends in the Las Vegas Closed City?"

"The Closed City? Are you kidding? That's the most dangerous migrant camp around. He was a strait-laced guy. Good family. Brother and sister in the military, too. His father is some bigwig with Westbrook Aerospace. Zach tried to get me a job there, made some inquiries with his dad. But Zach was told I wasn't qualified for the kinds of things they do. Which I thought was strange, given my job experience on the moon colony. Another blacklisting, I thought. Zach said they would put me on some kind of waiting list."

Armstrong checked his data-tab. "Okay, just a few minor little details to iron out. He's a family guy, you said? With a brother and sister? Castleton's military records say his parents are dead. He was raised in a federal orphanage, no siblings. And this dead dad of his was some bigwig in aerospace? There's no record of any employees with the name of Castleton working at Westbrook Aerospace, let alone running it."

"Wait—*what*? There isn't?"

"Seems your strait-laced lover-boy has the blood of a conman flowing through his cold evil heart. Love is blind. Do you need any more proof?"

Mackenzie's head slumped forward into her hands. She cried. Her body shook. "Look, I'll tell you everything I know about him," she sobbed. "I have nothing to hide."

"I think we can leave that to another day," Nikki said. "We've got the answers we need, right?"

Zharlev and Bryan nodded, yes.

"Hold on a second, doc—"

Nikki stood, grabbed Armstrong by the collar, and yanked. "Up, Major Doberman. She doesn't know where your guy is. She's co-operated—a lot. And she'll co-operate some more. But at another time. She's in no state to continue. Can't you see she needs rest?"

Armstrong muttered under his breath. "Okay then, another time."

"See? That was easy. You can do it if you try. It's always best to have the right attitude. Don't you agree, major?"

22 - THE DARK PLANET

The nightmare—surreal, abstract, ungrounded in earthly reality—paralyzed Chenzi with fear. Her subconscious fought the sleep-aides in her bloodstream and forced her awake. Drenched in clammy sweat, it took several fitful moments to understand where she was.

"Heart rate abnormal," Emma droned. "Pulse racing. Tranquilizer recommended."

"I just had one. It doesn't fix the problem. It makes it worse. I'll calm down. You should too."

Chenzi lay back on the pillow, afraid to close her eyes again.

Faraway worlds had once sent her soul into a state of wonder. Outside the ISO, a wormhole had turned that imagination into dread. Drug-induced sleep had failed to help a tired, anxious mind get much needed rest. Instead, it produced a nightmare—a terrifying flight into the wormhole's dark heart.

She'd dreamed she was outside the station on an EVA, but without a suit. A strange vibration surged through her body; a sensation similar to the magnetic field that had shaken the ISO. Passages in space-time opened up in all directions, tunnel-like mazes. Her body accelerated into the wormhole until her hands were a blur. Planets flew by at blazing speeds. When her journey finally ended, she floated above a world covered in an atmosphere of dark crimson gas. The planet hung in the heavens with a brooding, sinister presence, its clouds of gas churning plumes of hate toward the tiny human in its orbit.

Dark black, marble-like eyes stared up from its super-heated surface. She saw Marisol and JoJo enveloped in fingers of lava, crying out for help as they burned. But there was nothing Chenzi could do to save them.

An unwanted force suddenly pressed on her stomach, the same inexplicable force she'd experienced on the trail to Bonanza Peak. The pressure increased until pain filled her abdomen, the sensation so strong and so real, it jolted her mind into freeing itself from the nightmare's evil grasp.

She lay quietly, blood pounding through her temples.

A sudden chirp startled her.

The comms panel lit up.

She prepared to hear bad news. Marisol and JoJo had still not been found. With deep apprehension, she tapped the display.

It was ISO Ground Control.

"Chenzi, are you near a window?"

"Hold on."

"Look down. Report what you see."

She drifted over to the observation port. The oceans and continents below the ISO were fading into blackness as the sun fell below the curvature of Earth.

"Multiple patches of bright blue light."

"Location?"

"Three groups, nine or ten in total. The lights are moving. Over the Pacific, just west of Palos Verdes, heading east, toward land. They're moving very fast."

"Any others?"

"Over the Amazon Desert, east of the Andes. Two groups of four. What's going on?"

"Orient the station's cameras and follow them. Set radiation detectors to capture their electromagnetic signatures. Keep the UFOs under observation as long as possible. Record everything you can. These spaceships exited from the wormhole in the past hour. Didn't you see them?"

"I've been asleep."

Chenzi entered the Telescope Dome and pushed up to the cupola windows. "Control, do you see what I see? More of them are coming out of the wormhole and they're heading your way. Man, are they *fast*. I count five of them. Now...six."

"Copy that. Ground stations are picking them up."

After what Professor Temple had called the 'bench experiment'—flying an object, in this case a shuttle with an alien craft attached, into the center of the anomaly—the six alien craft working on the ring of exotic matter had returned to their mother-ship.

Crossbow-4 continued to sample the constituents of the energy field surrounding its central black void. The purpose of the ring, Temple had concluded, was to act like the frame of a door, a structural support to allow the wormhole to open and close.

The station shook and rolled.

"Oscillating magnetic field, strength 3.2 tesla," Boris announced. "Potential danger to structural elements."

"Auto-response override," Chenzi said. "Boris, do not shut down vibration-sensitive equipment. Emma, bio-protection please."

"Synthesizing benzodiazepine," Emma replied. "Nano-biocytes injected."

"Control, I'm getting ahead of this. No blackouts this time. I must have experienced these vibrations when I was sleeping. I thought I was dreaming, but it was real. These magnetic fields must occur when the wormhole opens."

The vibrations, and their sickening effects, ended.

"Boris, status."

"Magnetic field and gravitational waves have passed. Vibration damage minimal. Initiating auto-repair procedures."

"What next, Control?"

"Stay focused. Keep monitoring. Collect all the data you can."

"Am I in danger?"

"Everyone is in danger, Chenzi. The entire Federation is in a state of emergency. Your job is surveillance. There's nothing you can do except keep a close watch on the wormhole and let us know if more ships come out."

19 - BIO-MARKERS

The soft mechanical whine of a mobi-cradle's electric motor preceded the arrival of Lewis Temple. Nikki expected the Particle Physics conference room to be full. In her experience, the military populated events like this with a show of overwhelming force so participants wouldn't question who was in charge. But the briefing only had four attendees—the two doctors, Pavel Zharlev, and Professor Lewis Temple.

Professor Temple suffered from ALS, a motor neuron disease that caused atrophy of his muscles. Medical technology had learned to slow the progress of the disease but not alter its ultimate course. His legs were thin, virtual skin and bone under his clothes. His face had thinned around the cheeks, his hair and eyebrows wispy and gray. He sat with his emaciated arms crossed, motionless in his lap. The cradle's padded support propped up the professor's head and he breathed with the aid of mechanical ventilation through a tube implanted in his neck. However powerless he appeared to be from the neck down, it only took one look into his blue eyes to see the brightness of his genius shining out from a still very sharp mind.

Lewis Temple was a living legend within the scientific community. Most of what Nikki knew about him came from old videos of lectures he'd done when he was younger, when he had full control of an athletic body and commanded the stage with a magnetic and effortless performance. His knowledge and interests seemed limitless and his research ground-breaking. But he'd disappeared from public view over twenty years ago and now Nikki Akaju knew why. His deteriorating condition was a closely guarded Federation secret.

A data-tab sat upright on one of the cradle's armrests. Wires ran up to patches on the side of his head. Small speakers were attached to his neck brace. He spoke using his brain-waves, in a synthetic voice created from his own words, pre-recorded when he'd been able to talk.

"The danger we face is unprecedented," he said, in the voice synthesizer's stilted tone. "The final battle for the survival of humanity has begun."

"Please begin your briefing," Zharlev said. "Professor Temple's time is precious."

Nikki opened her data-tab. "The BioSciences unit here at Mead Canyon did thorough diagnostic tests on the human remains from the Caravan Park. Blood tests from the container ship crew and the survivors at the quarantine center were added to our data-set, as well as the medical histories of the marines at the drone base. We searched for anything common between these victims and survivors, and for anything different. Did the victims share any pre-existing conditions that might point to why they were susceptible and the survivors weren't? Without AI, that kind of data analysis would be like looking for a needle in a biomarker haystack. Thankfully, this place has the computing power to find that needle. And it might have found it."

She broadcast a series of tables and charts onto the screen. "AI flagged another bio-marker as statistically relevant. Maybe this new bio-marker is important, maybe not. We're not a hundred percent sure. All the victims, both military and civilian, had extreme magnesium deficiency. Interestingly, the survivors didn't have that condition."

"Magnesium deficiency?" Zharlev asked. "What illness causes that?"

"It's a nutritional deficiency, diet related, not something caused by a virus or other chronic disease," Nikki replied. "Beans and cereals are rich in magnesium. It's possible a poor diet is the cause.

But the SpacePort staff who died at the caravan park lived in communities where there's a good supply of vegetables and grains from their agri-domes. The military at Flagstaff were well fed too. These groups shouldn't exhibit a deficiency of magnesium, but they did. AI checked the victims' records for previous illnesses associated with magnesium deficiency—Crohn's disease, celiac disease, kidney disorders. But it didn't find anything. So, we have victims who lacked any of the symptoms of chronic diseases associated with severe magnesium deficiency, even though their tests showed they had it."

Professor Temple moved his mobi-cradle closer to the study results. His eyes darted from one chart to the next. "If you don't believe magnesium deficiency came from their diets or past medical conditions, do you have any theories about how this magnesium deficiency arose, Dr. Akaju?"

"No, but we haven't drawn a complete blank. Magnesium helps the body transport calcium and potassium ions across cell membranes, which is important for the transmission of nerve impulses. We know that magnesium deficiency can be a cause of seizures. I think that's where we need to turn our focus. Brain scans done at Malibu Heights on the patients from Ward 13 showed no previous neurological conditions that could have triggered their seizures. All of them tested positive for avian flu anti-bodies. I asked the hospital to re-run their blood samples. They also have magnesium deficiency, just like the victims who died from spontaneous human combustion."

"From what I understand," Temple said. "There were other people that night who were exposed to Jupiter clouds but did not have a seizure."

"I'm one of them, professor. I had my blood tested and I don't have magnesium deficiency. This is only one case so far, but it points to a causal link between having magnesium deficiency and having seizures. The next bridge we need to build is between that and the cause of spontaneous human combustion. We know the crew of the container ship suffered seizures in the days before their deaths. But what about the victims of combustion at the caravan park, the drone base, Adobe Park? Do we know if any of them previously had seizures?"

Pavel Zharlev squirmed in his seat. He glanced in Professor Temple's direction then his eyes wandered across the charts on the wall.

His timid disinterest to an important question raised a concerned look on Nikki's face.

"When we were on the container ship," she said. "The doctor from Vandenberg's Lab-15 brought Geiger counters with her to check radiation levels. I asked Dr. Veron point blank if she'd seen these seizures before and she didn't answer. I knew right then, she had. The military knows more than it's saying. It always does. You're not telling us everything, are you? What are you hiding from us?"

"Like you Dr. Akaju," Temple replied. "I'm stubbornly inquisitive. And like you, I don't suffer fools. Go ahead, Zharlev. Tell them."

"It's highly classified, sir. Shouldn't we get Military Council approval first?"

"Would someone please stop with this 'classified' bullshit. Sorry for the language, professor, but we're either a part of this team or not. If you're only telling us half the story, you'll not get the answer you're looking for. You'll get nothing. Because half a diagnosis is no diagnosis at all."

"I'm on the Military Council," Temple replied. "You have *my* clearance to tell her, Zharlev. Isn't that enough?"

Zharlev puffed his chest as if that would restore his credibility. "Yes, the container ship was hit by Jupiter clouds on its way into port. The seizures recorded on the CCTV coincided with the time the clouds were detected over the ocean."

"Damn, I hate being right. Veron knew exactly what she was looking for."

"We've been looking for answers, Dr. Akaju and we've not found any," Zharlev said. "These clouds have been hitting population centers, the migrant camps, the SpacePort. It happened before the riots in LA. And yes, we detected Jupiter clouds over Flagstaff and Santa Fe the day before the UFOs flew over."

"So those victims had seizures too?"

"We can't ask them. They're dead. But there's been widespread exposure to Jupiter clouds across all the Military Districts."

"What are they? Where do they come from?"

"Technically they aren't clouds, they're plasmas, similar to the exotic states of matter found when stars are born. They emit gamma rays—high energy photons, wave-like particles that move through solid objects. But that's not the only type of radiation in play here. Do you remember the humming Mackenzie Noor described at Whiskey Pete's Caravan Park?"

"She said it happened when the UFOs flew over, just before people combusted."

"Radiation sensors in the desert detected emissions of quasi-particles called phonons. You can think of phonons as quantum packets of sound waves, just like photons are quantized light waves. This wave–particle duality exhibits quantum tunneling that causes heat on a nano scale to flow between two materials."

"Is there an English translation for that?" Bryan asked.

"Sorry—phonon radiation generates heat on a sub-microscopic scale."

"Like between individual cells within the body? Radiation that could possibly trigger spontaneous human combustion?"

"It's possible that may be the mechanism. Until you uncovered this second bio-marker, we were struggling to find any link between what was happening to the human body and these radiation events."

Nikki's mind swirled with possibilities. "So, our victims received doses of radiation of two different types, at different times? First, exposure to these Jupiter clouds, where high energy photons caused seizures, then later, sound-based phonons which triggered human combustion. Am I getting that right?"

"Physics points in that direction," Zharlev replied. "The question remains: how do these two bio-markers make the difference between life and death?"

"Whatever is happening," Bryan said. "Maybe these Jupiter clouds are prepping the body for later destruction."

"At this stage, we have to put every hypothesis on the table," Professor Temple said. "The Jupiter clouds aren't a natural occurrence. They're the first stage in a concerted worldwide attack."

The room descended into a deep, eerie silence. Pavel Zharlev looked pale, exhausted. He rubbed his bushy brows as if his fingers could conjure up inspiration. Professor Temple sat frozen in place, his eyes not moving, a mannequin, empty of ideas.

"If seizures are the body's response to Jupiter cloud exposure," Nikki said. "Then avian flu must have previously increased the body's susceptibility in some way. Has avian flu infection damaged the central nervous system? Maybe, but if it had, we should have seen symptoms before people had this exposure. And what about magnesium deficiency? How does that trigger human combustion when a damaged body is irradiated by sound waves? Questions remain, but I'm open-minded about whether biological mechanisms are in play."

"The nature of discovery involves pursuing unlikely theories," Temple said. "That's how real progress is made."

"The scale of the problem we're facing is huge, professor," Nikki added. "Avian flu has been as common as the cold virus. And since no-one is routinely tested for magnesium deficiency, especially if they have no symptoms of illness, how do we know who is at risk and who isn't? If those spaceships return, we have no choice but to assume anyone exposed to Jupiter clouds is at high risk until we're proven otherwise."

"By now, that data-set could be in the millions," Zharlev said.

"Am I done here?" Temple directed his question to the two doctors. "You have more work to do, and so do I."

"One more thing," Nikki replied. "When we asked your AI to look for seizures in the medical histories, we came across a file labeled 'Leonardo'. It had top secret encryption. We couldn't access its contents. Who is Leonardo?"

"Yes," Temple replied, as he turned his mobi-cradle around and headed toward the conference room door. "We're done."

20 - INTRUDERS

Nikki gazed into the night sky from the observation deck on the roof of the Mead Canyon Research Center. The desert air was crisp and the evening cool. A light breeze caught her dreadlocks. High above, in the Milky Way, the constellations Cassiopeia and Sagittarius shone brightly. An unusual blue light shone to the left of Cygnus. A star? she thought. It's larger than Venus. She'd often star-gazed from the grounds of Malibu Heights, a way to decompress after a difficult day. But this new star was not part of any constellation she knew. The stellar object seemed to have a pulse, a throbbing glow, brighter than the crescent moon.

Footsteps approached across the roof deck. Bryan Leysson followed Nikki's eyes up into the sky. "I needed some fresh air too. But after Whiskey Pete's, I'll never be able to look at the stars the same way again."

Far to the west, the power blackout had begun in the Closed City of Las Vegas. "People will go to bed tonight as they've always done," Nikki said. "They'll wake up tomorrow with only one concern, is there enough food for my family to make it through another day?" She shivered. "This may be the last night for many of them."

The sat-link on Nikki's wrist flashed. "It's Muldoon." Headlights appeared on the far side of the darkened heliport. "He's here, in that jeep. What the hell? It's got a military transponder."

She opened an incoming message on a secure military frequency. Muldoon's hologram appeared. "Thing's are falling apart, fast, Nikki. There's been more UFO sightings and incidents like the caravan park."

"How do you know about that?"

He didn't answer her question. "Panic has set in throughout the Federation. The streets around Ward 13 have filled with migrants desperately wanting to find shelter inside. Brother Mikey smuggled your mom through the tunnels to Rossmore Station. I've arranged with Armstrong to pick your mother up and bring her here."

"You arranged with *Armstrong*? He doesn't appear to take orders from anyone."

"He does from me."

"You and Armstrong? What the fuck are you talking about? You can take the 'ex' out of military. Your cover is blown. Who the hell are you, Muldoon?"

"Yeah, okay. I'm both."

"Both *what*?"

"Both sides of the Barrier. I'm something different, whenever I need to be."

"What the hell does that mean? Shit, don't push me down another 'classified' rabbit hole, for fuck's sake."

"Look, your mother told me about that box, said something about Dante Parks and his research. Do you know what's in it?"

"If she's not told you, I'm sure as hell not going to."

"Someone has to. There's been a development. Armstrong's marines got a tip off about a fugitive, some guy named Zach Castleton, staying in the Jail Bait District inside Vegas. It's claim to fame is child prostitution. Armstrong raided the hovel where Castleton was hiding. But he'd already escaped, no doubt warned by someone with connections inside the military who wants to protect that dude from harm."

"Yeah, so? What's that got to do with my mother?"

The headlights of the jeep disappeared into the vehicle elevator.

"Armstrong found something there. Get down to the Physics Lab and I'll explain."

His hologram blinked out.

The hallways of the Mead Canyon Research Center—usually avenues of intense activity—were empty and quiet as they walked inside. The day workers had left. The labs were in semi-darkness to save power; only security lights were on. They took the elevator to Particle Physics. Muldoon was in the conference room scrolling through files on his data-tab. He was sweaty, his hair disheveled, his clothes dirty. His dress was 'desert nomad'—a hodgepodge of ripped khaki shirt and well-worn green combat shorts; a shoulder belt with pouches; and a camo scarf around his neck.

He broke his concentration as they entered and turned his data-tab around. "Armstrong found this." He showed her a scan of a crumpled piece of paper. "Yeah, it's paper, old-school, but impossible to hack. Castleton left in a big hurry and must have dropped it."

On the scan was a handwritten list of names. Nikki read through them and placed her hand over her mouth.

"What's wrong?" Bryan's eyes widened as he looked over her shoulder. "Holy shit, Nikki—your name, it's at the top. Do you know the other people on this list?"

"It's my family tree. Marcia Dos Monaga, my mother's maiden name. Adriana, my grandmother. Ana Estero, Grandma's mother. Zella Estero Parks, her aunt. Amare Parks, my great-grandfather. Oh shit, the Association has traced my family."

"Why?"

"Her connection to Dante Parks," Muldoon said. "This guy, Zach Castleton, he's Association. He must be. It explains a lot. Why he went AWOL. Why he has her family tree. They've been hunting for this research for decades. Her mother has a box that contains information about it."

Nikki gave the data-tab back to Muldoon. Red warning lights flashed in the corners of the conference room. The shrill sound of an electronic siren pierced the air.

Muldoon's sat-link lit up. He answered, then said to the caller, "Seal off the corridors. Lock down the facility. No one enters or leaves Mead Canyon. Security Protocol Lambda Max."

"What the fuck, Muldoon? You're in charge here too?"

"Temple is. I'm just his sword and shield. Special Protection Forces."

Muldoon tapped his data-tab. A split screen with four images appeared on the conference room's wall. The screens were views from the surveillance cameras in the corridors of the research center. Two figures dressed in black were running down a hallway. They disappeared from one screen, then re-appeared on another as they moved from one corridor to the next. The pair approached a glass security door, took aerosol cans out of the bags they carried, and sprayed foam on the glass. A wand ignited the foam and a shower of sparks ran around the pattern they'd sprayed. The intruders kicked the center of the door and a large section of glass collapsed. The pair stepped through the opening.

"Oh shit," Nikki said.

Pavel Zharlev appeared on one of the screens. He looked up at the camera and said, "They're on Sub-Level Four, two floors above you."

"Pavel, prep Professor Temple for evacuation," Muldoon said.

The pair of intruders reached a T-junction. One of them checked a device on their wrist and pointed to the right. They ran down the hall out of the camera's view.

"They're heading straight for the service elevator that opens into the Physics Lab," Zharlev warned.

"We're in Lambda-Max protocol," Muldoon said. "That elevator should be locked down."

"Hasn't stopped them so far. They got to Level Four by rappelling down the elevator shaft and breaking through the elevator's roof. Now they're headed to where you are. They seem to know exactly where Dr. Akaju is. How do they know she's even here at Mead Canyon?"

"Must be an inside job." Muldoon glanced back at Nikki.

"Hey, don't look at me like that, mountain man," she said. "You've got to be kidding, right?"

"That's not what I'm thinking." He pulled a device from a pouch on his belt. It resembled the grip of a pistol and had a small screen.

He approached Nikki and scanned her clothing. The light on the device turned red over the Temple Research logo on the front.

"Take off your jumpsuit."

"Huh?"

"Do it, now! Quickly. Let's go. You too, Bryan."

Nikki and Bryan unzipped their suits, stripping down to T-shirts and underwear. Muldoon grabbed the jumpsuits and ran out of the conference room as fast as he could. "Do not leave this conference room," he shouted back.

Muldoon returned, out of breath. "Tracking chips were sewn under the logo of the jumpsuits you'd been given. I was able to override the security lock-down on the vehicle elevator. Your suits are inside, on their way up. With any luck, they'll break into the service lobby, think we're in a vehicle, and follow the elevator up to ground level. That'll buy us time. Come with me and do exactly as I say, no questions. Just do it, okay?"

"I'm half-naked," Nikki said.

"Grab a lab coat on the way out. Let's go."

At the far side of the Physics Lab, Muldoon pointed to a large metal plate beneath their feet. "Stand there. Whatever happens, don't move off this floor pad!"

He touched the screen on his data-tab. The floor lowered with a mechanical whine. "This is how we get Professor Temple in and out of the lab without having to go through the rest of the facility. It connects to his private chambers, one floor below. Keep your arms by your side."

Once their heads fell below floor level, a panel closed above them. Small LEDs embedded in the metal floor plate lit the space. When the platform reached its destination, another lab emerged, lined with computer screens. A floor-to-ceiling window looked out over Mead Canyon. Stars outlined dark, craggy peaks.

"Through here." Muldoon motioned to a hidden door that opened as he approached it. They entered an adjacent hangar where a sleek four-rotor passenger shuttle was parked. A section of wall slid open on the other side of the aircraft. Professor Temple emerged in his mobi-cradle, Pavel Zharlev by his side.

"The Association has infiltrated Mead Canyon," Temple said, speaking in his automated monotone. "How did this happen, Muldoon?"

"I don't know, sir. My immediate priority is getting you to safety."

Muldoon tapped his data-tab and two massive sliding doors opened at the end of the hangar, letting the cold desert air inside. The floor of the hangar extended out over the cliff face, creating a short runway. A hatch on the side of the shuttle opened and a passenger ramp slid down.

"What about my mother?" Nikki said.

"I'll warn Armstrong not to land yet. Go with Zharlev and Temple. We're evacuating him to Vandenberg. I have to stay and clean this mess up."

Nikki frowned. "So, you're not the mountain rebel I thought you were."

"Let's say I have a very fluid job description. Professor Temple trusts me with his life. It's the only part of my job that truly counts. His knowledge may be the best hope we have."

21 - THE BOX

The skies over Vandenberg Air Base buzzed with military traffic. As ARVs took flight, Temple's shuttle was told to wait, hovering like a gull over the broad coastal scrubland that separated the base from the ocean. Once cleared to land, the craft set down on a pad beside the Aerospace Engineering Laboratory of Temple Research, a tall, pyramid-shaped structure in the middle of a hive of research buildings and rocket component manufacturing plants.

The group from Mead Canyon deplaned and Zharlev whisked Professor Temple quickly inside the building. Nikki squinted into the bright sky. An ARV with her mother on board appeared through the clouds, skimming the tops of the rugged mountains on the base's eastern border. The heavily-armed craft circled above the rolling waves of the Pacific and landed next to the shuttle.

Marcia Akaju had never flown before. When its ramp lowered, she looked pale. As she stepped onto the scorching concrete, the sudden rush of heat overwhelmed her. Nikki raced over and caught her before she fainted.

"They told me I'd be taken somewhere safe," Marcia said. "Then we were told it wasn't safe to land. What's going on, Nikki? I'd rather be back in Ward 13."

Major Ozzie Armstrong stood at the end of the cargo hold; arms crossed. "Welcome to Vandenberg, Dr. Akaju. Most secure facility in the Federation."

"Oh yeah, right. I've heard that one before," Nikki sneered. "Do you guys have some kind of competition? Was last year's winner Mead Canyon Research Center? Because two assassins ran rings around its security like a pair of angry squirrels. So, tell me, why should I trust Vandenberg is any better? Flying people into work every day was an open invitation to infiltrate that place. You're kidding yourself, Armstrong. My mom's right. Nowhere is safe anymore."

"Hey, fine by me. She wants to go back to Ward 13? Say the word and I'll take her, my compliments. It's her funeral, so I guess she gets to choose the flowers."

With that, Armstrong turned toward the flight deck.

Muldoon exited the ARV carrying a long, gray metal box, its lid securely taped.

"The secrets inside that box are no longer mine to keep, Nikki," Marcia said as he walked by. "And I'll be glad to get rid of them."

Across the runway sat a squat, gray, bunker-like facility, its facade dotted with blast windows, its roof decked with antennas. Camouflaged ground vehicles crisscrossed in front of the building in an endless ballet of military activity. "What the hell is that monstrosity?" Nikki asked as they walked to the entrance of the Aerospace Lab.

"The Acorn, headquarters of the Sequoia Forest Military District," Muldoon replied. "Constructed by the defunct Republic of California as an operations center for government in the event of nuclear war. They completed the Acorn just before the first missile exchanges between the Annapolis Convention and the Liberty Pact. It's a monster all right. Thick concrete that extends five floors underground."

"Where did they find the architect?" Nikki smirked. "At an undertakers convention?"

The ground in front of the Aerospace Lab shook. A thunderous sound rumbled in the distance. An expanding cloud of smoke, with a bright firestorm at its center, pushed out from a launch pad several miles south of the Acorn. The blue-gray hull of a spaceplane emerged from inside the cloud as it accelerated skyward.

"I thought they'd suspended launches," Nikki said. "They're still running them, despite everything that's going on?"

"Just unmanned ones. Edison Denard is not taking any chances. No pilots or passengers, nothing Jupiter clouds can mess with. It's a Pan-Lunar freight mission to the moon."

"He thinks the moon is a safer place than here?"

"Edison Denard is a bulldozer. He keeps plowing ahead with his plans until he clears every obstacle out of his way."

"You can't plow a Jupiter cloud."

"It doesn't stop him from trying."

Beyond the lobby, an elevator took them to the building's top floor, the apex of the ten-story pyramid. Pavel Zharlev greeted them inside a glass-walled conference room. A side-counter held trays of food.

Muldoon placed the old box on the conference table, the box's surface cleaned of compost, its lid pock-marked with rust. The oddly-shaped box drew everyone's eyes as if it had been recently unearthed from a Pharaoh's tomb.

Marcia Akaju walked over to the tall windows that looked across Vandenberg's landing pads to the white-capped sea. "I imagined many times where I would be when this day finally came. I thought it would be in a damp basement somewhere, in a safe house with candles for light, like the one poor Dante Parks stayed in, the night he died. My mother told me how sad and grim that day was. I thought that would be my fate too. I never dreamed I'd be way up here—bright sunshine, blue ocean, and the mountains, so majestic and grand. It's like traveling back in time, before the war, to lost years of peace, a childhood happiness I can barely remember."

Marcia shuffled over to the conference table. "Such a long time to wait."

"Sit and eat something first, Mom. Get your strength back."

"I'm not hungry," she said. "My stomach is in knots." She looked from face to face around the room. "Do you understand the responsibility you'll have once this box is opened? I don't think you do. How could you? Treasure that innocence, because it will soon be gone."

Muldoon untaped the box.

Marcia's fingers lingered. She took a deep breath and flipped the lid open. As she pulled out a photograph, her hand went up to her lips and her voice choked. "My mother. Bless her. With me, as a young child." Her eyes welled with tears. She passed the photo to Nikki. "Our past is now your future."

"Oh, Mom, please don't—" Nikki hugged her. "This is going to be so hard for her, Muldoon. Maybe we should do this later?"

"No," Marcia said. Her voice was firm. "These people have waited long enough to learn the truth, Dante Parks' truth. They don't need an old lady to slow them down. His secrets need to be shared with someone who'll know what to do with them."

Marcia took more photographs from the box, sorted them, and spread them across the table. "This is Ana, Nikki—your great-grandmother. With her sister, Zella. Taken in Brazil at the research clinic."

In the photograph, two young girls in bright floral dresses stood under tall banana trees. They were identical twins, early twenties; very pretty, dark complexion, short afro hair, big white smiles.

"And this one," Marcia said. "Ana with Amare Parks in the old city of San Francisco before he left for Japan. They didn't marry because they couldn't. He was already married. He may not have known Ana was expecting their child, my mother, before the Reborn murdered him."

Marcia retrieved other personal mementos and set them aside— her mother Adriana's medical ID badge and wedding ring; a necklace with Brazilian gemstones which belonged to Marcia's grandmother, Ana Estero. "The rest are old papers."

She removed a yellowed newspaper clipping with a note stapled to it. "It's in Japanese. The translation is attached. The year was 2006. The article tells the story of Dr. Amare Parks, an American who died on a bullet-train to Tokyo because he ate an improperly-cooked piece of pufferfish from a bento box."

"What's a pufferfish and what's a bento box?" Bryan asked.

"Pufferfish were a delicacy in Japan. But they had to be prepared by special chefs because their livers contained a toxin, a thousand times more poisonous than cyanide. There's enough toxin in one pufferfish to kill thirty people. Bento boxes were like lunch boxes, with compartments for takeaway food. Passengers bought them at food stalls in train stations. No one would suspect Amare Parks was given a bento box with a murder weapon inside. Because you would never find pufferfish sold in a bento box. His brother Dante was convinced the deadly fish was placed there by someone working for the Association."

Marcia took out a weathered notebook and carefully thumbed through its fragile pages. "These notes are Dr. Mitomi's, written during the research trip with Amare Parks to a remote village in the mountains of Japan. You should get them translated."

She described the notebook's contents, the story she'd been told by her mother about their interviews of the village women with superhuman fertility; the entries that documented the arrival of a spacecraft, and the alien who oversaw the birth of twins. The group's attention was riveted to every word she spoke.

"When my great-uncle Dante went to Japan to retrieve Amare's body, the police told him about UFO sightings the night his brother fled the village. People saw their jeep being chased by a spacecraft. It slid down a cliff in the torrential rain. Dr. Mitomi died in the crash but Amare Parks survived. He resurfaced in Hamamatsu a day later, then took the train to Tokyo and ate the poisonous fish."

She closed the notebook and patted its cover as if she'd finished delivering the final passage of a eulogy.

"These researchers witnessed the same things in Japan we're seeing now?" Bryan said. "Ninety years ago?"

"Yes. The arrival of these aliens and the brothers' research are inseparable parts of the same story."

Marcia lifted a dog-eared brochure out of the box. "The Adobe Park Fertility Institute in Santa Fe." She pointed to the group photo inside. "Dante Parks and his staff."

Pavel Zharlev asked to see it. "You said Adobe Park? In Santa Fe?"

"You know it?"

The photos in the brochure included an aerial shot of the Adobe Park campus with the fertility clinic and the other five buildings.

"That building's still there," Zharlev said. "Not as a fertility clinic of course. It's the admin building for the Adobe Park Desert Research Station. It doesn't look like that anymore. Most of the original building has crumbled, the parking lot is all sand, and cacti have taken over. But it's the same building, I'm sure of it."

"What about the one next door?" Marcia pointed to it in the aerial photo.

"Derelict. Beyond use."

"And the basement?"

"Probably the same."

"I hope not."

Marcia pulled out the last contents of the box—tattered old invoices for lab equipment, several scruffy manila files, and a large folded document.

"I know what you're thinking," she said, holding up the sheaf of papers. "How can this contain a whole life's work? It can't. So where is it?"

She unfolded the large document, laid it on the conference table, and smoothed its wrinkled surface. "This is what the Association has been looking for—the floor plan of the basement level of the Santa Fe College of Environmental Studies."

She picked up the old brochure of the clinic and pointed to the site map of the research park. "The Santa Fe Environmental College was the building next door to the fertility clinic."

"That's a strange thing to keep, Mom. Why was this blueprint so important Grandma saved it?"

"Before his death, Uncle Dante was worried his research archive would fall into the wrong hands. This floor plan holds the key to finding it. Only someone who knew what they were looking at, would understand how."

Marcia tapped the side of her head. "No explanation has ever been written down that could fall into the Association's hands. Not even now. Do you see these letters, the arrows that point to the letter A, and another set of arrows that end with the letter B?"

The group huddled around the tattered drawing.

"Some kind of route through the basement?" Nikki remarked.

"Yes, directions. It's a map. Looking at this diagram, you might think it's just an old maintenance record. Maybe it started life as one. Because of that, people would overlook its importance. If you knew what you were looking for, it's obvious what this blueprint means. But if you didn't know what the letters A and B represented, it was easy to dismiss this as just another useless piece of old paper. The dots marked A and B show the location of two hidden thumb-drives."

"What's a thumb-drive?" Bryan asked.

"An old form of storage device for computer files," Pavel Zharlev said. "A single drive the size of your thumb could hold an entire room full of paper documents. Terabytes of data."

"His research archives?" Nikki's eyes lit up. "Paper files would fill a room, but Dante Parks downloaded them onto these 'thumb-drive' things, then hid them in the building next door? So, if someone searched the fertility clinic, they wouldn't find anything?"

"Uncle Dante didn't hide them. He was too frail to travel back to Adobe Park. You asked why the blueprint was so important to your grandmother? After Dante Parks' death, it was your grandmother who created the thumb-drives, and she and your grandfather made the dangerous journey back to Santa Fe to hide them. The files on those thumb-drives explain what Dante Parks called 'astragenesis'—the Reborn are the product of generations of genetic experimentation by an alien race, a science he meticulously studied until he uncovered every detail of the things they'd done to us."

Marcia shuffled back to the window. "Whatever innocence you once had, has now gone. Those thumb-drives are like that old Greek myth. The Association doesn't want anyone to open Pandora's Box. Once its secrets are released, there's no way to put them back."

She placed her hand on the glass and stared out at the magnificent view, her eyes absorbing the sunshine of a forgotten childhood. "She made other copies of this blueprint. I don't know how many still exist. Your grandmother gave them to people Dante Parks trusted—his circle of medical colleagues. Most of them have now died of old age. But some of them disappeared without trace, probably murdered like Dante's brother. Your grandmother lived in fear for the rest of her life. The Association is still looking for these archives. That tells me no one gave up her secret. Maybe, this is the last copy. I don't know. Let's hope so."

Nikki picked up the blueprint. "That's why they've been hunting anyone whose family knew Dante Parks. If more copies of this blueprint still exist, we need to get to Adobe Park to retrieve those thumb-drives before the Association does."

22 - THREAT ASSESSMENT

An open-topped dune-jeep left the Engineering Lab and slalomed through a maze of parked ARVs until it reached the entrance to the Acorn.

After security scanned their faces, Nikki and Pavel Zharlev walked down a long, wide corridor to the office of General Wesley Ostergard, Commander of the Sequoia Forest Military District.

"I want to warn you," Zharlev said. "Ostergard loves engineers but has very little time for scientists. Talk to him about ion-pulse weapons or a new rotor design for his fleet of ARVs and you'll have his undivided attention. Talk to him about bosons and quarks, or biomarkers and antibodies, and you'll have to catch his head before it makes a big dent in the desk."

"Great. So why do we need to talk to him at all?"

"How else are you getting to Adobe Park? We need something Professor Temple's shuttle doesn't have—heavy armor. Santa Fe is a desert settlement. There's no law there without a gun in your hand. Military ARVs are precious right now. This will not be an easy ask."

"I thought this meeting was to brief General Ostergard on the incidents of spontaneous human combustion."

"He wants a threat assessment."

"I'm a doctor. I don't do threat assessments. What is a threat assessment anyway? We need to get to Santa Fe and get those drives."

Pavel Zharlev adopted a stony face. "Lewis Temple left for Denver late last night. The Military Council is in emergency session as we speak. The Council are discussing contingency plans if there's civil disorder. And if we don't find a way to protect our military when we try to fight back, we'll be exterminated. How's that for a threat assessment?"

The stark, featureless corridor echoed with the sound of military boots as they waited outside General Ostergard's office.

"How does Lewis Temple fit in all this?" Nikki asked. "Does he have any influence on the Military Council?"

"Professor Temple is at the intersection of everything. If it wasn't for Lewis Temple," Zharlev said, "the tension between the two Denard brothers would snap, and the balancing act between the politicians and the military would tilt toward self-serving disaster. Someone has to see what's good for the Federation as a whole, as opposed to what's just good for their own Military District. Lewis Temple isn't perfect in that regard, but there would be a tremendous vacuum without him."

"The Denard brothers? What about the government in Denver and Governor-General Addison Dray?"

"The appearance of democracy. The illusion of unity. The Military Council is the throne room of Edison and Ansel Denard, where their policies are blessed. The Denards are the one-two punch that makes this whole Federation tick. Edison Denard's corporations run ninety percent of the economy. Ansel Denard's research organizations provide the advanced technology that powers our military, our communications and infrastructure, and Lunar Base Imbrium. Without one, you can't have the other. Without the Denards, the Federation would revert to a three-ring circus with egotistical warlords fighting over which tribe should run the show. And of all the military commanders, Ostergard is the one the Denards trust the most. So if General Ostergard is pleased with what you have to say, you please the Denard brothers. That's how the system works."

"He's ready for you now," his aide said.

The general's office was lined with screens showing video feeds from countless drones and ARV patrols. Satellite maps marked the location of every military asset in play. The general, back turned, stared out the blast window at the vista that was Vandenberg Air Base.

"They conducted their initial series of tests," he said without emotion. "The container ship, the drone base in Flagstaff, and the desert research station in Santa Fe. They even checked the results on the ground at Whiskey Pete's Caravan Park just to make absolutely sure their test program was successful. A little gooey, but hey, it worked. Jupiter clouds have irradiated Greater Los Angeles, Oakland, and Denver. Someone—or some *thing*—either here, or watching from somewhere beyond Jupiter, is about to green-light this entire process and scale it up from a roadside barbecue to a Federation-wide pig roast."

General Wesley Ostergard turned away from the window. His eyes focused over their heads as if he were addressing an assembly of troops, not two lone scientists. Ostergard had no neck. It was just one continuation of thick muscle extending from his shoulders to his jawline. His shaved blond hair was so finely trimmed, sweat glistened between each strand like tiny diamonds. This was a man whose broken nose screamed, punch me again, I dare you; whose eyes do their own security check on yours with no need for a retinal scan. God help anyone whose light turned red.

"We know the weapons these aliens plan to use. What are our countermeasures?"

"We've analyzed the radiation spectrum of the Jupiter clouds," Zharlev said. "And the ARVs should be able to shield about ninety percent of it."

"What about the other ten percent?"

"We don't specifically know which component of radiation triggers seizures. We're working on that."

"Well, work harder. Get more specific."

"We can reduce the risk of seizures with bio-marker testing," Nikki added. "Your troops need to be tested for avian flu anti-bodies and magnesium deficiency."

He made fierce eye contact with Dr. Akaju. She took a step backwards. "Been there, done that, doctor. Tell me something new. Do you know how many marines have *not* had avian flu? Because I do. I have more grandchildren than that. I've ordered a rotation with Lunar Base Imbrium. That buys me a handful of pilots who haven't had avian flu before. Big hairy deal. That kind of screening doesn't make a dent in my problem. What about phonon beams and human combustion? How does that happen? How can I protect my pilots and marines from that?"

"We don't know, sir."

"Wrong answer."

Nikki gulped. "I wish I had the right answer. More research needs to be done. We're testing people who were exposed to Jupiter clouds but didn't suffer seizures. Their immune systems may provide a clue."

"A vaccine against radiation?"

"No, that's not possible, general. Radiation damage can't be vaccinated against."

"So, what has the immune system got to do with it?"

"We need to know what changes occur after exposure to Jupiter clouds. What happens inside the human body to make it susceptible to spontaneous combustion? If we can reverse that damage, we might find ways to protect your pilots and troops from phonon beams. The circumstances of the attack at Adobe Park would be useful to understand."

Ostergard glared at Nikki. "Adobe Park? Why Adobe Park?"

"We need to find survivors who were in the desert, had seizures, and escaped exposure to the phonon beams. To bring them back for testing."

"There are thousands of people who've had seizures, all over the districts and the migrant camps. They're sitting ducks for the next attack. Zharlev has the data. Haven't you seen it? You don't need to go all the way to Adobe Park to find test subjects, Dr. Akaju."

"Yeah, we could do that. But Adobe Park is...um...different." Nikki hesitated. *Shit, he's not buying Adobe Park.* "I still think we should go there. Santa Fe is the last outpost before the Nuclear Exclusion Zone. It would be a risky trip. There are desert nomads, bandits.

Can you provide us with armed transport? It would help if we had a dedicated ARV to get us around."

"And I presume you'd want a pilot who won't crash his ARV because he won't have a seizure after flying through a radiation cloud? And maybe some marines for ground security that are immune too?"

"That would be great."

"I suppose you'd want some picnic hampers? On board refreshments? Maybe video games to entertain you on the way?"

The general took a giant step forward. His eyes fixed firmly on Nikki's. He squinted in her face. The scan had begun. He pointed with an outstretched arm to the big military base just beyond the blast window. "What the hell do you think I'm running here? A holiday camp? The answer is, *no*. Absolutely not. Unless you haven't noticed, we're preparing for war. Against an enemy we have no idea how to defeat, no idea what other capabilities they have. And with military personnel who are one phonon beam away from becoming sandwich spread. So, I repeat, the answer is—no! *Capiche*?"

"Yes, general. Understood."

"Now, get out of here. Both of you. Go do some research. Come back with answers. I want solutions. I have plenty of problems."

23 - SANTA FE

A friendly face walked down the rear ramp of the ARV as Nikki and Bryan unloaded their duffel bags from the dune-jeep.

"There's a big guy inside with scars on his face who needs a valve installed in his head to let the steam out," Echo said. "He's with ten marines who would crawl into cracks in the floor if they could, to escape the explosion. Muldoon said General Ostergard punched a hole in the Acorn and shoved Major Armstrong right through it. How did you do that?"

Nikki cocked her arms and flexed her biceps. "Not bad, huh? But I have to thank Lewis Temple. He trumps any jar-head general, any day of the week. You're coming to Santa Fe with us?"

"I got this gig because I know that area well, places that aren't on any maps. After I quit the military, I thought I might find some peace living on a desert commune. Yeah, that didn't work out. They treated their women like sex slaves. But I left my mark behind. A few men in Santa Fe are missing vital parts. I consider that a win. So, what's this mission about?"

"Officially, we're looking for survivors of the Adobe Park incident," Nikki replied. "That's how we're going to keep Major Doberman and his band of werewolves occupied. Unofficially, I'm going to search the building next door, the former Santa Fe College of Environmental Studies. But I can't tell you what I'm looking for. Yeah, I know, more 'classified' bullshit."

"No worries," Echo said. "I'm cool with that. Glad to be on board."

A tall mountain man with a shaggy beard emerged from the cargo hold. "Zharlev won't be coming with us to Santa Fe," Muldoon said. "Something to do with the recent supply launch."

The heat of the midday sun sent rivulets of sweat running down Nikki's cheeks. "Can't wait to get inside and fire up the air-con."

Marine Major Ozzie Armstrong appeared at the top of the ramp. "Are you girl scouts coming, or what?"

Nikki saluted. "Aye, aye, Captain Hook. Whisk me away to Never-Never Land."

"Huh?" I thought we were going to Santa Fe?"

"You don't read much, do you, Tinkerbell?" Nikki hauled her duffel bag up the ramp. "All right, if you insist, we'll stop at Santa Fe first."

The ARV lifted off from Vandenberg and headed due east over the hills of the Los Padres Forest. It crossed into the Joshua Tree Military District south of Las Vegas and then entered the vast wasteland of the Great Texas Desert. Flight time to Flagstaff, the capital of the GT Desert Military District, was an hour and a half. They would land in Flagstaff to recharge the ARV's hydrogen fuel cells before the next leg to Santa Fe, three hundred and eighty miles further east.

Santa Fe, population three thousand, was primarily a security outpost, the most easterly town in the Federation. The Adobe Park Desert Research Station had a permanent academic staff of sixteen, working on drought-tolerant crops and the micro-mining of copper and precious metals. Twelve bodies—or what was left of them—had been found in two locations: in a mining camp in the Sangre de Cristo mountains to the east of Santa Fe; and in the desert to the south, near Adobe Park's agri-domes. Several people were still unaccounted for including a team of psychologists from Nova Mercurius; three student interns from Sagebrush University in Denver; and the two admins from the office building that had once been Dante Parks' fertility clinic.

At the refueling stop in Flagstaff, Nikki briefed the search team using a map projected onto the hull of the cargo hold. "Survivors of the attack at the agri-domes would have benefited from food and water availability. Why haven't they called in? Don't know. Comms are bad everywhere. We'll begin the search in the mountains first, fanning out from the mining camp. It's pretty rough terrain. Survivors may have hidden in caves."

"The search grid has been programmed into your heads-up displays," Armstrong said. "The ARV will be flying overhead if any of you get into trouble. Muldoon is coming with us. Dr. Akaju is too delicate for mountain rescue and will stay in the comfort of the research station at Adobe Park while you knuckleheads freeze your asses off in the dead of night, chasing ghosts on her behalf."

"Thank you for that, major. Much appreciated. My team will be interviewing a witness to the incident at the research station. Based on what we learn, we may need to gather intel from the people in town. It's a tough job, but someone with brains needs to lead that. In the meantime, I'm sorry, but you're stuck with Major Armstrong."

A few of the marines chuckled, but most knew better.

"Refueled and ready for takeoff, major," the pilot said as he walked up the ramp on his way to the flight deck.

"Wheels up, boys and girls," Armstrong barked. "Buckle in."

The ARV arrived at the Adobe Park Desert Research Station in Santa Fe just before 5:00PM. After dropping Nikki, Bryan, and Echo, the ARV's rotors churned the desert around Adobe Park into mini-tornadoes of sand as it left to search for survivors in the mountains.

The group were met at Adobe Park by six marines from the GT Desert Military District in their armored personnel carrier. The squad leader was Lt. Roosevelt Dowson, a lithe young officer with a stern non-nonsense face. He could have been a clone of Major Armstrong if he'd been a bit older.

The five other marines with him were much younger, barely out of their mid-teens. Remote outposts were a common first posting for new recruits. If they could survive the cruel environment of the Great Texas Desert—acting as the local police force in the scattered, lawless communities—then manning a guard tower on a Barrier would seem like child's play. The sparsely populated Great Texas Desert MD was essentially a giant boot camp for the other districts.

Nikki entered the research station's lobby. "Hello?" she shouted. A hollow echo ran through the empty hall. She'd been told an admin, a survivor from the attack at Santa Fe, would be waiting for them. The clinic seemed deserted. She called out again. There was no answer.

The building was unrecognizable from its former purpose. Rusty metal studs ran in a series of vertical lines to mark where the partitions for patient examination rooms used to be. Looters had stolen the original furniture decades ago. The space was stocked with an eclectic mix of desks made from reclaimed wood. A few coffee-stained mugs lay around. As the group wandered through, they found meeting rooms at the end of a corridor jammed with camp cots. The building was a ghostly open-plan relic, used more as a resting point between field trips than a place to conduct experiments. The evidence of human combustion still stained the walls even after the residue had been cleaned up.

"Split up, search the building and grounds," Dowson said to his squad.

"Bryan," Nikki whispered. "I'm slipping next door. Make some excuse if they want to know where I went."

"This place doesn't look like it has a functioning bathroom. Will that do?"

Nikki smiled. "Keep Echo with you. If you find that admin, you know what questions to ask. More importantly, keep the marines occupied while I search for those thumb-drives."

"Got it."

Nikki found a rear exit and slunk out of the research station. Nature had reclaimed the space between the old buildings. She navigated a difficult path through a dense thicket of junipers, desert willows, and cacti. Sagebrush and prickly pears blocked the side doors of the abandoned Santa Fe College of Environmental Studies. She made her way to the front. What had once been a two-story glass entrance was little more than a wrecked scaffold of rusty supports, the glass long since removed by scavengers. Tumbleweed littered the interior of the spacious lobby, which was coated in a layer of fine desert dust.

Nikki took out the old floor plan to find the way down to its basement level. Her boots shuffled through the dust-covered floor on her way to the back of the foyer. Several corridors ran in different directions. The light was poor and fading fast. She shone a flashlight down the hall. Much of the interior walls had collapsed, but one section had an opening with a metal surround. The door and its hinges were gone but under the flashlight's glare, the darkness lifted to reveal a staircase going down.

That's it!

Marked on the basement's floor plan was a maze of corridors, storage rooms, and closets. But that was a configuration that existed more than eighty years ago. Everything of value had been stripped clean since then—the wall boards and the metal studding that supported them; the pipes that ran overhead for the heating, air conditioning, and water supply; electrical conduits that contained power lines and computer network cables. The basement was just a large hollow shell with a three-inch thick layer of sandy dust over a concrete floor.

Her heart sank. How am I going to find those thumb-drives now? Perhaps they'd been stolen by looters? The only original features that remained were the large vertical concrete pillars that supported the floor above, arranged in rows and columns and shown as squares on the floor plan. None of the corridors existed any more, no jogs around storerooms or doors to open, nothing that resembled the winding route marked with arrows on the paper document.

Nikki checked the plan again for the location of thumb-drive 'A'. It corresponded to one of the squares that represented a structural pillar. She identified on the blueprint where the stairs entered the basement. By numbering the pillars in columns and rows from there, she created a set of mental grid coordinates.

Nikki trudged through ankle-thick dust along the first column of concrete pillars, turned down the row she'd calculated, and stopped where she hoped thumb-drive 'A' was located.

She shone her flashlight up and down the concrete pillar, a column about three feet square. Dust had settled everywhere, even on its vertical surfaces. She double-checked the floor plan. There was no doubt in her mind. This was the spot where thumb-drive 'A' was supposed to have been hidden. But where? Without its ceiling panels, the basement was at least twelve feet high. It had to be within arm's reach, she thought. It had to be easily accessible. No one should have needed a stepladder to retrieve it.

Nikki checked the diagram again. The 'A' was drawn on the outer surface of the pillar. She moved her hand across the column to wipe the dust away, working from above her head to her feet. Nothing. She repeated the process on the next side. Nothing again. But as she shuffled her feet to the third side of the pillar, her boot caught on something sticking out at floor level.

She knelt down and brushed away the thick layer of sand. She found a small stainless-steel plate, about four inches square, partially inset into the vertical concrete. It was stamped with the letter 'A'.

A small handle had been welded onto the plate. She pulled and the plate scraped forward. Behind it, the concrete of the pillar had been chiseled out. Inside the small cavity was a plastic tube. Nikki recognized it as the type of tube used to sample blood, a tube the fertility clinic would have had in abundance. The old brittle plastic shattered as she tried to open its cap. A thumb-drive fell into her palm. She closed her hand around it and clutched the object to her chest.

Found it!

Using her imaginary grid, Nikki navigated through the basement again and found thumb-drive 'B'.

What had hidden those metal plates in the past? Perhaps the cavities carved out of the concrete were behind a tool cabinet or a workbench, or under the back of a desk? Those things had long since been pilfered and after many intervening years, layers of dust and sand had hidden the plates from view. Dust was worthless to scavengers, but what the dust covered was more valuable to her than gold.

Nikki placed the thumb-drives inside the pocket of her jumpsuit and made her way out of the basement. As she exited the abandoned foyer, the sun had set and twilight had fallen. Across the scrubland of juniper and cacti, lights shone from inside the Adobe Park Desert Research Station, casting a faint illumination across the trail, back to the old clinic. More lights twinkled in the distance—the outpost town of Santa Fe, five miles away, down a wide desert road.

The stars above shone like diamonds on a blanket of black velvet. She spotted the unusually bright star she'd seen from the top deck of Mead Canyon. A dark shadow appeared in the sky, blotting out the mystery star.

That cloud is moving fast.

Nikki hiked down the rough trail. In the darkness, she stumbled on a rock and fell to her knees. Her hand reached out to maintain her balance and she caught the spiny pad of a prickly pear. Its needles embedded in her palm. "*Sh-shit!*" she yelled. "That hurts."

As she placed her flashlight on the ground to remove the needles, a wind arrived out of nowhere. It churned the desert dust and blasted gritty sand into her face. A sudden flash of bright blue light erupted in the crystal-clear heavens, spreading outward like a stone cast into a pond. Every shrub, every rock, every stand of cactus in every direction, lit up. Night had suddenly become day. A few seconds later, a sonic boom shook the ground. The air resonated with sickening vibrations. Nikki stumbled back onto the rocks.

The explosion of light faded, leaving a bright blue luminous ring high in the dark sky. Inside the ring, a stationary object appeared—an elliptical shape, backlit by moonlight. The ring of light collapsed inward until a blue glow clung around the spaceship's exterior. A structure of triangular panels peeked through the glow, a web-like pattern across its surface. Bands of blue electricity danced from panel to panel as the spacecraft moved slowly forward, dragging its thick envelope of cloud along.

More bright rings split the sky apart, their sonic booms echoing in the distance over the empty desert.

"No wings. No rotor pods," Nikki muttered, her speech meek and raspy. Her body shivered in fright. "Oh fuck, they're not ours."

She heard someone yell, "Nikki!"

The cry came from the entrance to the Adobe Park Research Station.

Her eyes dipped away from the looming spaceship. "Bryan?"

"We're coming. Stay there!"

Silhouettes raced out of the building and jumped into the armored personnel carrier. The six-wheeled tank kicked up dust and bounced down the desert trail toward her, smashing its way through the tangle of cacti and sagebrush.

Bryan leapt out of the back of the vehicle, grabbed Nikki by the arm, and pulled her toward the opened hatch.

Inside, a young woman huddled next to Echo, the girl's face a mix of confusion and fear. Nikki assumed she was the admin they'd come to interview.

The door had barely closed when Lt. Dowson ordered, "Go! Go! Let's move!"

Between the driver's compartment and the rear jump seats, a radar display swept past three distinct blips. Dowson pointed Nikki to the screen. "Three UFOs have entered Santa Fe airspace. We've been ordered into town."

"We can't be underneath those spacecraft under any circumstances," she replied. "You have no idea what you're dealing with. We need to clear out of this area as fast as we can."

"Wrong lady, we've seen them before." Dowson touched his headset, listened to the message, and said, "Whatever's in the sky isn't friendly, I got that. But Santa Fe is in danger and people need our help. I have my orders, and that's good enough for me."

"You were here during the first attack?"

As the armored personnel carrier bumped along the trail into town, Dowson pointed to another screen. "We saw the same kind of UFOs ten days ago. They have the same radiation signature. We were patrolling a valley to the north. The radiation alarm went off. This wheeled beast has all kinds of sensors and can survive a nuclear blast. So, if a detector warns us it's too dangerous to open the hatch, we pay attention. We were safe inside, but one of my men had already gone outside to relieve himself. Through the windshield we saw a strange cloud descending fast. It clung to him like ground fog."

"What color?"

"Blue. Weirdest looking stuff. Sparked like fireworks. Radiation readings were off the charts, so we couldn't risk jumping out."

"What happened to that marine?"

"He fell down and his body jerked. Then he went limp. There was nothing we could do for him. After the radiation cloud dissipated, our detectors said it was safe to go outside. We went to retrieve his body but he wasn't dead. In fact, he seemed just fine. Like he'd been sleeping. He couldn't remember anything. We took him to the medivac unit at base. The doc wanted to put him under observation in case there were side effects from the radiation. But he had no burns. Damnedest thing I ever saw."

"The rest of the squad was fine?" Bryan asked.

"Like I said, we stayed inside the vehicle. When we're trained to do something, we do it."

"Lieutenant," the driver said, as the personnel carrier arrived on the outskirts of the town of Santa Fe. "Looks like Major Armstrong's ARV has landed up ahead."

After leaving Adobe Park, the desert trail had been covered in darkness, but as they got closer to the small settlement, its homes and buildings were lit up as bright as day. Not from streetlights. A spacecraft hovered above the central plaza.

A small ARV had landed on a patch of ground on the boundary between the dark desert trail and the town.

"That's not Armstrong's," Bryan said. "Not big enough. Appears to be a reconnaissance vehicle."

"There's a scout squadron in Flagstaff," Dowson said. "We've not been notified they would be in this area."

Bryan climbed up next to the driver. "Holy shit, Nikki. The pilots. Recognize them?"

"Stop the vehicle, lieutenant," Nikki said. "Right now."

Dowson tapped the driver on the shoulder. The carrier slowed to a halt about fifty yards away.

"Do you have binoculars?"

"There's a night-sight on the turret." He pushed a button and a joystick popped out of the dash. "Optical, infrared, whatever you want."

Two figures stood next to the scout aircraft, one of them in conversation on a sat-link. Nikki used the night-sight to zoom in on their faces. "Oh shit, Bryan, what the hell? What are they doing here? Lieutenant, that man was in a land-cruiser that rammed us in LA, then shot at us with an RPG. And the woman? Her name is Dr. Liana Veron from Vandenberg's chemical warfare unit. But they're not in marine desert gear. What are those uniforms they're wearing?"

Dowson zoomed the night-sight to check their arm badges. "Federal Security Police."

"Like hell they are. Veron doesn't need a second job."

"I'll check them out." He input the images into the Federation's facial recognition system. "We got hits on both of them—the man is Lt. Zachary Castleton, military fugitive, multiple outstanding warrants, considered armed and dangerous. And the woman? Says here, Major Liana Veron, but the rest of her bio is classified."

"There can't be any valid reason for Veron to be chummy with a military fugitive who's a wanted terrorist. Those uniforms are either fakes or stolen."

"Whatever they're doing, they don't seem very bothered by what's going on in the sky above them," Bryan said. "I wouldn't want to be a looter right now, if that's their game."

"I agree," Nikki said. "Why the hell are they here?"

She turned the camera on the turret toward the center of town. "Geez, there's a small army of soldiers, police—whoever they are—bringing people out of their homes and marching them into the central square. That's the last place they should be."

"It looks like Liana is communicating orders to someone on her headset," Bryan said. "The security forces aren't meeting with any resistance from the residents."

"That's not surprising," Echo remarked. "If Federal Security Police knocked on your door and told you to evacuate, are you going to say no? You look up and see the danger in the sky, you can't miss it. The police say they have transport, they'll take care of you, get you somewhere safe. Cooperate? Sure as shit, who wouldn't cooperate? I'd kiss their feet if I wasn't so fucking scared. What the hell are the police doing with those folks?"

"I thought you were supposed to be the local law enforcement around here, lieutenant?" Nikki said. "Were you aware of this police operation? Have you been ordered into that square too? I bet you have. I wouldn't trust those orders. Not coming from those two."

"Yeah, something's not right. No way. I'll contact my base commander." Dowson got on his sat-link. "Shit. No response. Comms just went down."

Dowson gestured to the driver. "Sergeant, launch the drone. Get it over the square. I want to see what these police are up to."

The driver threw a switch on the instrument panel. A view appeared on the instrument panel from a drone that rose from a hatch outside the vehicle. The drone flew down the street. Its video feed showed the police conducting their door-to-door evacuation, then forming a cordon around the crowd they'd assembled in the central square.

"They're herding them," Echo said, peering at the drone footage on the screen. "God, Nikki, the motherfuckers are herding them! Right under that UFO."

Triangular panels underneath the spacecraft opened. Beams of multi-colored light shot down and struck the crowd. Flames appeared as people combusted and melted into the plaza's dust. The crowd attempted to flee but the line of police pushed them back.

Dowson squirmed in his seat. "Oh, *fuck*—"

"Lieutenant, if that crowd doesn't disperse, they're sitting ducks," Nikki said. "We need to break them up and get them moving—anywhere but that plaza. They can't stay where they are."

Dowson sat, stunned, mouth open.

"Lieutenant, did you hear me? Those people need to *move!*"

Dowson responded by throwing another switch. "Lady, mayhem is my middle name. Laser targeting activated. Launching tear gas into the square."

A muted *thump, thump* resounded above Nikki's head as the tank's mortars fired gas cannisters. A few moments later, multiple rounds fell from the sky, gliding on stubby wings toward red laser dots aimed at the ground from the drone. The cannisters bounced into the plaza and plumes of gas rushed out.

The spacecraft's beams continued to rain down on the crowd, but the tear gas had the desired effect. The scene descended into a chaotic rush to the exits that the gassed police couldn't control.

"Heads-up. That rotor-scout's taking off," Bryan said, pointing outside. "Our friends are leaving the party."

The scout vehicle rose vertically, banked hard left, and climbed into the darkness outside Santa Fe.

"Sergeant, target that spacecraft over the square," Dowson ordered the marine behind him. "Ground-to-air missile."

A whirring sound above their heads signaled a launch ramp rising from the top of the personnel carrier.

"Don't be stupid," Nikki shouted. "You'll just draw attention to us."

"Do it, sergeant," Dowson barked. "Fire!"

The contrail of a ground-to-air missile streaked from the personnel carrier into the sky. The missile was barely a hundred yards in the air when a bolt of energy struck it. The missile disintegrated into pieces, its fragments scattering like confetti.

"What the hell?"

"Nice job, lieutenant," Nikki said. "No one on this planet has technology even remotely close to theirs. So now you know what they'll do if anything attacks them. Please tell me you're not stupid enough to try that again."

"Shit, comm systems are still down," Dowson said. He retrieved the drone. "We'll head south, back to base. I'll need to get my next orders verbally."

"You need *orders*?" Echo scoffed. "How about this one, lieutenant? For fuck's sake, get out of that spaceship's cross-hairs!"

24 - EXODUS

The main base of the 7th Security Battalion, Great Texas Desert Military District, was located ten miles southeast of Santa Fe on fifty acres of high ground. The armored personnel carrier's bank of lights lit up the base's scorched remains. Lt. Roosevelt Dowson drove slowly through and stopped at what used to be the base commander's hut, now a burning clump of metal.

He ordered his squad of marines out. "Search for survivors."

It wasn't clear if the base had put up any fight. As flashlights scoured the grounds, dozens of sooty patches lay beside smoldering vehicles, marking the places where marines had been incinerated. The comms tower was down. The radar dome had exploded.

Nikki slumped to the ground and leaned against the carrier's huge tire. Its warmth drove away the chill of the desert night. In the distance to the north, she could see several patches of blue light on the horizon. One by one, the spacecraft departed, darting vertically into the heavens. The last craft extinguished its wide spotlight over Santa Fe and rose above the destruction. It shrunk to a speck, then disappeared completely.

"Job done." Tears welled up in Echo's eyes and slowly trickled down her cheeks. "Fucking bastards." Her voice choked. "Armstrong's ARV, did they escape this? Is Muldoon—?"

"Try not to think about it." Nikki put her arms around her. "In my line of work, death comes with the job, so you learn to sanitize your feelings. It's hard, I know. But you've got to do that right now."

"I've seen plenty of death," Echo said. "But this? This is on a whole different level altogether, Nikki. It sends ice running through my veins. My mind can't cope with all this mindless killing. Is there any hope of getting through this?"

"We have to keep hoping. We don't know what's happened to Muldoon. The ARV is shielded. If they got back to it in time, then maybe—we have to hope they did, that's all." Nikki stared at the strange star shining above the desert. "Bryan, remember the first time we met Liana Veron? On our way to the container ship?"

"I still can't believe she was involved in what happened."

"She always struck me as a cold fish. Something about her eyes. Emotionally dead. Sociopathic. *Major* Veron? I wonder what rank she has in the Association? She was really interested in my mother. They were looking for her, and damn it, I led them straight to her house in West Garden Grove. I even told her how to get there through Rossmore Station. How stupid was that? My mother kept telling me to be careful who I trusted."

"Hey, don't torture yourself," Echo said. "When I first met you, you had no idea who the Association were. How could you have suspected she was one of them? Just be thankful we rescued your mom when we did. If we hadn't helped her escape that night, you wouldn't have known about those thumb-drives."

Nikki rubbed her face, deep in thought. "They've done this before. Zach Castleton was at the Flagstaff Drone Base. He must have directed that attack. He must have helped the Ceruleans target the caravan park. Veron knew where the container ship crew had been sent. General Ostergard was right. Between the two of them, they've been helping the Ceruleans conduct a series of tests. And now Santa Fe. But that was no test run. That's what we can expect from now on."

"Once we get comms back, we need to tell Zharlev and Temple what we saw them doing in Santa Fe," Bryan said. "Maybe Vandenberg can track where their scout craft went."

Footsteps clanged down the ramp of the personnel carrier. The young woman from Adobe Park—the girl who Nikki thought was its admin—stepped into the freshness of the cool night air. Tall, fit, with wild, short brown hair, she was dressed in cargo trousers, loose fitting linen shirt, and a camo neck scarf.

Nikki extended her hand. "Dr. Nikki Akaju. This is Dr. Bryan Leysson. And this is Echo."

"Yeah, we've met," Echo said. "This is Dixxie. She came to Adobe Park to be interviewed."

"I thought Vegas was dangerous," Dixxie said, shaking hands. "But *this*? Makes Vegas look tame. Yeah, I know, I'm from *that* place."

"So, you were an admin at Adobe Park?" Nikki asked.

"No, a second-year intern," Dixxie said. "Sagebrush University, Denver. Nutritional biosciences. I got in through a visa program for migrants. They've just expanded it to the Vegas Closed City. There weren't many of us considered, as you might expect. Getting security clearance was harder than the university's entrance exam. But a ticket out of Hell is a ticket out, so I took it. Then I landed in *this* shit. What an absolute cluster."

"You'd gone walkabout next door at the college, Nikki," Bryan said. "When Dixxie arrived with the admin of the research station. But as soon as Dowson's marines showed up, the admin took off in her vehicle, scared as a rabbit and just as quick."

"Sharleen—that's her name, the admin at Adobe Park," Dixxie said. "She's been weird ever since I arrived for my work term. She's a former migrant like me, but we never connected. She was distant, strange. I thought maybe it was because I was Vegas and she was South LA. Or maybe, it was because she had Eastern heritage in her blood and my family were Liberty Pact. But that's not even a thing these days, especially between people my age. At least not in Vegas."

"Weird? No, it was more than just weird," Echo said. "It was weird as in—two Association goons playing air traffic control, that kind of weird."

"You think Sharleen warned the Association?" Nikki said.

"What association?" Dixxie asked. "The only association I know in Santa Fe are the researchers. Are they all dead? What about the other interns? Can we go back and find them?"

"There's an ARV of Federal Marines searching the area around Santa Fe. But we can't go back. We survived that attack and that's the most important thing."

"That's twice now. I just hope my luck hasn't run out."

"You were in the first attack on Santa Fe?"

"Sort of. I was at the agri-dome when I was sent into town for supplies. On the way back, this small spacecraft appeared. Much smaller than the ones tonight. It followed me, like it was hunting me. I tried to lose it but it changed course faster than I could. It was super rough, off-road terrain. My dune-jeep crashed into a ditch. I took cover in a cave and watched this UFO circle around before it gave up and headed south. One of the jeep's struts had broken. Since I was closer to town than camp, I waited until nightfall when it was cooler, and walked back to Santa Fe. I stayed with Sharleen. The next day we heard about what happened at the agri-domes. Just gruesome, like tonight. But she didn't seem to be worried, didn't bat an eyelid. Like maybe it had happened before? How can you get used to something like this?"

"Or, she knew it was going to happen," Echo commented.

"Were you exposed to any strange clouds before that spacecraft chased you?" Nikki asked.

"You know what, yeah, but not that day, earlier. I was in Santa Fe with Sharleen. My first day, just arrived from Denver. My memory of what happened—it's like really vague. I kinda recall this blue cloud, like the one the lieutenant talked about—you know, his marine, outside the tank."

"They're called Jupiter clouds," Nikki said. "What we saw tonight was a different kind of radiation. It seems military vehicles like this one provide good protection."

A trio of flashlights wobbled toward them from the darkness on the other side of the base. Lt. Dowson was talking into his head-set as he approached. He ended the conversation and said, "We found a mobile comms vehicle in decent shape, so we've restored some links, local signals."

He pointed in the direction of the road they'd followed out of Santa Fe. "See those vehicle lights in the distance? Survivors. Don't know how many. They set off an emergency beacon and have comms. They have badly injured people. We're going back to help them. You stay here. We'll need as much passenger capacity as possible."

Headlights turned around the corner of the destroyed barracks.

"We found another operable personnel carrier, so we'll take that with us too."

"You mean you're leaving us? Here? *Alone*?" Dixxie cried out. "You can't do that. We've got to be inside one of these tanks. I mean, if those things come back, they'll—we'll get fried!"

"Look, you don't have a choice. Got it?"

"No!" Dixxie jumped up. "You can't leave us here. We're survivors too."

She ran up the ramp of the armored carrier and called from inside, "You'll have to kill me to get me out of this thing."

Dowson put his hands on his hips. "Fucking civilians."

"Nikki and Bryan are emergency doctors," Echo said. "If there are injured people, they should go with you. I'll stay behind and look after Dixxie."

Dixxie yelled from inside the APC, "I said—I'm not going to be left outside!"

"I assume you can rustle up medical kits from somewhere?" Nikki asked Dowson.

"Sure, if they're not melted. The medivac tent is right over there."

"Let Dixxie come with us. Dr. Leysson and I will need help. She seems smart and energetic. I'll take responsibility for her. I'll ride back to the base on the outside of the tank if there isn't room inside."

Dowson hesitated. The APC's hydrogen-cell engine buzzed alive as his marines prepped it to leave. The second APC, parked behind it and idling, was ready to go. "Alright, you win."

He got on his head-set again. "Bring the comms truck up here."

He turned to Echo. "Stay here with the comms team. They'll look after you. Just don't get in their way. And you two—" He pointed to Nikki and Bryan. "Find some medical kits fast, and then we roll, okay?"

***

Two sand-buggies led the refugee convoy, pulling flat-bed trailers. Children and the injured rode on top of a mound of backpacks strapped down with crates of food and cans of water. Seven quad-bikes ran alongside the trailers, overloaded with whatever gear they could scavenge during the escape from Santa Fe. Hundreds of yards behind the front column, those fit enough to walk struggled to keep up. The arrival of two armored personnel carriers halted the slow-moving convoy's advance.

Nikki counted thirty-two people, including eight children, some as young as three. "Please don't tell me this is all that's left of Santa Fe, Bryan."

"There's some flat ground over there for a triage area. I'll get set up."

Most of the injuries were cuts and broken bones, caused during the melee in the center of town. But a few had suffered heart attacks, one of whom had passed away enroute.

"This guy has a really bad leg wound," Bryan said. "I'll need help to replace the tourniquet or he may bleed out."

"Can't do it, Bryan. I have a young boy with a collapsed lung. If he turns blue, we'll lose him."

"I've patched up people after knife fights," Dixxie said. "I can help Dr. Leysson."

"Go, quickly. Do exactly what he tells you." Nikki turned her attention to the young boy. "Does anyone know him?"

A woman with dark hair covered in dust said, "I'm his mother. My name is Marisol. He's my son, JoJo."

"How old is he?"

"Six. We hit a pot-hole in the road. JoJo fell off the trailer and landed chest down on a rock. He only started wheezing about ten minutes ago."

"He's got a broken rib which has collapsed his lung. I need to aspirate his chest cavity. I'm going to give him a shot of morphine so I can feel for the best place to insert a tube." Nikki prepped his chest with antiseptic. "It would be great if you could reassure him."

Marisol cradled JoJo's head. "The doctor is going to give you something that will make you sleepy."

The boy coughed. "Will I dream of Space Mommy?"

"Maybe. Shh, no more talking." Marisol stroked his hair. "Close your eyes, hon. You'll feel a tiny prick, but when you wake up, you'll feel much better."

Nikki administered morphine into the boy's vein. "It's quick acting. It needs to be. Poor guy, he must be in a lot of pain."

JoJo's body relaxed. Nikki aspirated the trapped air and inserted a tube for drainage.

"Is he going to be okay?"

"As far as the collapsed lung, I think we got to him just in time. The biggest risk will be infection. You see that young girl over there? Her name is Dixxie. If he gets in distress, tell her and she'll get me."

"Thank you."

"I'm curious. Who's 'space mommy'?"

"It's a long story. About why we're here and why she's up there." Marisol pointed to the night sky. "I shouldn't have brought JoJo with me. I didn't expect—I didn't know—I mean, what were those things?"

"It's not anyone's fault. You're lucky you were able to escape."

Nikki left the boy with his mother to examine the other injured. As she treated them, they recounted stories about strange blue clouds that had descended in waves on Santa Fe in the days before the attack. It took an hour for the two doctors to stabilize their patients.

Lt. Dowson approached with a man who walked with a limp.

"We buried the dead guy," Dowson said. "We have no way to keep the body cold. His wife is distraught about it, but hey, we're doing our best, right? As soon as we hitch the trailers to our APCs, we'll ditch the sand-buggies and bikes and move out. You gotta have a word with everyone about leaving their vehicles behind. They don't like that idea. You can explain it better than I can."

"Got it." Nikki replied, her eyes fixed on the massive man standing next to Dowson.

"This is Izak Windsong. I've known him for a long time," Dowson said. "He's the owner of the hardware store in Santa Fe, the unelected leader in the outpost, and the guy these people look up to more than anyone else. He can help get the message across."

Windsong was a physical giant of a man, even taller than Muldoon. You had to be big in every sense of the word to survive in the Great Texas Desert. It was the fringe of civilization. One bad decision might mean dying from heat stroke or starvation, or being murdered by armed nomads.

"It took muscle and brains to get these folks out of harm's way," Dowson added. "And Windsong has both."

"You're hurt," Nikki said, noticing the limp. She examined his torn pants. "You're bleeding. Let me clean this up."

"It's nothing. After the police threw tear gas grenades, people scattered. In the rush, I fell. Why did the police confiscate our weapons then open fire on those who tried to flee? A few of us had hidden our pistols, so we returned fire. Makes no sense. We had to fight our way out of town. Our own police? Shooting people they'd come to rescue?"

"I'd like to know those answers too," Nikki replied. "Just know, they weren't there to rescue you."

"Hey, we've gotta get moving." Dowson said.

Nikki informed the survivors about the consequences of traveling in open-top vehicles. People grumbled, as they always do, but understood. Izak Windsong convinced several young bucks, in his gruff down-to-earth style, to abandon their wheels. Being inside a radiation-sealed military vehicle was better than trying to outrun a UFO on a quad bike.

Lt. Dowson and his marines loaded the wounded into the two personnel carriers. The fittest, like Windsong, rode on the trailers. Nikki was the last on board the APC. The tanks moved out; every seat taken. "We'll pick up the others at the base," Dowson said. "Load up the comms APC, head south, and follow the old highway trail west to Flagstaff."

"That's quite a hike, isn't it?" Nikki said.

"Nearly four hundred miles. It could take twelve hours or more. It'll be sunrise soon. We should make it there after sunset."

"Twelve hours is one thing for marines, but we've got children and injured. We'll need breaks to check up on the most critically wounded. Bandages will need to be changed. Your time-line is super-optimistic."

"Lady, we're going to move as fast as we can. But all bets are off if those UFOs come back."

***

A spray of bright orange sunlight rose over the hill country to the east of the marine base as the two armored personnel carriers arrived with the survivors from Santa Fe. The marines Dowson had left behind had been busy overnight, rustling up what remained of the food, water, and medicine from the ruined camp. Spare fuel cells had been found, loaded on a trailer hitched to the comms carrier, a rugged, six-wheeled tank with room for more refugees.

Turnaround at the base would be quick. But just as the three vehicles were due to leave for Flagstaff, Dowson received a call on his headset. Dowson's face turned grim as he gathered his marines for a briefing.

"What's going on, Nikki?" Bryan asked as they looked on from a distance.

Dowson dispersed his marines and walked back slowly. His expression was sullen. "That was Military High Command in

Denver. Change in plan. We're heading to Roswell instead. You'll be happy to know our journey's been cut in half. Should take us six hours, marine time."

His face had turned pale. He wobbled on unsteady legs.

"You look like you're about to faint," Nikki said. She caught him from falling. "Take off your headset. Sit down. Doctor's orders."

Dowson slumped to the ground.

She handed him a canteen. "Water. Drink. You look dehydrated."

He glugged half of it, poured some in his hand, and wiped it over his face. "I'm fine."

"You look like you've seen a ghost," Bryan said.

"I have." He buried his face in his wet hands, swiped them through his hair, and rubbed the back of his neck. "Flagstaff's gone," he replied. His voice choked. "Gone. Everything. *Fucking gone*. We're talking thousands of military casualties and thousands of civilians. Reconnaissance said they couldn't see any survivors."

Nikki gasped. "Oh, geez." She kicked the dirt. "Goddamn it! We've got to find a way to fight back, and fast."

Lt. Dowson put his headset on and rose to his feet.

"Roswell?" Nikki said. "There's a military base at Roswell? You sure?"

"Look, sister. I'm in the military. The uniform's a big clue, right? I didn't think there was a base at Roswell either. But they sent me its coordinates and ordered me to go there. Someone knows better than me. That's how it works. We're all saddled up. Get your ass on board and let's find out."

***

One hundred and ninety miles southeast of Santa Fe, a large missile-armed drone buzzed the convoy, darting from one vehicle to the other as a camera suspended beneath its dome-shaped underbelly spun side-to-side. The drone finished its reconnaissance, dipped its front rotors, and whizzed off.

"Lieutenant Roosevelt Dowson, Charlie Squad, 7th Security Battalion, Santa Fe Forward Operating Base," Dowson said into the comms panel inside the APC. He pressed his index finger onto a small glass screen. A red laser scan activated. He repeated that with his eyes, then transmitted the voice recording and ID scans to Roswell.

A few moments later, an AI response came back. "Identity confirmed."

It was 4:17PM. The journey had taken eight and a half hours, breaks included, tired survivor time.

Dowson's personnel carrier crunched to a halt on the bed of a hard, dried up salt lake, its stark flatness a contrast to the mountains around it. He climbed up through the front driver's hatch. A blast of searing hot air blew into the cooled cabin. "Well, these are the coordinates I've been given," Dowson said, climbing back down and shutting the hatch. "We're here. Wherever 'here' is."

"Lieutenant," the driver said. "We have company."

Through the windscreen, a blurry image appeared inside the bands of heat haze rising from the dry lake bed. The fuzzy shape got larger as it approached. A two-person scout-car pulled up next to Dowson's carrier, its occupants in fluid-cooled desert jumpsuits and black-visored helmets. A platform behind the front cab held a missile-armed drone securely in place.

"Follow us," was the comms message.

The scout-car reversed and turned around. The three APCs followed. In the middle of the flat desert, the scout-car dipped suddenly as if it was going down a steep hill. A wide section of the lake bed had dropped away. The convoy was led down a thirty-degree inclined-ramp into a dark subterranean chamber.

"No lights," was the next message.

In about a hundred yards, the floor leveled off, and the three APCs entered a huge well-lit garage. Six scout-cars and a slew of other menacing armed vehicles sat parked in a row. The convoy of personnel carriers lined up side by side, disconnected their trailers, and opened their rear hatches. A mechanical sound echoed inside the garage as the ramp they descended rose up to seal the garage again.

Weary refugees walked down the ramps.

The occupants of the scout-car removed their helmets. "Yes, we do exist," one of them said. "Lt. Antony Chesnid, Roswell Special Operations. Your group will be segregated from the main base. If any of you want to step one foot inside, you'll have to get security clearance. And I don't care what forms you've signed before."

"Do you have medical facilities?" Nikki asked.

"The best. We can perform brain surgery if needed. And we've done it. Once. Hopefully, we won't have to do that again. Why do you ask?"

"X-rays? I'll assume that's a 'yes'. How about CT scans and MRI?"

"All of the above. Did you pass any hospitals on the way? Didn't think so. We're it. Who the hell are you?"

"Dr. Nikki Akaju. No doubt you have a fancy data-tab to go along with that fancy missile-packing drone. Swipe it. Check me out."

Lt. Chesnid was a clean-shaven, shaved-head, walking bullet. He tapped on his data-tab. "Akaju, can you spell it?"

She did. "Doctor, Nikki. That's me."

He brought the data-tab up to her face, did a retinal scan, grabbed her finger and did a fingerprint scan, checked the results, and said, "You don't need to sign any more forms."

"Didn't think so. Does it mention Lewis Temple?"

"I get it. You're a big shot."

"The biggest."

"What can we do for you, Dr. Akaju?"

"Everyone needs to have some food, have a shower, be given some kind of scrubs or hospital gowns if you have any, including children. I need a comfortable waiting room near your X-ray and CT scan facilities, one that can accommodate at least ten people at a time and has three desks. And fuck your restrictions on their movement. Because right now, I'm in charge."

"This is Dr. Bryan Leysson. These are my assistants, Echo and Dixxie," she continued. "They'll need data-tabs loaded with Federation medical record forms to process my patients. I need your radiography techs or medics, or whoever runs those machines, to be put under my command. And finally, I need an uplink to the Temple Research Engineering Lab at Vandenberg. Oh, and I need everything done as quickly as possible—no, check that, I needed it yesterday."

"That's all? Shit, give me something hard to do."

"One more thing. Do you know what a thumb-drive is? And how to read it?"

25 - FACES

"Boris, I need a 3D print of hose connector number 47-G."

"Sintering of titanium alloy commenced."

"A type-BN oxygen sensor is burned out."

"Spare identified. Parts locker 91."

"Auto-retrieve, please."

The part was extracted from storage and delivered on a small self-propelled tray.

"Thanks, Boris. How's that connector coming?"

"Connector fabrication at twenty percent. Estimated completion three minutes, forty seconds."

"ISO Control, this is Chenzi. This station has been shaken so many times by magnetic fields, it's a cocktail of micro-cracks waiting to open up. Warped oxygen manifolds are losing their seals. Life-support systems are on a knife's edge of failing. Electronics malfunctions are everywhere. I've shut down the No. 4 bank of solar panels until I can do another EVA. The ISO is on sixty percent power. If it weren't for built-in redundancies, I'd be sent crazy with alarms. Boris doesn't help. As soon as I fix one thing, he scrolls down his infinite to-do list and tells me something else is faulty."

"Chenzi...Simon Belledeau here. We've made a decision. We're arranging a shuttle to take you off station tomorrow. It's not optional this time, Chenzi. The ISO needs a complete overhaul. We're sending a construction crew from Lunar Base Imbrium for EVA repairs you're not trained to do. They'll need to exhaust the atmosphere in the ISO to conduct pressure checks after that. We don't want to risk you staying on board if something serious develops. Time for some R&R. The ISO's solar panels are not the only batteries needing a re-charge."

"Roger that, Control. The emotional side of me says no effing way. The logical side says it's time to stop being a jerk and get in the lifeboat."

"In the meantime, there's been a new development," Director Belledeau said. "In the past hour, Crossbow-4 has picked up signals coming from the wormhole."

"What kind of signals? More spaceships?"

"We don't think so. It's a repeating pattern of fast radio bursts, similar to the signature of a neutron star. The signals are accompanied by an audio stream on a frequency used by our shuttle comms, like beeps from one of our transponders. Hurry up with that repair, Chenzi. Ensure Leonardo is properly aligned with Crossbow-4, in case the wormhole opens up again."

"No arguments there. It sounds like I should stay a bit longer."

"Negative. When the construction shuttle arrives, we'll put the ISO in robotic animation while repairs are made."

"Oh geez, Boris has all the fun."

"You've had more than your fair share of that, Chenzi. We need to reunite you with your family."

"Roger that, Control. You've found them?"

"Not yet. But don't you want to be on the ground when we do?"

Several days had passed since the wormhole opened and a fleet of Ceruleans spaceships had descended on Earth. From that point forward, no further alien activity had been observed near the ISO. The mother-ship loomed over the smaller space station like a resting alligator, eyes open, body at the ready, its next moves unpredictable but bound to be deadly.

Chenzi fitted the oxygen sensor into the life-support equipment inside Module Alpha and moved into the Telescope Dome to check Leonardo's AI programs.

"Boris, I need auxiliary power to extend the boom of the gamma-ray detector."

"Power re-routed."

"Open infrared and visible light imaging modules. Set primary focus at fifty percent by radius from the anomaly's core."

"Positioned."

"Activate the ISO's radio-wave node and connect it to the Earth array."

"Node connected. Note: gamma-ray detector boom has fully extended."

"Good. Set detection cone across the full diameter of the anomaly and commence gamma and X-ray scanning."

"Activated."

"Control...alignment of Leonardo's imaging modules has been completed. Performing calibration protocols. Gamma-ray data being streamed. Leonardo is also tuned to receive radio-wave frequencies. We're set to go up here. Now what?"

"Roger that, Chenzi...just take a break and wait for the shuttle."

***

Alone in the quiet of the Telescope Dome, Dr. Zhu Chenzi closed her eyes and let her body drift slowly up to the cupola windows.

"Do you want a sleep injection?" Emma asked.

"That's a negative. No more nightmares, thank you."

Her body was tired, but more than that, her hyper-active mind was totally exhausted. Freedom from gravity made tasks easier, tools lighter. But when asleep, she lost control of where that weightlessness might take her, journeys into the darkest places of her sub-conscious. In the silence of the empty space station, she attempted meditation, her body nestled next to one of the windows. Eventually, her exhaustion overcame her fear of dreaming and she drifted off to sleep.

Her mind took her inside the egg-shaped object that had attached itself to the shuttle. A veil of vaporous blue light covered her. When the vapors parted, she was face-to-face with its alien occupant—black eyes, blank expression. An overwhelming sense of invasion rushed through her body, like something was burrowing inside. That gnawing feeling of being coveted, of being owned, returned.

Her adrenaline blended with terror, a toxic mental cocktail. Chenzi woke with a scream—a scream nobody heard but her.

As she opened her eyes, the Telescope Dome was bathed in light. Outside the dome's windows, three small alien craft circled the ISO, multi-colored beams penetrating the station from all angles. The craft were miniatures of the mother-ship, elliptical in shape with triangular patterns on their outer skin, their surfaces coated with a plasma of sparkling blue energy.

"Control...," she murmured, half awake.

"We see them, Chenzi."

"Detecting rapid heart palpitations," Emma noted.

"Try to stay calm, Chenzi," Director Belledeau said over comms.

"Easy for you to say."

Beams entered the Telescope Dome and probed Leonardo's consoles, searching every corner of the chamber. The beams reached her and stopped moving. Chenzi froze with fright, held in their grasp. A sharp pain entered her head, as if her skull had been pierced by a needle. The pain moved down her spine and settled into her abdomen. Her lower body burned with an intense warmth as if two tiny fires had been lit. After a few minutes, the beams went out and the stark white of the Dome's walls returned.

Chenzi crept to the window. The small spaceships had retreated and were flying toward the mother-ship. A panel underneath it opened, and they flew inside.

"Chenzi, we lost communication with the ISO for a few minutes. Are you okay?"

She gulped. "I hope so. I feel weird. A bit nauseous. The ISO is in a magnetic field again."

"There's been an intensification of the radio-bursts," Director Belledeau said. "We think—"

"Heads-up, Control. Looks like the wormhole's about to open."

Chenzi scooted away from the windows and checked Leonardo's consoles. Data streamed down its displays. Images of the wormhole appeared on monitors, taken in various wavelengths from infrared to X-ray. "Imaging modules are operational, Control. We should get a good look when it opens."

"Do you want an anti-nausea injection?" Emma, her DOC, asked.

"Not now, Emma."

"Detecting hyper-activity in the anterior pituitary gland," Emma said. "Excess production of luteinizing hormone."

"For fuck's sake, Emma. I said, not now."

Strands of energy spiraled like a kaleidoscope as they stretched the black void in the center of the wormhole. A moment later, the wormhole exploded in a flash of blinding, white light. The inside of the ISO lit up. The nova-like explosion quickly collapsed inward. Chenzi glanced across the monitors. An object appeared in the afterglow—a spacecraft, long and cylindrical in shape, about a third the size of the alien mother-ship, covered in the same vaporous blue plasma. The ISO and a nearby communications satellite turned their cameras toward the newly arrived spacecraft. Beneath the vapor, the craft's fuselage twinkled with sparks of white energy. The ship flew toward the bigger craft and stopped underneath it.

A panel underneath the mother-ship opened.

"Are you seeing this, Control? It's docking."

"Affirmative."

The blue plasma that coated the cylindrical craft drifted away, exposing the craft's hull, a transparent glass-like tube. Inside the tube were seven egg-shaped pods lined up end-to-end. One end of the glassy cylinder opened and the line of eggs moved forward. An egg emerged into the vacuum of space, its surface sparkling with tiny lights. A beam shone out from the underbelly of the mother-ship, caught the egg, and pulled it inside.

"Control, I see—" Chenzi choked up. "I mean—no, it can't be."

"Chenzi, what's going on?" Belledeau asked.

"You can see them, right? The egg-shaped objects contain—no, that can't be true. There must be another explanation. Boris, analyze the feed from the visible light cameras. Conduct biometric analysis on the shapes inside those egg-like objects. "

"Analyzing," Boris chirped. "Anthropometric checks complete. Facial construction, limb proportions, and body shape identical to homo sapiens. Requires genetic analysis to confirm. Preliminary conclusion: the shapes are 99.9% anthropologically identical to Earth humanoids, pregnant females. Estimated gestation: eight to nine months."

Another egg-pod emerged from the tubular hull and was drawn into the opened panel on the underside of the mother-ship. The process repeated until all seven egg-shaped objects had been removed from the docked craft. The panel on the mother-ship closed. Blue plasma enveloped the smaller craft and it detached from its dock.

"Cargo," Chenzi muttered.

"Say again, ISO."

"It's a transport, a cargo ship. It was transporting—I'm lost for words. I can't believe this. I need a second opinion, Director Belledeau. Boris, relay the biometric data to ISO Ground Control."

"Transmitting anthropometric analysis with annotated observations. Do you want facial recognition checks performed, Dr. Zhu?"

"Say again?"

"The visible light images are ultra-high resolution. Enhancing the light curves of the recorded images has a 99% probability of success in producing recognizable facial profiles. Objective: determine identities of humanoid lifeforms."

"*What?* What the hell are you saying, you stupid program?"

"Humanoid lifeforms are only known to exist on one planet and its satellite moon. Unidentified spacecraft has unknown origin. Facial recognition may assist an investigation by authorities to determine if criminal activity has occurred. Unauthorized detention of humans suspected."

"Criminal activity, Boris? Out here? Oh geez, that's fucking absurd. Artificial intelligence? You're an oxymoron. Control, did you hear that?"

"Roger that, ISO. Proceed with plan."

"What plan?"

"You may initiate facial recognition."

"You can't be serious."

"Proceed, ISO."

"You *are* fucking serious."

Oh my god, they can't be serious, can they?

"Okay, what the hell. Boris, capture facial profiles of presumed humanoids and send them to Ground Control."

"Initiated. Facial analysis complete. Profiles generated. Data transmitted."

"Chenzi," Director Belledeau said. "Set all consoles for remote monitoring. Get into your flight-suit. Perform station decommissioning protocols and wait for the construction shuttle to arrive."

There was silence from the International Star Observatory.

"Chenzi, do you copy?"

"Something's trying to get inside, Control." Her voice cracked with fear. "Something mechanical has clamped onto the window. Oh shit, it's drilling a hole."

"We can see it on the boom camera."

"It's injecting something through the window." Chenzi's video feed jerked as she scrambled away. "*Oh geez*—what is that thing? It's like a jellyfish."

Chenzi pushed away from Leonardo and scampered into the tunnel that led to the Docking Bay. "Oh, no—*oh fuck, no!* Get off me, you motherfucker!"

"Chenzi, what's happening?"

"It's on my suit. It's grabbed onto—no, you don't—*oh fuck!*"

"Chenzi?"

Silence.

"Chenzi, come in."

Silence. Painfully long silence.

"Boris, medical assessment, please...Science Officer Zhu Chenzi."

"Analysis requested," the AI droned. "DOC-Emma, report."

"Science Officer Zhu Chenzi, medical status," Emma replied. "Heart rate stable. Pulse indication: at rest, sleeping. Blood glucose level high. Elevated hormone secretions from anterior pituitary gland, adrenal gland, and hypothalamus."

"Emma," Director Belledeau said. "What is your diagnosis for Science Officer Zhu Chenzi's condition?"

"Situation dynamic. Accelerated production of human placental lactogen detected. Increased blood flow to uterine wall indicates placental growth has occurred and is advancing rapidly. Condition has changed again. Detecting second heartbeat. Hyper-accelerated embryonic development indicated."

"Say again? Two heartbeats?"

"Comparison of Science Officer Zhu Chenzi's anatomy to her baseline indicates a major medical anomaly is occurring, not previously documented in homo sapiens. Detecting a third heartbeat. Diagnostic analysis points to dual fetal gestation equivalent to four to six weeks in earthbound females."

"Emma, you're not making any sense. Boris, verify the integrity of Emma's programming interface and correct any logic damage."

"Scan of interface complete," Boris responded. "DOC-Emma's operational codes do not show any faults. No logic discrepancies detected in her active programs. Performing a secondary audit of subject's medical data stream. Reprocessing. Audit complete. Emma's diagnostic conclusions have been affirmed. Science Officer Zhu Chenzi is pregnant with twins."

26 - ROSWELL

Inside Roswell's radiology lab, Echo and Dixxie cradled steaming mugs of coffee like they were their newborn. "I gotta join up again, Nikki," Echo said. "Special Forces. That's the gig. Real coffee. Not that chicory shit."

"How did it go with Vandenberg?" Bryan asked.

Nikki took him by the arm into the corridor. "I didn't want them to hear." She shut the door. "This base is a world away from what's happening. Given what they've already been through, they don't need to hear this."

"That bad?"

Nikki's face quivered. She fought back tears. "It's a shit-storm out there, Bryan. Refugees are streaming out of the desert. The urban centers are barely hanging on. People are being turned away because food is running out. Panic is sweeping through the migrant camps. The Barriers might not hold."

"I've seen that look on you before, after the ambush in Ward 6. You said you were coping back then and I gave you a pass. Right now, I'm not sure. After Santa Fe, I'm at the end of my tether. You look like your grip's about to fail."

Nikki leaned against the corridor wall. "We might be the lucky ones but that doesn't mean we're entitled to jack-shit. I'm not about to quit. How are we doing with the scans?"

"Just getting started. Dixxie is right on top of everything. The radiology techs think she's a qualified medic."

"Living in Vegas makes you grow up fast."

"What are we hoping to find?"

"Anything. Nothing. I don't know anymore." She pulled her data-tab out of her jumpsuit. "Their bloods came back. Some of them have magnesium deficiency, but not everyone. That's interesting. We may have lucked out with a baseline of patients who either weren't exposed to Jupiter clouds or were immune to them. With these scans, maybe we can figure out what's going on internally."

Lt. Chesnid bounded down the long empty corridor. "Yo, Dr. Nikki. I've been chasing you all over the place. Those thumb-drives? Our tech has the data. When do you want to see it?"

Nikki's face lit up. "Are you kidding? Like, right now. Bryan, are you done here?"

"Yeah, everything's all set. It's just scheduling. Echo and Dixxie can handle it. I'll tell them."

Special Forces Base Roswell was all on one level, a large square complex dug out of the salt, forty feet underground. They followed Chesnid to the base's communications center.

"Any news about Armstrong's ARV, lieutenant?" Nikki asked.

"Comms are down across most of the Great Texas Desert. Vandenberg lost radio contact with them, not even a ping from their transponder. I'm sorry I haven't got better news."

"How come Dowson didn't know about Roswell? What's this base for?"

"Vandenberg said I have to crawl across broken glass if you say that's what you want me to do. That means giving your team all the coffee you want, and all the help you ask for when you need it. Which is what one of my best tech guys has done. Thumb-drives, right?"

"You haven't answered my question, lieutenant. I've just gone through hell and back to get those thumb-drives. Dowson may not need to know who the hell you are, but I do. The data on those drives needs the highest level of comms security."

"Shit, lady, I don't know who you are either. I just know Vandenberg thinks the sun shines through your...whatever. But it doesn't count for everything. Releasing information about this base requires Military Council authorization. Do you want to see what's on those drives or not?" Lt. Chesnid gestured to a door. "Because we're here. Central Comms, Special Forces Base Roswell. After you."

Inside the Comms Center, a dozen marines sat in front of an array of surveillance screens showing video feeds from drones out on patrol. Access to the base's electronics lab was through a door at the far end. By the look of the devices on the lab's workbenches, Roswell could repair anything that had electrons flowing through it, from drone circuit boards to fuel cell control modules. Nikki spotted her small thumb-drives cradled in clear plastic holders, laying on what looked like an inductive charging pad.

"You're the lady with the files?" the tech said, in front of a display monitor.

Nikki sat down beside him. "This is an encrypted military server, right?"

Chesnid huffed. "Lady, you're inside a Special Forces base whose existence we can't confirm. And next door, there's a room with a dozen screens showing video footage that doesn't exist from drones that don't either. What do you think?"

"I get it, lieutenant."

"She doesn't think our servers are secure enough," Chesnid said.

The tech smiled. "Once the data is on our servers, only two other people have biometric clearance to access it, Lewis Temple and Pavel Zharlev. I mean Professor Lewis Temple? Whoa, lady, there must be some hot shit on those drives. Anything you want them to see, swipe the data into that folder in the corner and it's sent to Vandenberg. But nothing's retained here at Roswell once you do that. You won't be able to see it again. The data will only be on one server at a time."

He stood up and pointed to the screen. "All yours. I've downloaded the data into directories marked 'A' and 'B' for each of the thumb-drives."

"I'm worried about the original devices. They're small and portable, which makes them too easy to steal. If we've uploaded the data, they should be securely destroyed. How?"

"It's pretty archaic technology," the tech replied. "Simple. You just smash the shit out of them."

"Okay, do it."

The tech swiped his hand over icons representing the drives on the bench. "That external data has now been shredded. But just to be absolutely sure—" He took the thumb-drives out of their cradles, placed them under a laser soldering tool, and zapped them into two blobs of gold-circuit-encrusted molten plastic. "That should do it, unreadable. Data gone to cyber heaven."

"Slick. I like it," Nikki said.

"Keep them as good luck charms." Chesnid gestured to the Comms Center. "If you need help, my guys will come running. But ask that question again and they'll arrest you."

"I'll take those lumps of plastic. My advice, lieutenant? Everyone here on this base—a base that doesn't exist—should find a good luck charm of their own."

Lt. Chesnid nodded, then he and the tech left.

Nikki tried to sync her data-tab with the screen. 'Access Denied' popped up. "Their encryption is as good as they said it is. I just hope we haven't uploaded all this stuff onto an Association server."

"What are we looking for?"

"Not sure. But if we lose access once the files are transferred to Vandenberg, let's at least see if there's something useful to us here. We should focus our search on references to phenomena like Jupiter clouds or spontaneous human combustion."

Dante Parks had cataloged his work using topics and dates in the file names. Drive 'A' contained research started by Amare Parks in 2001 and continued by Dante into 2010, four years after Amare's death in Japan. The second thumb-drive was the largest, nearly two terabytes, containing the work Dante Parks did after that, until his death in 2070 at the age of ninety-seven—sixty more years of research, saved by Nikki's grandmother.

Nikki segregated the larger 'B' directory into two parts. "I'll start with 'A', Bryan. You take the first half of 'B' and see what you can find."

The pair spent the next hour scrolling through the massive archive, from the earliest profiles of the brothers' patients in Brazil to the genetic sequencing that mapped the progression of alterations to the patients' DNA from one generation to the next.

"Some of the twins were dying from diseases that are not normally fatal," Nikki said. "And it only happened with twins, no other children in the village. After Amare's death in Japan, Dante compiled a record of UFO sightings near the clinics in Brazil. Many of his patients claimed to have been abducted, like the villagers in Japan. He correlated those sightings with his clinical data. He found the more recent births had fewer abnormalities and there was a decline in sickness and death in older twins. The quality of local medical care couldn't account for that result. Genetic sequencing highlighted significant changes in the DNA of the children over time, in sync with the appearance of UFOs."

"He definitely changed focus," Bryan said. "In drive 'B', it's less about superhuman fertility and more about techniques for the biomedical enhancement of the human genome. He was trying to track what the Ceruleans were doing, but was always one step behind their results."

"Makes sense. Over time, the Ceruleans got better at preventing birth defects and they'd adjusted human DNA to resist the infections that were killing the children. If we went back over the history of Ward 13, maybe we would see the same pattern, a transition away from what Echo said were their 'rejects' to what she said were their successes."

"There's a section of files in 'B' drive that are gigantic, Nikki. Nearly a terabyte. From the date codes, it spans more than thirty years. I've opened a few folders. Looks like it contains the technology of gene editing he used to replicate what the aliens had done."

"Replicate? He did his own experiments on the human genome?"

"It seems so. It's no wonder the Association wanted to bury it."

After another hour of intense study, Nikki got up and stretched. "The second half of 'B' drive is a dead-end. There's nothing new, just more of the same. A ton more. I have a decent grounding in genetic engineering but the terminology has gone way beyond anything I can understand."

"Same here. None of the UFO sightings refer to what the Ceruleans are doing to us now. Jupiter clouds seem to be something new, something Dante Parks hadn't experienced at all."

"That's really disappointing. There's a folder of personal emails I've kept until last. They're labeled with my Grandma Adriana's name. It's a window into her life as a doctor. I'd really like to read through them before we stop. She was in her eighties when I was in med school but her mind was still sharp. It was like having a private tutor."

"Well, I need a break." Bryan massaged his stiff neck. "And more coffee. Want some?"

"Do they have anything stronger?"

"Not officially. But I can check around. Someone in the Comms Center must have a magic potion to take the edge off. Video surveillance is even more boring than this."

"Forget anything I ever said about wanting more 'boring'. I take it all back."

While Bryan went for coffee, Nikki opened the folder with Dante Parks' personal emails. He was a regular participant in family gatherings. As the years went by, messages celebrated her grandmother's thirty-fifth birthday, then her mother's twenty-fifth, and baby Nikki's first. They were clearly very close to their great-uncle even in his advancing years.

Bryan returned with two mugs and a wry smile. "Marines will never let you down, Nikki. Remember that. Sip it slowly. Might knock you out."

"I'm not even going to ask. As long as it's not fatal."

Tired faces bathed in the mist rising from the mugs. The coffee had a pleasant kick from its mystery ingredient.

"Did you find anything interesting about your grandma?"

"She was much more involved in his research than I thought, most of it before my mother was born, so it's no wonder Mom didn't recall it."

Nikki scrolled through to the end of the email folders, warmed by the spiked coffee and her memories of a grandmother she loved dearly. She was about to close the directory when she spotted a sub-folder that stood out from the rest.

"Hold on, Bryan. Geez, check this folder out, it's labeled— *Armageddon*."

The sub-folder was a month-by-month chronicle of the Constitutional War, from before its start in 2035 through to its grim conclusion in 2038.

Nikki and Bryan sat transfixed as they read articles collected from news sources on both sides of the conflict, the Southern States of the Liberty Pact and the Eastern States of the Annapolis Convention.

Dante Parks had also saved his proposed testimony to Congress, scheduled for May 12, 2035. The file included his prepared opening remarks and was titled, *The Association of the Reborn: Its Origins and Organization*.

"He wanted to get their attention," Bryan said. "And reading his draft, he sure nailed it. I mean how much clearer can you get than this… Alien manipulation of the human genetic code has reached a dangerous crossroads. The ultimate purpose of the Association of the Reborn is unknown but it is scientifically beyond doubt this secretive organization consists of the human descendants of a program of genetic engineering conducted over decades by extra-terrestrial beings. This is the greatest threat to the existence of the human race since the Ice Age and requires an urgent response."

"The continent descended into nuclear madness just as he was scheduled to testify," Nikki said. "If you ever wondered what a shout would sound like in the middle of a nuclear explosion, this is it."

They read ashen-faced through the chronology of hostilities in the Armageddon file. By 2036, the Constitutional War had entered the second year of conventional warfare. But toward the middle of 2037, the Liberty Pact, fearing imminent defeat on multiple fronts, used aircraft from the former Strategic Air Command to launch coordinated nuclear strikes on Washington, New York City, Boston, Pittsburgh, and Philadelphia.

"Holy shit!" Nikki pushed back from the desk. She stood, palms clamped on her face, eyes glued in disbelief. "It can't be true. This is sickening. It wasn't an *accident*, a one-off mistake that started the war. Just the opposite. These nuclear attacks happened *years* later. Some sick fuck gave the order, crossed the line. All the history we've been taught about that war, Bryan—every last word—it's a flat-out lie."

Article after article described how the Eastern States of the Annapolis Convention responded—retaliatory strikes that were swift and above all, merciless. Liberty Pact cities were hammered by the East's nuclear arsenal—Dallas, Houston, Atlanta, Nashville, Charlotte, St Louis. The nuclear exchange escalated as out-of-control computer algorithms on both sides gamed the next steps.

Missile strikes took out Chicago, Indianapolis, Cincinnati, and Detroit. Bombers launched revenge on Kansas City, New Orleans, Oklahoma City, Tampa, and Miami. In a matter of days, every state east of the Mississippi had been turned into a radioactive wasteland.

The continental weather systems pushed nuclear fallout from west to east, and from north to south. Deadly clouds of radioactive isotopes drifted outside America's borders, decimating eastern Canada and the islands of the Caribbean.

It was unclear what stopped the carnage. What was clear, was the mass migration of survivors that began soon after the last bomb was dropped. Martial law was declared in California and the other secessionist western states. By 2042, the Federation of Western Military Districts was formed.

"No one needs to imagine how horrible it was. They can read it in black and white," Nikki said. "Big cities, a pile of ash. Water and food contaminated by radioactive fallout. Starving people by the millions. Roving militias bent on revenge and genocide. That's even before anyone risked migrating across the Great Texas Desert. It's all here. Every gory detail."

"In this article," Bryan said, "a journalist exposed oligarchs in the West who provided covert military support to both sides, depending on where their previous loyalties had come from."

"Why should we be surprised by that?" Nikki paced the room. "What we've been taught about Western neutrality is a whitewash of the truth. Old state borders couldn't separate innocence from guilt, no matter how much independence was declared. It wasn't that simple. I never expected we would find all this. I thought these thumb-drives would be all technical stuff, dull science. There's a massive amount of that for sure, but this shit about our history— it's been erased from our school texts as if it never happened. I don't know what else we're going to find in these files, but it's just *way* too intense."

"Your mother was right. These files will change everything. Everyone knows that brutal war had two sides. But in school, we were never taught why the war started, or how it progressed."

"Which makes this history so dangerous," Nikki said. "The Federation claims it was lost in the fog of war but there's got to be a computer system somewhere with this information—data that traces everyone's family members back to the war, what side they were on, what they did, and to whom. That knowledge is power. How much of that power was used in the past as blackmail? Think of the corruption, the leverage someone could hold over district governors, police chiefs, anyone in charge of anything, who had something to hide. Once someone knows what your family did in that war, you're caught in their web. But who's the spider?"

"The newest generation of migrants should never be told the whole truth, Nikki. That would revive the cycle of hate, a recipe for all of it to happen again. This information is explosive in so many ways."

"I thought you weren't into politics."

"I'm into survival. So where do we go now with these files?"

"I'm done with all this shit. I'm exhausted. I vote we swipe them over to Vandenberg."

"All of it? We'll lose access. It'll be buried again."

"Good. Maybe it needs to be. Right now, this political shit doesn't help anyone. Whoever climbed that power ladder is already there. And very soon, it will become irrelevant. As far as the genetic research, yes, I found the thumb-drives, but I don't need to read absolutely everything on them. I don't understand most of it. There's a huge amount of work needed back at Vandenberg to decipher it. What does it mean? How can it help us? We need a major deep-dive into that, not just the two of us poking around at random like this. A team of genetic scientists needs to take it from here. And quickly. Time is not on our side."

"I was wondering when you'd come to that conclusion."

"I need more of that spiked coffee."

Nikki sat down at the monitor. "I'm doing it, Bryan." She swiped both master directories over to Vandenberg. The files no longer resided on Roswell's servers.

"What a huge relief to get rid of that," she said. "At some point very soon, someone will have to step back from all this history and science, and give me the answer to a fundamental question about where we are, right now, today. Why would an alien force—an advanced civilization so interested in studying us they took great effort to tamper with our genome—why are they now in the process of exterminating us?"

"I don't think knowing that answer will help us. We just have to find a way to resist them and fight back."

"I think you're wrong. I think that answer is very important. There must be an end-game. And I have an idea what that is."

"In the tunnels on the way to Ward 13," Nikki said. "Muldoon gave me a cryptic lecture on how he thought the Constitutional War ended. At that moment, I had no idea what the hell he was talking about. I think I do now. He said the Association took back control from those who'd lost it. He said they wanted to halt an uncontrolled extinction-level event. We now know, in graphic detail, what that looked like. Uncontrolled extinction was counter to their aims. It didn't fit their plans. What aims? Whose plans? He wasn't referring to the civil war, Bryan. I realize that now. The suggestion that some kind of rational diplomacy could resolve things after all those cities were incinerated, is just not realistic. He was right to scoff at that, said the war had gone too far by then, that hatred had sunk in too deeply. He specifically used the term, *uncontrolled*. Once a nuclear war starts, 'uncontrolled' is a pretty damn good characterization of what follows."

"Well, I don't follow where you're going with this."

"What if the problem is not with the idea of an extinction-level event, but that it's an 'uncontrolled' one?"

"Meaning?"

"Indiscriminate nuclear attacks were leading to self-extinction all over the world. The Earth was becoming uninhabitable. If the Association had worked to end the Constitutional War, and other wars around the world, then what just happened in Santa Fe? That was an extinction-level event, for damn sure—but with a huge difference. The Association's operatives disguised themselves as police to round up people and lead them to their deaths. What we saw was a pre-planned set of executions, coordinated from the ground to the air. Those exterminations in Santa Fe were not indiscriminate. They were targeted and well-organized. They were *controlled*."

"What are you saying?"

"The Ceruleans have produced enough Reborn to start the next phase of their plan—the complete replacement of the old human race with their new species. These attacks are the beginning of a new extinction-level event, a *controlled* one, not indiscriminate. The Association's main mission has changed from breeding—to speeding up our annihilation."

27 - THE CAPITAN MOUNTAINS

After more spiked coffee, Nikki and Bryan had fallen asleep, heads slumped on the desk in the electronics lab.

A loud thump on the door woke them. Lt. Chesnid barged in, urgency in his voice. "We've received an encrypted voice message," he said. "Do you know someone named Muldoon?"

Nikki moaned, opened her eyes, and squinted. "You've found him?"

"A microwave tower picked up a voice transmission from his sat-link. If you don't come quickly, we might lose it."

"Bryan," Nikki said, pushing his shoulder. "Lieutenant, he's out cold."

"Leave him." Chesnid hustled her groggy body out of the lab into the Communications Center. "We've triangulated the signal's location." He pointed to a pulsing red light on a satellite map. "The trace is moving at about thirty miles an hour, so he's in some kind of vehicle, heading south from Santa Fe, about seventy miles due west of Roswell between the Capitan Mountains and the Snowy River Caves. That's a pretty rugged area. Most of the old road system is impassable, blocked by sand dunes."

"Have you been able to talk to him?"

"Not yet. The signal came via an encrypted voice channel. We pinged it to track its location, but the signal's been getting weaker. His sat-link may be losing power. The number it's been calling belongs to you. But calls are being re-routed to a server at the Malibu Heights Hospital."

"Our answering service. Call-forwarding."

"We retrieved the last message he left on that server. That's how we know it was sent to you from a person named Muldoon. We intercepted it about five minutes ago." He played the message. 'Nikki, this is Muldoon again,' the voice recording said. 'God, I hope you're still alive. I'm in the desert south of Santa Fe. We're lost. We need help. No one is answering. Tell my wife Echo that I love her. Please call if you can.'

"That's a really weird message," Nikki said. She activated the call log on the sat-link around her wrist. "Oh shit, more messages. Four of them. Since they were messages forwarded from Malibu Heights, I ignored them. I mean, I can't be dispatched from here, can I?"

"Can we hear the other messages?"

"Sure, can I patch them through to your speakers?"

Message 1— "Nikki, pick up. This is Muldoon. I'm safe. I'm with three of Armstrong's marines. I'm banged up, but okay. I need to talk to you."

Message 2— "Nikki, Muldoon again. Please say you're safe. Where are you? Why haven't you called back?"

Message 3— "Nikki, call me. It's Muldoon. I need to know where you are. Is Echo with you? You remember her, right? She's my wife. Is she with you?"

Message 4— "Nikki, this is Muldoon again. God, I hope you're still alive. I'm in the desert south of Santa Fe. We're lost. We need help. No one is answering. Tell my wife Echo that I love her. Please call if you can."

"In those last two messages, he said several times, 'his wife Echo'. Echo's not married to Muldoon, her partner is a guy named Mikey. Muldoon knows that, and he knows I know that too."

"He's trying to tell you something."

"He sure is. Someone's forcing him to send those messages, someone with a gun to his head. He's giving us misinformation, to tell us something's wrong. It's a heads-up, something I would know isn't true, but whoever he's with, wouldn't be able to tell that. Which means only one thing. There's this terrorist group—the Association—they've got him. He's a hostage. But they really want me, and they're using Muldoon as bait."

"Because?"

Nikki pointed to the electronics lab at the other end of the Comms Room. "Because I've got the files from those thumb-drives."

"Not a big deal," Lt. Chesnid said. "Lady, this Association, whoever they are, are messing with the wrong people. He's with three marines, but they're bad guys? I'll put a squad together and whoever's got your friend, we'll seriously fuck them up. Just say the word and we're there."

"How can you guarantee his safety?"

"We'll do a recon. Set up sniper points. Pulsed particle beams. Laser targeted. Speed of light. We can castrate a coyote at a thousand yards. No, seriously, we've done it. If someone's literally got a gun to your friend's head, their brain wouldn't be given a nanosecond to pull the trigger."

"Okay, you've got the word—go. But I'm coming with you."

***

Four special ops vehicles drove through Roswell's underground roads and entered a large hangar. Three were jeeps equipped with missile-armed drones, each of these scout cars with a sniper and a drone operator. Nikki and Lt. Chesnid were in the fourth vehicle, a personnel carrier.

Inside the hangar, the four vehicles mounted individual platforms with rotor engines at the corners. Clamps locked the vehicles' undercarriages securely in place. Control systems connected the platforms to the vehicles' instrument panels, turning each driver into a pilot. The roll-on/roll-off platforms, Chesnid explained, allowed Roswell Special Forces to get airborne quickly, land virtually anywhere, and drive off on ground patrol.

As soon as Lt. Chesnid gave the signal, the roof of the hangar parted and the night sky appeared above. One by one, the task force—code-named Eagle Flight—lifted off, en route to the Capitan Mountains.

"Switching to night vision," Chesnid said as Eagle Flight formed up. The windscreen in front of them turned a ghostly green.

"Muldoon said he was with three people," Nikki said. "But could there be more?"

"We sent a drone ahead with infrared heat sensors." Chesnid checked the comms screen. "It's above the arranged rendezvous now, near the entrance to the Snowy River Caves."

An aerial view of a stationary jeep appeared as a hologram. Four heat sources were illuminated: three people in the vehicle, one moving on the ground beside it. "You said Muldoon was a big guy, right? Looks like he's the one sitting in the front passenger seat."

Nikki checked the display. "Yeah, I'm pretty sure that's him."

"The scouts will split up, create sniper posts. Once they're in position, we'll land, roll-off, then proceed to the rendezvous point."

The formation flew over a pitch-dark landscape of empty desert. An undulating series of hills soon emerged on the night vision windscreen, the lofty peaks of the Capitan Mountain Range behind them.

Chesnid slowed the command craft to a stationary hover.

"Eagle Flight...break, break," he ordered.

The three scout-craft separated from formation, accelerated, and flew ahead.

"Time to build the trap. Make another call to Muldoon. Get a status check, chit-chat, anything. Just stall for time until my snipers get in position."

"Got it." Nikki tapped Muldoon's number on her sat-link.

"Nikki—" he answered. He cried out in pain. "Ah shit, that hurts."

"Muldoon, are you injured?"

"Broken leg. One of Armstrong's marines did a field splint and gave me some morphine, but it's wearing off."

"Is Armstrong with you?"

"No. I got separated from his patrol. That's when I fell into a crevice. Then—well, I can't—"

"I understand. Your wife, Echo, sends her love."

"Yeah, Echo—okay, thanks."

"Are you with survivors from Adobe Park?"

The line went silent.

"Muldoon? You there?"

"Yeah—not survivors. I'm with three of Armstrong's marines."

"What happened to his ARV?"

Another pause. "Don't know. They said it crashed north of Santa Fe."

Nikki went on mute. "Muldoon took the hint about Echo. He knows we understand he's been taken hostage. The so-called marines who are holding him must be telling him what to say."

"Okay, relay the plan."

Nikki continued the call. "We have your location, Muldoon. Once we land, we'll be approaching from the east. Our vehicle will turn on searchlights. Sit tight and wait."

"That's great. We're not going any—"

The call ended abruptly.

"He cut me off. That's not like him."

"Your Association friends have the information they need, so why prolong the call? They're showing who's in control. At least, they think they are."

After a tense twenty minutes, the last sniper team reported in. All had clear lines of sight on the jeep and they'd launched their armed drones. Inside the command craft, the instrument panel displayed visuals from each new eye in the sky.

The command craft left its stationary hover and flew toward the LZ, one mile from the Snowy River Caves. Chesnid checked the comms link with Special Forces Command at Roswell and said, "Operation Eagle is now active."

The command craft landed and the personnel carrier rolled off its platform into the hilly terrain. "Eagle Leader is on the move."

A rough desert trail led over the dunes at the base of the Capitan Mountains. The personnel carrier dipped into a shallow gully and drove up the other side.

Nikki shifted in her seat. "Call it intuition, lieutenant, but I don't trust this. So far, things have been way too simple. It smells of a trap, like Santa Fe. What if they hijacked Armstrong's ARV? Could it be hiding somewhere in the mountains, ready to pounce on us? It's got some serious firepower."

"Roswell has a satellite over our position." Chesnid tapped the comms panel. "Roswell Command, this is Eagle Leader. Can you confirm any hostiles outside the targets' perimeter?"

"That's a negative, Eagle Leader. Sat comm shows no air traffic. Ground scan also negative. Just you, a jeep, and the targets."

"Roger that, Command." He turned to Nikki. "See? No cavalry is around the corner to save their asses."

The entrance to the Snowy River Caves came into view. Chesnid stopped and flashed the vehicle's searchlights.

"Eagle Leader...this is Eagle-4," said a sniper. "One of the targets has gone into a cave. I do not have a shot. Repeat, no shot."

Chesnid checked the drone feed. "Copy, Eagle-4...prep a missile to fire into the mouth of the cave on my command."

"Roger, missile system activated."

"Oh my god," Nikki said. "I just realized; how do we know Muldoon's sitting in the front passenger seat? Maybe I'm wrong. Maybe it's not him. He could be in the back seat and the person in the cave has him in his gunsight in case we try something. Muldoon could be any one of those people in that jeep. Your snipers could kill the wrong guy!"

"Shit, you're right." Chesnid paused. "All units, stand by."

"We need to confirm where he's sitting," Nikki said. "I know him well. I can approach the jeep and identify him."

"Outside? Are you kidding? That's very dangerous."

"They want me, lieutenant, and probably alive. The thumb-drives are history. That data is safely on the servers at Vandenberg. But they don't know any of that. This isn't about me anymore. Muldoon saved my life, more than once. It's the least I can do to save his life now."

Chesnid tapped nervously on his knee. "Okay, I'll give you a flashlight to use as a signal. Hold it to the ground until you reach the jeep. Raise it, scan all their faces, then point the flashlight to the ground again to signal you know who's who. Raise the light one more time and shine it directly into the face of the person you think is Muldoon. Hold it, okay? Right on his face. Leave the rest to my snipers. Your signal will determine who gets whacked and who doesn't, so you'd better be right. Don't worry, we've done this before, same tactic. I've never lost a hostage and I'm not going to this time."

He handed Nikki a flashlight. "Ready?"

"Oh, shit." She steadied her hand and drew a deep breath. "Okay, I'm ready. Let's do it."

"Eagle-2, have you got a clear shot on the driver?" Chesnid said.

"Affirmative, I have the shot."

"Eagle-1, do you have a shot on the front seat passenger? Will your shot pass through to the subject in the rear seat?"

"Affirmative, on the front passenger. That's a negative on the pass-through, Eagle Leader. My shot's clean."

"Eagle-3, your target is in the rear seat. Have you got eyes?"

"Affirmative. I have the shot."

"Eagle Team...hostage protocol. We're going to ID the hostage with a light. On my command, hold fire on the hostage, take your shots on the others. Eagle-4, on my command, fire a missile into that cave and smoke whoever went inside."

"Copy that," came the replies.

"That's it, Dr. Nikki. All set." The carrier's door slid open and cold air rushed in. "Go! No time to waste."

Nikki leapt out of the vehicle into the chilly desert night. Wind whistled through the mountain pass as the sound of her footsteps crunched across a field of gravel. She gripped the flashlight tightly and pointed it to the ground, her heart pounding.

"Muldoon!" she yelled. There was no reply from the dune-jeep.

She yelled louder. "Muldoon!" Still no reply.

Nikki quickened her pace until she was close enough to shine the light into the faces of the three people sitting in the jeep. "Muldoon? Why aren't you answering me?"

"Muldoon's a bit occupied," a voice from the darkness said.

Scan the faces.

Hold the flashlight to the ground.

Then back up to Muldoon.

Muldoon was sitting in the front passenger seat. His face flinched in the bright light; a sniper's red laser dot centered on his forehead. She moved the flashlight from one face to the other—more dots, targeting two men dressed in marine uniforms, one in the front beside him, the other in the back seat.

Nikki lowered the flashlight to the ground, hesitated, then whipped her arm up. She caught Muldoon's face and held the light steady. The person in the back seat jerked as a white-hot ion-pulse pierced one side of his head and exited out the other. His limp body hit the post of the jeep's roll-bar and slumped sideways. A second ion-pulse struck the person sitting in the driver's seat. He fell out of the jeep to the ground.

The sky above the jeep lit up with a bright flash. Eagle-4's drone-fired missile streaked overhead. The missile was an instant from entering the mouth of the cave when a bubble of blue energy burst out from inside. The energy bubble rippled over the missile, freezing it in the air, then the bubble expanded in all directions, engulfing the jeep and the drone above it.

A blue electric haze swept over Nikki and cocooned her, prickling her skin. Her arms and legs stiffened. Her spine locked in place, making it impossible to move. Her body rose slowly in the air. The desert floor disappeared under a layer of sparkling mist.

A dark silhouette appeared at the cave entrance, backlit by a pulsing blue light. A tall, lanky alien with long thin arms and a bulbous head emerged, covered in a shroud of blue vapors. A band of energy swirled around Muldoon; his body also paralyzed.

The Cerulean moved toward him with an unearthly fluidity and raised its hand. Thin, webbed fingers sent out beams of white light. As the beams coalesced around him, Muldoon's body levitated upward, out of the jeep. The Cerulean placed its thin fingers on Muldoon's chest. The creature's hand moved silently across him, touching every inch of the human in its grasp. Muldoon flinched in pain.

The alien finished its examination, left Muldoon frozen in the air, and slunk over to the bodies of the slain marines. Its hands lingered over their faces. Finding no signs of life, the Cerulean turned toward Nikki in her floating electric prison. It stared into her face with cold, haunting, black-marble eyes. The creature had no nose or mouth. A layer of bluish plasma clung to leathery skin.

Nikki gasped for air, struggling to breathe, fear closing her throat. Her stomach tightened under a rush of nausea. Slowly, the Cerulean raised its hand. A beam of light emerged and pierced Nikki's forehead inflicting a sharp, searing pain as if an incision had been made.

She closed her eyes. Memories expanded like slow-moving fireworks, appearing out of the darkness of her mind. Images glowed bright and large, then faded away—childhood memories, her mother tending her garden, the trauma of the call-out that nearly snuffed out Nikki's life. Her brain felt like every nerve cell was being interrogated, every memory stripped of information; the essence of her soul sampled and pieces taken away. Blood dribbled out of her nose, its sickly metal taste coating her lips.

Suddenly, the pressure inside her head eased and the images vanished. The pain was replaced by a euphoric calm, a soothing warmth, like the wound in her head had been treated and healed. She opened her eyes. The Cerulean had finished taking whatever it wanted from her, and with its strange fluid gait, had re-entered the cave.

The rock face above the cave's entrance opened like a giant hatch. There was no sound. Pieces of rock, bigger than a jeep, floated silently away until the blue glow from inside the cave shone out into the night.

A cobalt-blue cylinder of light descended from the sky into the opening. An egg-shaped pod rose from the cave, bands of energy shimmering across its translucent surface. Inside the pod, the silhouette of a tall, thin alien, with its distinctive bulbous head, towered over of a smaller shape, a human shape, sitting cross-legged.

The pod ascended up the beam; the cylinder of light retracted into the sky; and the opening above the cave closed. Massive rocks re-assembled like a giant jigsaw puzzle, as if time had reversed.

With a startling suddenness, the energy fields that surrounded everything dissolved. The vaporous ground fog dissipated and the cocoon of swirling blue plasma around Nikki unzipped. As the pressure clamping Nikki's body melted away, she fell six feet to the hard desert floor, pain shooting through her legs.

She wiped the blood from her nose with the back of her hand, raised her head, and stood up. She winced as she walked toward Muldoon. He lay on the ground near the jeep, grimacing in pain after falling on his broken leg.

"Nikki, watch out!" he yelled. "Get down!"

Above their heads, a billowy contrail signaled where the once-frozen missile had been freed to pursue its original course. It entered the cave's mouth. Less than a second later, a fiery explosion erupted inside. The blast wave knocked Nikki off her feet. A dust cloud rushed out from the cave's entrance. She rolled onto her face and covered her head. Small shards of rock rained down around her.

The dust cleared. Coughing, she crawled toward Muldoon. "Are you okay?"

His face was cut from flying debris. His nose was bleeding like hers. "Fuck no," he moaned. "Have I died? Is this Hell?"

Nikki examined the splint around his injured leg. It was still intact.

A rumble like a peal of thunder shook the ground. Nikki and Muldoon looked skyward as a cloud consumed a large elliptical spacecraft. The craft ascended and the cloud dissolved until all that was left in the heavens was the starry night.

Nikki's lips trembled. "I thought for sure that alien creature was going to take me away, like that marine that went into the cave."

"She walked in there in a trance, like she'd been turned into a robot," Muldoon said. He glanced at the dead bodies around the jeep. "There was something odd about all of them. I knew as soon as I met them, they were Reborn."

Nikki nestled into his beating chest. All she wanted to do was sleep and forget.

"The power those aliens have—it's unimaginable," he said, wrapping his strong arms around her. "They know precisely what they're doing, but we know nothing about them. We just stumble from one ambush to another like a herd of frightened deer. And these Association operatives, they're in lockstep with what's going on."

Bright spotlights penetrated the lingering dust cloud, turning night into day. Gravel crunched, the sound of racing footsteps coming from all directions.

"What the fuck just happened?" Lt. Chesnid said. "What was that thing?"

Nikki stood up, her face twisted in anger, and pushed Chesnid hard in the chest. "I thought you said the airspace was clear?" She thumped him again. "I thought you said no cavalry was hiding around the corner?"

"Lady, we've got to recalibrate—every single fucking thing. Standard tactics clearly no longer work."

"No shit."

28 - THE MECHANISM

Dr. Mateo Toschi, a short man in his late sixties with a prominent nose and a receding hairline, ran nervous fingers through his salt and pepper beard as he waited in the consultation room of the medical wing at Roswell.

Nikki's mobi-cradle entered.

"How's the pain, Dr. Akaju?" he asked.

"Manageable, thanks. A six-foot drop onto packed desert gravel would test anyone's weight-bearing bones. Better to find out now that my previous stress fracture hadn't fully healed, than to rely on my foot later and be caught out when those creatures return. I don't like being confined to this cradle thing, but your orthopedics doctor said the bone would heal quicker this way, at least for a few days, then I'll be up again with a boot."

Bryan Leysson strode through the door. "Sorry I'm late. I was checking up on that kid with the collapsed lung. He's doing really well."

"I'm the medical director here," Toschi said, extending a hand to Bryan. "I knew your father. We were student interns together in the Civil Defense Corps before I went to med school. Long time ago."

Behind Dr. Toschi, a wall-high video screen held a series of MRI and CT scans. They grouped around the first set of scans as Toschi explained what they were. "Your refugees from Santa Fe represent every condition you could hope for. Some were exposed to Jupiter clouds, but not all of them. Some had avian flu, but not others. Some lived on a commune outside of town but although they're unvaccinated, none of them caught avian flu. These scans are representative of three distinct patient groups with identical internal pathology, no exceptions. As soon as I saw these scans, I alerted Vandenberg."

Toschi opened the comms feed to Vandenberg. A conference room of white-coated personnel surrounded Dr. Pavel Zharlev.

"Everyone has a theory," Zharlev said. "We'll give you a few minutes to look over the scans, then we'd like yours."

Nikki moved the mobi-cradle along the screens, browsing from one set of scans to the next until she'd seen all three. She returned to the middle patient group. "Do you see it, Bryan, the tumor on the adrenal gland?" She reviewed the scans representing the last patient group. "But in this case, the tumor, or what's left of it, is flattened, like it's burst."

"It's unmistakable, very distinct features in both cases."

"So, the first patient group is our baseline?" Nikki asked.

"Correct," Toschi replied. "The scan of an unvaccinated settler from the desert commune—no avian flu, no known exposure to Jupiter clouds."

"And also, no tumor. What group does the middle patient represent?"

"Someone who's had avian flu, but not yet been exposed to Jupiter clouds. I've never heard of tumors like this occurring after contracting avian flu, have you, Dr. Akaju? There are children in this group too, with the same scan results."

"Tumors in general are not associated with viral infections and adrenal gland tumors are more common in older people, not children. Usually, adrenal tumors are benign and small, less than a centimeter. But what I'm seeing here is a large, bulbous sac. You can't miss it. And in that last patient, we've got a different picture. The tumor appears to have burst."

"The last set of scans are from the patient group who have had both avian flu and exposure to Jupiter clouds," Toschi said.

Nikki moved closer. "I can imagine what speculation this has created at Vandenberg, Dr. Zharlev. Does this mean, in those people exposed to Jupiter clouds, the radiation has burst their tumors? But seizures and memory loss are neurological effects, and these tumors are associated with the endocrine system not the brain or central nervous system. So, what's the connection? Do you have a theory about that?"

"No, nothing definitive," Zharlev replied.

"The first step is to determine if these tumors are cancerous," Nikki said. "We need biopsies done, fast."

"I don't have enough surgical staff or operating rooms to conduct that number of biopsies," Toschi said. "Not if you want them done quickly. We need to transport your patients to Vandenberg."

"Why not send medical teams with mobile operating theaters to Roswell?" Zharlev said. "The military keeps field hospitals on standby, packaged, and ready to be deployed. If we requisition some of them, we can get medical teams airborne in less than two hours. We need to get on top of this development."

"Sounds good to me."

"And Nikki, the BioSciences Lab has been studying the files on those thumb-drives. What a huge amount of research to comb through."

"Any conclusions yet?"

"Only one. No more spiked coffee naps for you," Zharlev said. "Not for anyone."

"Yeah, I kinda got that."

***

Transports from Vandenberg arrived at 21:00 hours with three mobile operating theaters and within two hours, the additional surgical teams got to work. The next morning, Nikki briefed Lewis Temple and Pavel Zharlev on the biopsies done on the refugees from Santa Fe.

"The adrenal gland tumors are not cancerous," Nikki informed them. "But the tumors' biological makeup is unlike anything anyone has ever seen."

She displayed photographs from the surgeries. "In this shot, we see intact tumors removed from several patients who had avian flu but weren't exposed to the Jupiter clouds. Inside these tumors are hundreds of thousands of tiny hard-shelled cysts. Magnesium compounds from the bloodstream, bones, and tissues have been concentrated in these cysts until most of the patient's supply of magnesium has been locked up. This group of refugees displays the same levels of magnesium deficiency we found in the victims of human combustion."

"Cysts inside tumors?" Professor Temple asked. "Has that ever happened before with other diseases?"

"Not in that same way," Nikki replied. "Parasitic organisms like amoebas use a similar shell-like coating to survive outside the body. In those cases, cysts form a protective shell to the external environment. When people ingest the cysts by eating contaminated food, the shells dissolve in the stomach to release the parasites. But in this case, the hard shells are doing the opposite. They are protective when *inside* the body. They keep the magnesium compounds trapped inside the tumor. Roswell's AI program searched the medical journals and there's never been a disease that manifests itself like this—until now."

"What purpose does this trapped magnesium serve?"

"We asked the AI program," Bryan said. "What would happen if these cyst-filled tumors were exposed to radiation from Jupiter clouds? Would those radiation levels be strong enough to rupture the tumor's membrane and release the cysts into the body? The AI's answer came back with a firm, yes."

"The surgeons from Vandenberg removed deflated tumors from patients who were exposed to Jupiter clouds," Nikki said. "The biopsies confirmed exactly what AI predicted. Radiation exposure has burst the tumor sacs. The surgeons found the cysts had traveled through arteries and veins and settled like blood clots everywhere including the brain."

"The presence of cysts in the blood vessels of the brain will disrupt its normal functions," Bryan said. "That's why people exposed to Jupiter clouds suffered seizures and memory loss."

"As far as spontaneous human combustion," Nikki continued, "we're not sure what mechanism is in play. If magnesium-rich cysts are deposited throughout the body, what happens when they're exposed to phonon radiation? We know magnesium metal ignites in the presence of oxygen, but that's sitting on a lab bench, in room air, with a source of ignition. Magnesium compounds in the body are a completely different issue. Could phonon radiation cause organic magnesium to ignite?"

"Once we get samples of those cysts," Zharlev replied. "We can run experiments to test if phonons will ionize the magnesium and cause the combustion of human tissue. Possible? Who knows? Everything has been a long series of one-of-a-kind medical mysteries."

"The Weapons Lab at Vandenberg has been working on body armor to shield the military against phonon radiation," Professor Temple commented. "In the meantime, can you develop a surgical procedure to get rid of those tumors?"

"That's not going to be easy, professor," Nikki replied. "For patients with intact tumor sacs, we have to be careful the surgery itself doesn't leak cysts into the bloodstream. For patients with ruptured tumors where the cysts have spread, we don't know if that process is reversible with treatment. The cysts are larger than blood cells, so maybe we can filter them out of the blood using a dialysis machine. Roswell has only one dialysis setup. To try different blood-filtering techniques, we need a lot more."

"You'll get them." Temple reversed his mobi-cradle. As he left the conference, he said, "Good work."

The video feed ended.

29 - MARTIAL LAW

Dr. Nikki Akaju limped forward on her strapped leg and pulled back the curtain around one of the medical bays. At six-foot-ten, Izak Windsong made the gurney look like a bed sized for a toddler. She adjusted the IV line and wrapped a blood pressure collar around Izak's massive arm. "Any bigger and we'd have to have one custom made." She pumped the collar up and read his systolic pressure. "How are you feeling, Izak?"

"Like I constantly need to pee." Windsong pointed to the bag draining urine from his bladder.

"Good, that's what we want. The bag's nearly full so we can send it off for analysis. We'll check if any cysts have passed into your urine. Blood samples will tell us if any remain after the dialysis."

"So, I don't have to worry about that horrible body-on-fire thing now?"

"We hope so. But everything's still experimental."

"Hey, no arguments here. I'm game for anything. Just get this crap out of my body as fast as you can. That's all I care about."

"You're a real trooper, Izak." Nikki removed his urinary catheter. "I haven't thanked you for what you did, escaping Santa Fe. You took a significant risk to help a lot of people who are alive today because of you."

"Can you tell me what's going on out there? Have there been more alien attacks? There's a ton of speculation. This base is a dead zone for information. I can quiet things down if I knew what to say. The Santa Fe people look up to me. They trust me."

"I know. But I'm afraid I can't really help. I don't know everything that's going on either. And what I know, I can't share. Not because

I don't want to, but because it's only a small part of a bigger picture. Bits of information taken out of context can be a problem. It just creates more fear. We have plenty of that. All I can say is, we're getting ready to fight back. And that's progress."

"Good to hear. Our people are desert settlers by birth, but we stayed in the desert by choice. We've been fighting for our survival all our lives. We know how to do that, and we're good at it. This is just one more challenge, I guess."

"That's the best attitude to have right now. Let's make that spirit infectious, okay?"

"You got it, doc."

"Hang in there, Izak. I'll check back soon."

Nikki closed the curtain and delivered the urostomy bag to Dixxie. "Can you get a nurse to draw his blood, please? How are we doing with the surgical patients?"

"No complications," she replied. "Dr. Leysson is fantastic. He let me watch the procedure to remove a tumor."

"We need more doctors. You're a smart girl. Thought about changing professions?"

"I'd need a sponsor. I'm a migrant, remember?"

"You got it, kid. My pleasure. Hey, where is Bryan?"

"Still in theater."

"If he's looking for me, tell him I have a call with Vandenberg. I've got to go. We'll talk again later."

In the conference room, Nikki uploaded the results of the surgical and dialysis treatments. When Professor Temple and Pavel Zharlev joined, she noticed expressions of concern. "We haven't had an attack in several days," she said. "Is something imminent?"

"The aliens' tactics have changed," Zharlev replied in a subdued voice. "Spacecraft are searching out small groups of refugees fleeing the countryside for the larger towns. They've been abducting women of child-bearing age. Once the Ceruleans are finished, the military expects a much larger, more devastating attack."

"How much is left of the world for them to destroy?"

"Communications outside the Federation have always been difficult. But we've been able to track the flight paths of their spaceships using satellites. Their movements provide us with a map of where the remainder of the world lives. It's revealed a few surprises. We're not sure what the global population count is anymore. Previous estimates of less than a billion people might even be too high. We know from merchant sailors many places are so tribal and primitive, they're still at war with each other. It's unlikely whoever's left overseas has the technology to cope with their attacks and organize any kind of effective military response."

"So, we're it? We're the only ones who have the ability to fight back? No one else?"

"It would seem so."

"There was no mention in Dante Parks' files to connect avian flu with what's happening now," Nikki said. "Our pandemic started decades after his death. He couldn't have known about it."

"The BioSciences team have come to an astonishing conclusion," Professor Temple said. "The Ceruleans genetically engineered avian flu to weaponize the infection once they knew how virulent the global pandemic had become."

"They did—*what*?" Nikki stepped back from the screen. "They *engineered* it?"

"All viruses mutate over time, but a particular feature of the AVF-7 variant was the emergence of a new spike protein that didn't make any contribution to increased viral load or replication. When AVF-7 became the dominant worldwide strain, no one suspected it was an engineered form of the virus. This spike protein was thought to be a non-functional mutation, a biological redundancy. We ignored it as an area of medical concern. In hindsight, that was a mistake. But how were we to know?"

"The BioSciences team infected adrenal gland cells with this spike protein," Zharlev added. "That protein is far from redundant, Nikki. It produces a new type of adrenal gland tumor. All subsequent variants of avian flu now have this spike protein. Nature is not getting rid of it."

"And what about the cysts? Did you find any connection with spontaneous human combustion?"

"In the lab, we successfully used phonon radiation to ignite the cysts. The quantum-tunneling effect of phonons produces the micro-heat needed to split organic compounds of magnesium into free-radical magnesium ions. In contact with oxygen in the blood, there's a violent reaction. The Ceruleans re-engineered avian flu as a mechanism for our extermination."

"Doesn't that seem like a complicated way to kill us?" Nikki asked. "Create adrenal gland tumors from a flu virus, burst them open when exposed to one kind of radiation, then ignite the body with another kind of radiation. I'm not a military strategist, but that seems like a very inefficient way to kill your enemy. Why not just expose us to lethal doses of radiation, all in one simple step?"

"The Ceruleans observed the effects of our nuclear wars," Zharlev replied. "The Reborn are intermingled with us in our communities. That kind of blanket nuclear radiation would kill them too. No doubt a lot of Reborn were lost during those wars. The madness had to stop and they made that happen. Dante Parks' research proves the Ceruleans genetically engineered the Reborn to be immune to viruses like avian flu. So, they made a version of avian flu that was deadly to the rest of us. In the bodies of the Reborn, the process of tumor growth never gets started because they never get infected in the first place."

"Selective extermination."

"Correct. If you want to eliminate a weed, you use a weed killer that doesn't harm the plants you want to grow. AVF-7 avian flu is that weed killer. And we are the weeds."

"How are the treatments on your patients working?" Temple asked.

"So far, so good, professor. Robotic surgery is delicate enough to remove the tumors without rupturing them. And in the other patients whose tumors have burst, results after dialysis show levels of distributed cysts that are no longer measurable. If any cysts are still present, we can only hope the quantities are so small, any exposure to phonon radiation might cause localized tissue damage but not death by total combustion."

"That's a great result."

"I have a bigger worry, professor. With nearly universal exposure to avian flu, most of the population must already have these adrenal gland tumors. Because they remain asymptomatic until they burst, these tumors have been overlooked as a medical condition. Let's assume we're ready to roll out these treatments. Now we're talking about a medical emergency requiring—I mean, I can't even imagine—a *massive* demand for surgical and post-op facilities, blood dialysis wards, diagnostic scans and tests. If we were just talking about thousands of people, the path forward would be tough enough, but we're talking *millions.* I have a hard time getting to grips with the scale of treatment required to fix this problem."

"We'll start planning, using whatever resources we have. That's all we can do," Temple replied. "We'll prioritize treatments to the military, the security forces, and essential workers."

"Everyone's an essential worker, professor. The military still needs to be fed, right?"

"Unfortunately, someone has to have the lowest priority."

"I know exactly how that works," There was a hint of venom in Nikki's voice. "The wealthiest and most privileged first. The educated and skilled next. Any places that are left will be fought over by the rest of our free-citizens. By that time, those who've already had a lifetime of bad luck—the migrants—will have been reduced to ash by the Ceruleans' phonon beams."

"What else do you suggest, Dr. Akaju?" Professor Temple's voice echoed with a harsh mechanical tone. "If the Ceruleans accelerate their attacks, we'll have more than just a mass casualty event, we'll have panic and civil disorder in the Western Districts like they had during the Constitutional War. Which means total anarchy. Only now, we don't have anywhere else to migrate to—nowhere to escape this cataclysm except the Pacific Ocean."

"I don't have any suggestions, professor. I'm sorry. I'm physically and mentally exhausted. The big picture is overwhelming."

"Then don't think about it. You're a doctor. Rest up. Focus your knowledge and skills on what you've been trained to do. That's all we're asking of you. That's all we can ask of anyone right now. You have a hard-working, expert medical team at Roswell. There's still a lot of work ahead of you there. I have to brief Ansel Denard in a few minutes. Then we'll be conferencing with the Military Council in Denver to discuss tactical options to counter the ongoing threat from the Ceruleans. That includes a contingency for martial law. We'll talk again soon."

As usual, the meeting ended abruptly. Professor Lewis Temple didn't indulge in idle chit-chat or long goodbyes.

Nikki limped out of the conference room. Special Forces marines scurried past her on their way to an increasingly more frequent schedule of patrols.

Declare martial law when we're already run by the military? What exactly will that look like?

30 - THE HELIOS DEVICE

Little flecks of undigested food floated in front of Chenzi's face, escapees from the loose space-sickness mask that clung to her cheeks. The rush of yet another nauseous episode overwhelmed her throat.

Emma administered a dose of antihistamine to combat the nausea.

As the space station completed its orbit, there was no such thing as 'morning' in the Earth sense, nothing except the natural rhythm of GDF15 hormones that spiked as the twin fetuses grew inside her.

Chenzi disposed of the bag of effluent. Without the other crew members, waste management on the ISO was the least of her worries. There was plenty of empty capacity on board.

As far as 'it' was concerned, 'it' had been disposed of—the slug-like translucent green bio-aberration that had crawled through the hole in the station's titanium-glass windows. It had pursued Chenzi through the station's access tunnels in a circus act even Chenzi's best flips couldn't evade. It had burrowed through her jumpsuit until it latched onto its target—naked skin; any skin, anywhere, it didn't seem to matter to the tentacles that pumped infernal jelly into her until the aberration had shrunk to a quarter of its original size.

What remained outside Chenzi's body was a limp blubber that could be easily plucked off her skin, a hopefully dead remnant she'd imprisoned in a bio-hazard container. But Dr. Zhu Chenzi had absolutely no interest in becoming the researcher who would later dissect it in the name of science. That revolting thought made her even more sick.

"Blood sugar levels indicate a need for nutritional sustenance," Emma chirped. "Re-hydration is also recommended."

"Fuck off."

"Synthesizing Vitamin B6. Injecting 20 milligrams of nano-biocytes."

Chenzi moaned and attached a new sickness bag to her mask. "When will this ever end?"

"Average daily occurrence lasts for a period of fourteen weeks. Accelerated gestation in this case indicates a potentially shorter duration of symptoms. Do you want another ginger biscuit?"

"Oh Emma, please fuck off and leave me alone."

Chenzi wretched again.

The comms panel in Module Alpha lit up. "How are you feeling today, Chenzi?" Simon Belledeau asked.

"Not you too. Would everyone please treat me like the astrophysicist I am and not some invalid."

"Roger that, Chenzi. We have some news that's bound to cheer you up. Your partner Marisol and son JoJo have been found, and are alive and well."

Chenzi's eyes watered. Teardrops drifted around her face. Her hands formed fists and punched the air.

"Are you there? Did you hear me?"

"Oh god, did I ever! That is so great. Where are they?"

"The military rescued them near Santa Fe. They've been recovering at a base near a place called Roswell. JoJo has a cracked rib but he's stable and doing fine."

"Docking sequence initiated," Boris announced. "Docking ring engaged. Locking hooks secured. Docking sequence complete. Opening airlock to Pan-Lunar Shuttle-483."

"The construction shuttle has arrived." Chenzi removed her space-sickness bag. "I'm more than ready to go, Control. I'm done here. Truly done."

"Chenzi, the repair crew aren't staying," Belledeau said. "They'll secure the ISO as best as they can and return with you to Imbrium."

"Why? I thought they were here to overhaul it. What's going on?"

"Do you remember the Helios Device?"

"How could I forget? Some crazed lunatic's theoretical idea you could blast an asteroid into pieces. Somehow the thermonuclear impossibility of a contained anti-matter explosion wasn't included in his desire to spend a shitload of money."

"That lunatic is Edison Denard."

"I was referring to Dr. Koop Van Stratton. His tokamak design struggled to produce an anti-matter particle long enough to get it on the surface of an asteroid."

"Van Stratton incorporated all your ideas, Chenzi and his tests so far are promising. The plasma generated by his new tokamak is stable. The device has been miniaturized since the last time you worked on it during your posting at Imbrium. Professor Temple wants a word with you about it."

Temple's image appeared on the display. "Chenzi, the Helios Device has not yet been validated for asteroid mining, but we have another purpose for it. The Cerulean mother-ship is an elaborate refueling station and logistics hub. We noticed a depletion of electromagnetic signals from the spaceships after their missions. Whatever propulsion system powers their spaceships, they return to the mothership frequently. That energy is restored after they've docked for a while. The cylindrical cargo ships you observed delivering pods with abductees have been returning back through the wormhole with further people they're taking from Earth. We have to stop both processes. Destroying the mother-ship is paramount. Our other main objective is to disrupt or even eliminate transit through the wormhole."

"And you think the Helios Device can do that?"

"Van Stratton has been working hard to build a second prototype at his Deep Space Exploration Lab on Imbrium," Pavel Zharlev said. "Once your construction shuttle is halfway back to the moon, we'll launch both Helios Devices. You will see them zip past you. We know the Ceruleans employ defensive mechanisms to protect their ships. We're disguising both Helios Devices inside shuttles. If they're curious and don't perceive a threat, we may be able to get one close enough to the mother-ship to detonate it before they react. Simulations indicate the explosive blast should penetrate through the ship's defensive plasma barrier. Whether that's enough to destroy the mother-ship is a big unknown, but we have to try."

"You mentioned a second device?"

"The other target is the exotic matter ring surrounding the wormhole entrance. If the ring acts like the frame of a door, we're hoping an anti-matter explosion will break its continuity. Maybe the door will collapse and shut the wormhole. We considered flying it straight into the anomaly's center, but we're not sure if the Helios Device would just get swallowed up before it detonated. Maybe that would cause damage wherever the wormhole takes it, while leaving the entrance intact at our end. Targeting the frame is the goal."

"That's an ambitious plan."

"It's more than ambitious, Chenzi. If it works, the anti-matter explosions near the mother-ship will likely take out the ISO or knock it out of stable orbit so it burns up on re-entry."

"We can't wait until the station is on the other side of Earth?"

"We're going to try, but the ISO might also be hit by a debris field from the mother-ship or enter an electromagnetic storm left behind when we attack the wormhole. Either way, the risks are too great to leave anyone on board."

"I hope your plan works," she replied. "Knowing Van Stratton like I do; his tokamak contraption could be a wet firecracker and fizzle into nothing."

"We have to take that chance, Chenzi," Professor Temple said. "We have no other options. The Helios Device is the only readily available weapon that can put a stop to our annihilation."

31 - PROJECT ASTRAGENESIS

Three weeks later
Joshua Tree Military District

Fierce gusts swept across the airfield at the Mead Canyon Research Center, sending sand and gravel hundreds of feet into the air. The ARV from Vandenberg tipped at an acute angle as it tried to land in the wicked crosswind. Nikki grabbed the straps of her jump seat and imagined something pleasant to steady her nerves—a happy thought before they crashed. Struggling, the ARV righted itself and aborted its approach. Rotors roared as it made a rapid ascent to clear the sandstorm.

"We're going to circle over Vegas until this wind subsides," the pilot announced.

Pavel Zharlev and Professor Temple were being tight-lipped about something they'd called the Helios Device, detonated in space several weeks ago. A general communique from the Military Council said the Federation had delivered 'a major blow' to the Cerulean invasion. Whatever that blow was, it wasn't enough to slow down evacuation plans. Phonon beam attacks had ended immediately after that, but recent sightings of spaceships, although less frequent than before, indicated the threat remained.

The ARV banked over the agri-settlements that surrounded the Closed City of Las Vegas. In all four directions of the compass, military vehicles escorted ragtag convoys of land-trains and buses. The first evacuations were nearing completion: a logistical nightmare to relocate free-citizens from across the Districts to safer accommodations, mostly old nuclear missile silos in the grasslands north-east of Denver, and fallout bunkers in the mountains west of the Sagebrush MD. Once those spaces were filled, people would be sent to the military's storage caves in the mountains of the Sequoia Forest, as far north as the border with Cascadia.

Arrangements for the evacuation of skilled work-visa migrants were being put in place. But the bulk of the migrant population remained where they were, above ground in the Wards, vulnerable and exposed. Should these migrants be moved, or just left behind, abandoned, and unguarded? That question had swirled around every briefing Nikki had attended, without a firm resolution.

The most dangerous exercise in people-rustling had been in progress for the past two weeks. The military had long wanted a reason to disperse the population of the largest and most lawless migrant camp in the Western Districts, the Las Vegas Closed City. Short-term priorities within the stretched military budget had always taken precedence over finding a long-term solution. This crisis had sliced through that bureaucratic log-jam like a hot knife. The question had always been, where could these migrants, most of them hardened criminals, be sent?

The military's solution involved carving up the inhabitants of Vegas into manageable bite-sized pieces and sending them to various prison camps and detention centers. But given the Closed City's hidden arsenal of old weapons, the security forces had to disarm its criminal factions first. A campaign by the military and police of door-to-door searches and forced evictions had resulted in brutal street fighting where only one side was bound to prevail, and it did. The success of the 'Vegas Dispersal Strategy', as it was called by the Federation's central government in Denver, established the blueprint for the evacuation of the other migrant wards once their turn came.

Below the ARV, convoys appeared and disappeared in a maze of dust clouds rising up from the parched earth. All across the Districts, the fates of millions of souls were being blown by seasonally cruel winds. Adequate food distribution and the availability of clean water in the shelters would become the next challenge. Inevitably, Nikki thought, some of the people the government wanted to save would perish by other means—starvation, disease, especially the sick and elderly. But the military didn't care. Avoidance of an armed revolution, regardless of the human cost, was their primary goal. Preventing violence through violence was their plan. That had been a theme throughout the Federation's history. Why change now?

Nikki had been the last member of the emergency medical team to leave Roswell for Vandenberg. She'd made a point of visiting every survivor from the Santa Fe attack before her departure. Patients with bodies eviscerated by deadly magnesium-rich cysts had received several dialysis treatments and as far as this evolving science knew, were now clear of contamination.

Her own terrifying ordeal with the Cerulean had produced no adverse effects from the radiation exposure she'd received. The stress fracture in her foot wasn't as serious as first thought and had healed. But during her medical, Dr. Toschi had discovered, that although she'd suffered a mild case of avian flu in the past, no adrenal gland tumor had grown inside her. The reason was another medical mystery.

After an hour circling Vegas, the ARV was cleared to land at Mead Canyon. The facility was once again staffed and operational, although with far fewer project teams. Security had gone into overdrive. Pavel Zharlev was waiting on the other side of yet another checkpoint. As they proceeded to his laboratory, the difference inside the research center was striking—corridors of dark, empty laboratories and conference rooms.

"Where is everybody?" she asked.

"We think it's still too dangerous to shuttle personnel from Nova Mercurius every day." Zharlev's voice held a hint of defeat in its tone. "The research departments have been dispersed. The Astrophysics, Meteorology, and Aviation Technology groups have gone to Vandenberg. Crop research to the agri-domes in Nova Mercurius. We've kept the BioSciences team here because their delicate instruments don't transport well. The particle accelerator can't be moved, so my Physics Lab is staying too. We've created shelters for the lab techs. People have grumbled. It's not the luxurious accommodations they're used to in Nova Mercurius."

Zharlev made an unexpected turn and proceeded down a corridor away from the Physics Lab until they arrived at a glass-paneled security tunnel. Another facial scan opened a darkened glass door. Across the threshold was a large, bright, starkly white laboratory with rows of genotype sequencing instruments that filled every work top from one end of the lab to the other.

As the pair entered, the staff stopped their work.

The hum of a mobi-cradle announced the arrival of Professor Lewis Temple.

"Welcome to your new home, Dr. Akaju," he said. "We've started some of the research without you. Hope you don't mind. But time is precious."

"What will I be doing here?"

"Hopefully, running the place." Temple had a rare twinkle in his eyes. "Come into the conference room and I'll explain."

The conference room was large with circular walls that held curved screens and holographic projectors. "You will be leading the brightest minds from our BioSciences Division for this project," he said. "It has the highest priority within Mead Canyon. Whatever you need, you will get it. We're calling it Project Astragenesis."

"All *this* has to do with what you found on those thumb-drives? Dante Parks and his research?"

"Yes. Everything in the lab has been assembled with the specific intent to advance his work. He spent his entire life documenting the science and genetic engineering behind the aliens' experiments. But he went further, as we'll explain. His research provides exciting new avenues to follow. The BioSciences team did autopsies on the two Reborn operatives killed by Special Forces in the mountains. You'll be interested in the results."

A hologram of a DNA's double helix appeared in the center of the conference table.

"It's clear the Reborn have a unique genetic makeup."

The rotating DNA strand had numerous color-coded sections.

"They're a totally new species of human," Temple said. "The Reborn share only ninety-six percent of our DNA. Their DNA's unique genetic sequences are shown in this model. As you know, even a small difference can have a profound effect on how the body functions."

"Reborn DNA falls into two groups," Zharlev added. "The first group—they refer to themselves as 'rejects'—found their way to Ward 13. The changes in their DNA are not as advanced as the other group, represented by the Association. One group is benign. They co-exist happily with us. But the other one? Well, you know what they're willing to do. They are enablers of genocide. We know the two groups are different, not just from us, but from each other. It's imperative we understand genetically what those differences mean."

"So, our assumptions and theories are true?" Nikki said. "The Ceruleans kept going until they perfected their new master race?"

"Yes. Not only that, but the aliens seem to have a way of coercing the Reborn into doing their bidding. We don't know how. We need to find ways to identify the Reborn among us, another area of research Project Astragenesis will set as a priority."

"It's as important to understand how the aliens failed, as it is to understand how they succeeded," Professor Temple said. "With your leadership, Nikki, this lab is where we can make that happen. We trust your inquisitive mind more than anyone else's. We also trust you to protect the project's secrecy. Our work on astragenesis cannot be sabotaged by the Association."

"We have recent evidence the Ceruleans have progressed the science of human fertility to a darker, far more ominous phase," Zharlev said. "They've developed parthenogenesis, the ability of the female of a species to reproduce asexually, something Dante Parks had not discovered before he died."

"You mean fertilization without a male?" Nikki gasped. "In humans? Oh my god."

"It's not unheard of in the natural world," Zharlev continued. "Climate change and nuclear contamination have destroyed so many ecosystems, many species are now extinct. Nature has been forced to adapt. We have more insects, reptiles, and fish capable of asexual reproduction than ever before in our natural history. Mammals are adapting too—reports of tigers and leopards in post-fallout Asia, polar bears in the north of Cascadia, solitary animals with large ranges and limited opportunities to mate. Females are reproducing without a male. It seems the Ceruleans have taken parthenogenesis one step further, with humans."

"A major objective of Project Astragenesis," Temple said, "is to find out how this is being done."

"You said you have *evidence* of parthenogenesis?" Nikki's face turned quizzical. "What evidence?"

"A patient, a pregnant patient. Her name is Chenzi. You'll get to meet her soon," Zharlev replied. "It's imperative we develop a proactive genetic response to defend ourselves against the Ceruleans' biological threats."

"A proactive response?" Nikki's tone was skeptical. "We have corrective medicine—surgical removal of tumors, dialysis of the blood. So far that's all we've got. Maybe that's all we'll ever have in the short term. We're quite some distance away from being medically *proactive*, let alone having a 'genetic' response. What does that even mean?"

Pavel Zharlev's blank eyes disturbed her. He seemed resigned to some dire inevitability; the look of a scientist whose discoveries may soon change the world as we know it.

"Wait. Oh, no, you're not suggesting? You are, aren't you? The next step Dante Parks didn't live long enough to pursue? You want to create your own version of a new master race—one protected from the Ceruleans, a genetically protected version? At least you hope it will be. A new 96-percent, but of *our* creation?"

There was silence.

Nikki stepped back. "I don't think I can participate in that."

"You don't have a choice," Temple said.

"What are you going to do, professor? Torture me to co-operate? You're not the Association. I won't help you create your new Frankenstein's monster. No...*I won't*. Definitely not."

"Interesting analogy, but that's not what I meant about not having a choice."

"So, what did you mean, professor?"

"No doubt you've wondered why that Cerulean didn't abduct you?"

"I don't even want to remember what happened that night," Nikki said. "That creature looked me up and down, poked my head, and said, no thanks, you're not for us. It took someone else instead. None of that has made any sense to me. Still doesn't."

"The Cerulean who examined you made a conscious decision to leave you behind," Temple replied. "And we think we've found out why. It comes from your family's medical history."

"What's my family got to do with it?"

"The records on those thumb-drives document how Dante Parks altered the DNA of your grandmother's fetus before her birth and when her child grew up, Dante Parks genetically engineered the fetus of your grandmother's pregnant daughter as well."

"Her daughter? You mean, my *mother*?"

"Over a period of nearly thirty years, your grandmother Adriana helped the elderly Dante Parks conduct fetal DNA alterations in pregnant volunteers. In the final years of his life, your grandmother oversaw her own daughter's pregnancy to ensure the genetic engineering secrets he'd learned were carried forward one more time, even better than before, three generations later. That ensured the legacy of Dante Parks would survive after his death. It's all documented in the thumb-drives your grandmother hid, until now."

"What legacy? What was carried forward?" Nikki was taken aback. She mulled over his words, confused. "Wait, you said, her *own daughter*'s pregnancy? No, you don't mean—but that's—you mean, *me*?"

"Dr. Akaju, Dante Parks developed methods of genetic engineering he practiced from one mother to another, techniques that ultimately re-engineered your own genetic makeup," Professor Temple said, his mechanical voice an emotionless acknowledgment of a new scientific truth.

"He made you immune to the growth of adrenal tumors and possibly to a host of other endemic diseases and cancers that have plagued us throughout history. He couldn't have known what was going to happen, but he prepared you and others, genetically, for the dire possibilities that might befall humankind in the future. He wanted to ensure our continued survival, despite how we were destroying the world. Your genome is one of the 96-percent too, but different again from the Reborn. That was his legacy. You are immune to the spike protein the Ceruleans created to exploit our inherent genetic frailties. Because of that, your genes have protected you from the mechanism of tumors and cysts they're using to exterminate the rest of us. Don't you want others protected like that too? People you love? Their children?"

Nikki was stunned into silence.

"That night in the desert," Professor Temple continued. "When a Cerulean was looking to abduct a female specimen, it rejected you and took someone else, one of their own Reborn. Why? Whatever that genetic reason was, it may be critical to the survival of the human race. You were no longer a suitable candidate for their asexual insemination. Your genetic makeup wasn't right. This entire laboratory is dedicated to finding out why."

Professor Temple moved his mobi-cradle closer.

"You, Dr. Nikki Akaju, *are* Project Astragenesis."

ABOUT CHARLES A CORNELL

When I'm not trying to survive the chaos of everyday life, I'm dreaming up all kinds of crazy fiction. To say I have an overactive imagination is an understatement. I specialize in science fiction, science fantasy, dieselpunk, and steampunk.

My goal is to thrill and amaze my readers with dynamic plots, unusual twists, interesting characters, and worlds of wonder. I do this from my writer's den in a small village in North Lincolnshire, England with the occasional interference from my ginger tabby cat who claims to be from another dimension and will push me through a wormhole if he is not fed on demand.

My first published novel, *Tiger Paw*, won the 2012 Royal Palm Literary Award for Best Thriller from the Florida Writers Association.

My dieselpunk work, *DragonFly* is a retro-futuristic collision of science fiction and fantasy with a generous dash of alternative history. *DragonFly* was a 2014 Royal Palm Literary Award Finalist in Science Fiction, has received two prestigious Reader's Favorite Five-Star Reviews, and won the 2018 Reader's Favorite Silver Medal in the Young Adult - Action category.

To keep up to date with my novels and short stories, visit my website:

Cornell-SciFi.com

MORE FROM
CHARLES A CORNELL

STEAMPUNK AND DIESELPUNK

The Most Peculiar Tales
DragonFly
Die Fabrik / The Factory

MYSTERY THRILLER

Tiger Paw

NON-FICTION

The Character Quad: A New Tool for Writers
A Survivor's Guide to Working at a Big Corporation

SATIRICAL FICTION

Harvey Drinkwater and The Cult of Savings

DRAGONFLY

DragonFly explores the incredibly turbulent times during the 1940s and the 'what ifs' that might have been. *DragonFly* follows the journey of Veronica Somerset as she battles the odds to become Britain's first female fighter pilot.

Packed with full color illustrations and black and white 'retrographs', *DragonFly* conjures up a whole new world of fantastic technology, dangerous fighting machines, and wizards battling across the boundary between good and evil in a World War re-imagined like never before.

The characterization is top-notch! The heroine's character development intensifies with every turn of the page. The inclusion of the photography is icing on the cake in this extraordinary narrative. Insightful, creative, and unique—be ready to be shocked and awed by *DragonFly*!
— Cheryl E. Rodriguez for Readers' Favorite

DragonFly by Charles A Cornell is an extraordinary novel. The story is extremely entertaining, but it also made me think. It is indeed a truly adventurous tale: I could not put it down and read it in two days! The pace of the story, the superb illustrations, and the style of the author all make this novel a must-read!
— Marie-Hélène Fasquel for Readers' Favorite

"*DragonFly* is brilliant! The Golden Age of Science Fiction is alive and well!"
—Carol Kean, book reviewer for Perihelion Science Fiction Magazine and an Amazon 'Vine Voice'

"A gripping and fast paced new adventure series..."
—Five Star Amazon Review

"I want to commend the author for writing a compelling and strong female lead... It's characters like Ronnie and the courage of authors like Cornell (to write such characters) that will help change the face of the sci-fi/fantasy/dystopian genre."
—Five Star Amazon Review

"It has something for everyone. History wrapped in mystery draped in Sci-Fi makes *Dragonfly* a fast-paced winner!"
—Five Star Amazon Review

"The thrilling climax... outdoes any big action flick for sheer sweep and menace. Cornell hits a home run!"
—Ken Pelham, award winning author of the mysteries, *Brigand's Key* and *Place of Fear*

"There is a lot to like about *Dragonfly*... surprises... intrigue... in a world that doesn't particularly follow the history that we know."
—Lewis Knight, author of *The Haven World* novels.

"It was fantastic ... Charles has done a wonderful job blending alternate history with the mystical. His characters are well developed. I was disappointed when it ended."
—John Charles Miller, author of alternative history novels

For more on DragonFly visit:

Cornell-SciFi.com/Science-Fantasy-DragonFly

THE MOST PECULIAR TALES

Does your heart beat faster in the dark than in the daylight?
Do your hands tingle under the touch of copper and brass?
Then *The Most Peculiar Tales* are sure to satisfy.

Six paranormal tales set in a steampunk world:

The Reversible Man... A mad scientist creates a trail of murder and larceny. Professor Carr must capture The Reversible Man before the professor is sent to the gallows for a crime he didn't commit.

Suddenville... A sleepy coastal hamlet is terrorized by daemons. Why are they abducting the villagers and can Professor Carr reach beyond our dimension to get them back?

A Most Peculiar Time... The haunting of a castle on the borders requires opening portals to heaven and hell in order to save a family from three dueling spectres.

The Darwin Room... A creature is unleashed by a twisted experiment that attempts to advance the theory of evolution.

Soul Ripper... A young girl has been taken hostage and her soul ripped from her body. Professor Carr enlists the help of a most unusual psychic medium to bring the culprit to justice.

Theatre Macabre... An assassin stalks the theater in a plot to kill a member of the Imperial Family. With help from a magic hummingbird, Jeremiah must intercept the anarchist before he prevails.

Cornell-SciFi.com/Cornell-Steampunk

BV - #0016 - 020824 - C0 - 216/138/16 - PB - 9781068734403 - Gloss Lamination